"America lost some of its best mho chose exile. . . . Jack Todd's [voic[ ]] other experience this nation had, :]es Carroll, author of *An American R*[ ]

"[*Desertion*] is a powerful book: fr[ ]]unching, courageous, affecting. . . . From writers like Caputo and Herr and O'Brien we have the stories of those who went to Vietnam and died or were wounded. From Jack Todd we come closer to understanding the terrible costs to those who stayed back and survived."—*Quill & Quire*

"Jack Todd has written a deeply personal, wholly compelling memoir about a time in American history that haunts us all. We can only be grateful for the power and straightforward honesty of his writing."—Robert Kotlowitz, author of *Before Their Time*

"*Desertion* is an intensely moving, unique war story. In a voice that captures both the moral stalwartness and impetuousness of youth, Jack Todd delineates the hidden costs of the Vietnam war, how it not only tore apart the lives of the men who served, but equally derailed the life of one man who refused to serve."—Jill Ciment, author of *Half a Life* and *Teeth of the Dog*

"Jack Todd, in his remarkable, harrowing tale, shines light on an all too easily forgotten aspect of the Vietnam era, with the immediacy of a journalist and the lyricism of a novelist. *Desertion* is a fascinating read, all the more so for its being true."—David Rakoff, author of *Fraud*

"This book deserves a high place in the literature of America's war in Vietnam. Gracefully and eloquently and honestly, without falling into the traps of self-pity or misspent anger, Jack Todd has written a stunning account of his desertion from the U.S. Army in 1969. I doubt that Mr. Todd would call himself a hero— certainly most so-called 'patriotic' Americans would not—but having read this frank, beautiful memoir, I can think of no better term to describe a man of such incredible integrity and moral courage. In tight, powerful prose, Mr. Todd captures the terrors and doubts and humiliations that must necessarily accompany such acts of spiritual and political valor."—Tim O'Brien, author of *The Things They Carried* and *Going After Cacciato*

"Award-winning *Montreal Gazette* columnist Todd has written a moving memoir focusing on his decision to desert from the U.S. Army because of his opposition to the Vietnam War. . . . *Desertion* is a powerful, well-written account."
—*Library Journal*

DESERTION

in the Time of Vietnam

DESERTION

in the Time of Vietnam

A Memoir

Jack Todd

With a new introduction by the author

UNIVERSITY OF NEBRASKA PRESS

LINCOLN AND LONDON

First Nebraska paperback printing: 2012

Library of Congress Cataloging-in-Publication Data
Todd, Jack, 1946–
[Desertion]
Desertion in the time of Vietnam: a memoir /
Jack Todd; with a new introduction by the author.
p.   cm.
Originally published: Boston: Houghton Mifflin, 2001.
ISBN 978-0-8032-3981-4 (paper: alk. paper)
1. Todd, Jack, 1946– 2. Vietnam War, 1961–1975—
Desertions—United States. 3. Vietnam War, 1961–1975—
Social aspects—United States. 4. Americans—
Canada—Biography. I. Title.
DS559.8.D4T63 2012
959.704'38—dc23   2011041453

AUTHOR'S NOTE:
This is a memoir, not a work of fiction. I have made every effort to recover
it accurately from memory, checking my own recollections against notes and
surviving manuscripts from the time and against the memory of others. In
a very few specific instances, the names and identifying characteristics of
people mentioned in this book have been changed to protect the privacy
of individuals I was unable to contact.

Introduction

In early May of 2001, I was on a brief tour of the eastern United States to promote this book. In Washington DC, an appearance on the *Diane Rehm Show* on National Public Radio had left me drained and exhausted. After so many years, the emotions surrounding the Vietnam War were as powerful as they were in the late 1960s and early 1970s, when the conflict overseas was tearing America apart at home. No matter which side of the argument callers were on, their words were emotional, heated, inevitably sad.

From Washington, I went on to New York City. I arrived early for another NPR interview in Lower Manhattan, so I stopped for a light lunch in a restaurant in the bowels of the World Trade Center. Four months later, I watched in horror as the towers collapsed on that basement, marking the beginning of a new kind of war.

The decade since this book was first published has brought two lengthy, costly, deadly, and ultimately ambiguous conflicts. There are more American boys coming home in body bags, although the people who wage these wars have learned, since Vietnam, how to manage public opinion: now they keep the dead discreetly offstage, to avoid offending the sensibilities of folks eating dinner in front of the six o'clock news. The real cost of war may be hidden, but the dead are no less dead because their bodies are off-loaded at remote landing strips in the wee hours of the morning.

Vietnam was different. It was a national trauma, played out on the nightly news. Because of the draft, virtually everyone had a son or a brother or a husband who might end up in the line of fire. By the time Saigon fell in 1975, the war had scarred thousands of American families (not to mention the horrors suffered by the Vietnamese people) and opened deep wounds on the cultural and political landscape at home that have not healed to this day.

The Vietnam War was wrong. Morally wrong, ethically wrong, politically wrong, murderous and quite possibly illegal. More than fifty-five thousand Americans and at least one million Vietnamese were sacrificed for no reason at all except that the leaders in Washington were too stubborn and too narrow-minded to understand the magnitude of their folly before it was too late. The war was wrong in the global scheme of things, and it was wrong from the narrow perspective of American self-interest. If that was not entirely plain in 1968 or 1970, it is absolutely clear today, after such prominent architects of the war as Robert McNamara admitted it was a tragic mistake. You can't drop napalm on people one day and win their hearts and minds the next day. You can't destroy a village in order to save it.

For young men like me who were caught between the draft, our own deep patriotism and hunger for the perceived glory of other wars, and the pressures from our families and peers, the Vietnam War was a constant, gnawing dilemma. What was our draft status going to be? What would we do if the day came when we were classified 1-A and we received our draft notice in the mail? Would we have the moral courage to go to prison? To give up our country for our beliefs? Or would we simply take the line of least resistance, allow ourselves to be drafted, and hope for a desk job?

Like most wars, Vietnam was a rich man's war but a poor

man's fight. America's battles, by and large, are fought by African Americans, Hispanics, and poor whites. I fell into the latter class, the poor white trash who have formed the backbone of the military at least since the Civil War. George W. Bush and Dick Cheney found a way to avoid Vietnam. For young men like me who came from the wrong side of the tracks, there was going to be no easy way out, no matter how ardent our opposition to the war.

This book is the tale of one man's transformation from gung-ho Marine officer-in-training to reluctant army draftee to deserter—of the emotional and political conflicts that led to a decision that has haunted me ever since. Not because it was politically wrong (it wasn't) but because the personal price was so great. It would have been so much easier to simply go with the flow, to be a rear-echelon clerk or a journalist for *Stars and Stripes* (I had not been assigned to infantry training), serve my two years, and return to the *Miami Herald*. Instead, in the span of less than three months, I lost everything: family, girlfriend, career, job, country. Between the end of October 1969 and January 1970, I went from promising young reporter at the *Herald* to denizen of Vancouver's Skid Row. It would take me at least twenty-five years to recover, and in truth, it was probably not until the publication of this book, thirty years after I went AWOL from Fort Lewis, Washington, that I was able to put it all behind. To this day, I miss the badlands country of western Nebraska, where I was born and raised.

From the beginning, my aim with this book was to use the particular to get at the general. It is not, given the subject, a particularly political book. It's rather a portrait of a time, of individuals caught up in a situation that required a moral choice, of the different ways in which we made that choice and the consequences we suffered as a result. It's my story, but it is also the story of my best friend, Sonny Walter, who served in Vietnam and was ultimately destroyed by the experience. I make no judgments on those who, like Sonny, chose to serve: we all had our private anguish, our own ways of sorting out the truth. By 1968 it was a painful process, no matter which side you were on.

For those struggling with current and future wars, perhaps this book will be of some use. It tells a story that, in the mass of literature on the conflict in Southeast Asia, has seldom been told, although an estimated one hundred thousand American war resisters chose Canada over service in Vietnam.

The Vietnam War threatens to become, like World War I, a very literary war. For those who want to pursue the subject, there is now a solid bookshelf of important works, from nonfiction such as Michael Herr's brilliant *Dispatches*, Frances FitzGerald's *Fire on the Lake*, Bernard Fall's *Hell in a Very Small Place*, and Stanley Karnow's *Vietnam* to a long list of fiction titles, some of which have become classics, such as Tim O'Brien's *Going After Cacciato* and *The Things They Carried*. For a powerful reminder that American troops weren't the only ones who suffered, I would direct readers to Bao Ninh's *The Sorrow of War* and Duong Thu Huong's *Novel Without a Name*. From the American perspective, the most recent entry is the massively detailed and powerful Karl Marlantes novel *Matterhorn*, which graphically illustrates the sheer hell and stupidity of war while attempting, simultaneously, to glorify the exhilaration of combat.

Marlantes attempts to have it both ways, but it's a gulf that cannot be crossed. In times of great moral crisis, you have to choose. During the Vietnam War, the choice was stark: between a conflict that was wrong in every way and prison or exile. I chose exile. For that, I have been condemned as a coward. But every human being, deep inside, knows the truth. And the truth is that my decision to resist the war by leaving my country is the bravest thing I have ever done.

For Jesse and Tyler

———

DESERTION

in the Time of Vietnam

Prologue:
Waiting for Charlie
Nebraska, 1958

SONNY IS TEN, I am eleven, and we have a plan. We're going to kill Charlie Starkweather.

It's almost the end of January 1958. One of those dead cold winter days when there is no snow on the ground and the pale brown grass in the morning bends under a white frost and goes snap-crackle-pop as you walk. The sidewalks are slick with frost, so you can run a few steps and slide, run and slide all the way to school, your breath making little white puffs in the cold blue air. After you run awhile the cold glues your nose shut and you pull your jacket up and breathe inside it, warm secret breaths like under the covers in the morning, when your mother says you have to get up but you burrow down deep under the pillow and try not to think about the way the cold floor is going to feel when it hits your feet. Every time we stop to catch our breath we stand and whisper, making plans for Charlie.

The rumor is all over town: Charlie Starkweather is coming to Scottsbluff. To our jail. To our little jail, in our little town. Starkweather and his girlfriend, Caril Ann Fugate. Not prowling for kids to kill this time but prisoners now, in handcuffs and leg irons, surrounded by deputy sheriffs and cops. This, we are sure, is a temporary condition. True desperados can't be held in something as small, as fragile, as inconsequential as the Scottsbluff jail. Their escape, the escape that will be on every radio station in America tomorrow, vibrates like death in the air, like an arrow so close you hear it hiss before it bites deep into the bark of a cottonwood tree and sticks there, quivering. If our plan works, Sonny and I will make the front page of every newspaper in America with our pictures under big, black headlines screaming "Hero Kids Foil Starkweather Escape!"

The first time we talk about getting our guns, Starkweather and Fugate have already killed ten people, starting with her parents and baby sister in Lincoln and a kid working in a gas station who wouldn't let Charlie buy a stuffed animal for Caril Ann on credit. They're being hunted all across the state and up into Wyoming. Pop has to walk my sisters across the street to church because they're scared Starkweather will get them. Pop was a boxer, a pro with a big right hook. His hands are broken and his nose is bent up and he's almost sixty, but he still knocks people out when they cross him. He's not afraid of Charlie Starkweather or anybody else, so when Pop walks the girls to church we know it's serious.

We're scared first and then angry, the way people are when they're frightened. We know as much about Charlie as we know about Superman. He's a nineteen-year-old garbageman and Caril Ann is his fourteen-year-old girlfriend and you spell her name "Caril" with an "i" not "Carol" with an "o." Starkweather is five foot two in cowboy boots and has bright red hair which he combs like James Dean's, and he wears pegged black pants and a leather jacket. He can't see anything without his glasses, which are so thick it looks like his eyes are swimming back there somewhere, goldfish in an aquarium. In our nightmares he's the killer with the Coke-bottle eyes.

Charlie Starkweather can't be held in a small-town jail. Anyone can see that. He will bust out with a pistol in each hand and jump in that big shiny black 1956 Packard he stole after he killed the rich guy in Lincoln. The car will be waiting just outside the jail and Starkweather will come flying down West Overland Drive past our house with the cops in hot pursuit, like on *Highway Patrol* with Broderick Crawford, and we'll be waiting for him. We're going to get Starkweather before he gets us.

We take our time walking home from school, working out the details. Sonny has a .410 shotgun and I have a .22 single-shot rifle. We both have plenty of ammo because it's winter and we don't shoot much in winter. We'll do our homework, eat supper, meet on the street, and wait for Starkweather, because for sure he won't break out until after dark. We have the perfect place to hide, where they dug the holes for new houses and sewer lines across the street. The backhoes piled up big heaps of dirt and when winter came they left a trench where we play World War II, fighting the Nazis from our foxhole. It's perfect. The hardest part will be explaining to our parents why we're taking our guns out in January. That's all we have to do, get out of the house with our guns and our ammo. If we make it that far, when the jailbreak happens we'll be right there, waiting for Charlie.

"You're not going to shoot that thing tonight," my mother says. It's a question, not an order, so I keep on cleaning the single-shot Savage .22 rifle in our kitchen, liking the smell of cleaning solvent and gunpowder, the way you push the rod through the barrel with the little white cloth patches on the tip that come out the other side black and then less black until the rifle is clean. Working in the light from the single bright bulb dangling from the buckled and swaybacked ceiling over the cracked linoleum floor, the cord that holds the bulb wrapped all the way down with black electrician's tape over the frayed spots where the wires stick out. My mother doesn't like the .22, never did. She gives me a look over the top of her glasses, busy with the dishes, not liking the rifle in her kitchen.

"Just going to shoot some targets with Sonny."

"It's awfully cold out there and it's pitch-dark."

"I know. We just want to do some target practice. We ain't going to be long and we got streetlights now."

"You're not going to be long and we have streetlights now."

"Yeah. We're not going to be long."

"Is your homework done?"

"Yep. I done my homework and I done my chores."

"You did your homework and you did your chores."

"Yep."

She won't stop me. Pop would, for sure, but he's asleep in the chair next to the heater in the living room, and everyone will be quiet and let him sleep because the one thing we're afraid of more than anything on earth, even Starkweather, is waking him up. He had way too many fights when he was boxing, so his brain is a little fuddled and if he hears a noise he'll come up out of the chair saying, "What-what-what-what the goddam hell?" and he'll have his fists up, ready to punch somebody. He never hits us even when we're bad, but he's so scary we go around on tiptoe even when he's awake.

I don't lie to my mother, exactly, I just don't happen to mention Starkweather or Caril Ann Fugate or the plan to shoot Charlie when he comes barreling down our street. I finish cleaning the rifle, take a box of .22 long-rifle shells from the cabinet on the back porch, pull the bolt back, and slip one into the chamber as soon as I step out the door. Sonny comes sauntering up the street, shotgun over his shoulder, grinning the way he always grins when we're out after magpies or rabbits. Sonny has even done a little planning—he's slipped out of the house toting a couple of sleeping bags.

We walk back up the far side of the street away from our house so Mom won't see us if she happens to look out the kitchen window. We find a place where the backhoe has piled the dirt up high and we dig in behind it so no one can see us. We both know this is a little bit pretend and a little bit real, but it feels a whole lot more real once we start making a comfortable space for ourselves, with the .22 and the shotgun pointed out so we can cover the street. The ground is hard and cold, but we're warm enough after we crawl down into the sleeping bags. We pull them tight around our shoulders but don't zip them up because we want to be able to move quick in case we don't get Starkweather with the first shot and he climbs out of the car and comes after us. We're close to the corner so we can see the traffic on West Overland, and any cars coming down Avenue F will come right past our little dirt bunker, where we can get a good look at the driver and pick him off clean.

We try sighting our guns on the street, figuring the most likely distance for a shot and where we can squeeze it off. We have to get the sights set right for the distance and figure out how far ahead of him we'll have to aim if he comes fast, and how much lead it will take if he's slow, thinking it will be better to take him through the windshield when the shot is head-on instead of waiting until he's closer, when it'll be like trying to shoot a rabbit zigzagging through the brush, when all you can see is a flash of cottontail. It's cold and our breath makes little white clouds that hang in the air and we're shivering already, even though we're both wearing parkas and stocking caps and gloves and we've put on long underwear and two pairs of socks. Mittens would be warmer, but with mittens on you can't squeeze a trigger.

"You OK?" Sonny asks.

"Fine. But if they're going to come I hope they come quick. It's cold out here."

There's no traffic at all at first, only cars that go by on West Overland without slowing down, nothing at all that looks like a big black '56 Packard. Finally a station wagon passes, and we can see we have a problem. Cars turning right off West Overland shine their headlights into our eyes, especially if they have the high beams on like the station wagon, and the light blinds us for a couple of seconds. By the time we can see again the car is right there, fifteen feet away, so if it's Starkweather we have to shoot as soon as he turns the corner or take our chances up close.

After the station wagon it's quiet for a while until old Tom Martin makes the turn in his pickup truck. Once the headlights are out of my eyes I can see Tom chomping his cigar the way he always does, never lighting it but just chewing it up, with flecks of tobacco stuck to his lips and to the stubs of his dark brown teeth, where he still has teeth. I can't see his teeth, but I can see the cigar all right once the headlights are past, which means I'll get a clear shot if the driver is a killer in a black Packard.

We wait a long time, shivering, talking in whispers, trying to keep warm. Finally a black Dodge comes up West Overland slow and turns right and comes toward us in low gear.

"'Fifty-two Dodge!" Sonny whispers.

I nod and tighten my finger on the trigger. There's something wrong about the way the Dodge is moving, slow and like the driver doesn't know where he's going. Maybe Starkweather couldn't steal the Packard so he grabbed this Dodge. I raise the .22 and get him in my sights, get the spot weld on the stock with my cheek the way my brother Red taught me, take a deep breath, let it out, hold it. Don't jerk the trigger, just squeeze. Don't breathe at all, just hold it real steady and squeeze till you hear the shot go off bang! then breathe and throw the bolt and reload, wishing now more than ever that I had a repeater in case the first shot doesn't get him and we have to keep firing. The headlights are in my eyes and for two or three awful seconds I'm blind, not knowing who or what is on the other side of those lights, not knowing whether to shoot or run, hide or freeze. Then the Dodge is right beside us and I can see the driver, a fat old man hunched down over the wheel, looking back and forth like he's lost. I take a deep breath and lift a stiff finger off the trigger. I can hear my heart pounding whoomp!-whoomp!-whoomp!-whoomp! even through the parka, so loud I figure Sonny can hear it too. I'm sweating, cold as it is, and I feel like I'm going to pee my pants. The black Dodge turns into a driveway and the driver kills the engine. I hand the rifle to Sonny.

"Keep the street covered. I have to pee."

I scramble down the pile of dirt and over to the far side of what will be the basement when a house goes up here next summer and pee in the corner, shivering from cold and fear and that strange thrill you get when you're a kid and you go outside at night, looking up at the stars.

"This is dumb," Sonny says when I get back. "They ain't gonna come."

"You don't know that."

"They ain't gonna come."

I know he's right but I don't want to give up. A big car comes barreling down West Overland going way too fast. We don't get much of a look but I say I thought it was a Packard and for sure it was black.

"If that was him, we missed him," Sonny says.

But if that was him we'd know it by now. There would be sirens, police cars screaming by, lights coming on all over the place, people wanting to know what was going on and wondering if Starkweather is on the loose. Instead there's nothing at all. Just the night and the chill and the cold stars a billion zillion miles away, tiny like the light you see when a guy strikes a match on the far side of the river. Finally my mother starts calling. We ignore her, but a couple of minutes later Pop steps out onto the porch in his slippers and hollers, "Jackie, get the goddamned hell in the house!" and I'm up and running, Sonny's footsteps fading down the street as he runs too, both of us sprinting for safety.

"What on earth were you doing out there all this time?" my mother asks.

"Nothin'."

It isn't a lie. We haven't done a thing except wait, holding our guns, cold and scared. Mom makes me a hot chocolate and sends me to bed. I stay awake a long time, listening to everybody snore, waiting for the police sirens which will mean Starkweather is on the loose, figuring out exactly how I will get the .22 and slip a long-rifle shell into the chamber and go back to my post to wait for the killers in the Packard. I know I won't do it, though. I'm fresh out of brave.

The next day all the papers run a picture, Starkweather handcuffed and smirking and surrounded by cops, still trying to do the James Dean look even though he's a dead man, bound for Lincoln and the electric chair. We can't believe how short and harmless he looks. Later they'll call him the "natural-born killer" and write songs and make movies about him and Caril Ann, making it like Charlie Starkweather is some kind of twisted American hero, but really there's nothing deep about him. He's just a vicious little schnook who kills people for no reason at all.

We're quieter walking to school. More grown-up, closer to being men because we almost did something very stupid together. Closer to each other, too. Not talking about the guns and the way we waited, because when you really do a thing you don't talk about it. Proud anyway because if Charlie Starkweather came down our street in Scottsbluff that night, we were ready to fight.

Part I

TENDING TO RUIN

AT DAWN, ragged webs of rain hang over the Atlantic. The breakers off South Beach run ahead of the storm, dark waves ripping to white foam on wet sand as the clouds lock in and the rain takes hold down the length of the Florida peninsula. The deluge pounds the tile roofs of the homes in Little Havana, the glass and steel bank towers downtown, the yachts moored in Biscayne Bay. Lizards hunker down in the trees, the numbers man in Liberty City takes refuge in his rusty pickup truck, commuters stuck on I-95 curse and crawl, the tourist from Ohio calls home to say this vacation is a real waste and what's the point of Florida if you can't get a suntan—? The rain pounds palm fronds off the trees and sends them skittering down the street, lost in the flood. Streets vanish under the rush of water, cars stall, a soggy American flag on a rusty pole hangs limp over a used-car lot. Someone has picked up the Atlantic and tilted it over Florida, and when it stops the ocean will be dry as a drinker's throat on New Year's Day.

It's Halloween 1969, and if the ghosties and ghoulies and long-leggedy beasties are out and about, they must have gills. Rained out of one last morning on the beach, Mariela and I pull into ourselves, into a raw nub of sadness. The weatherman says we can expect seven inches of rain on North Miami Beach. It seems impossible, but as we drive through Miami,

I feel a tug and the car drifts twenty feet, floats with the current right through an intersection. Mariela's strong fingers tighten around mine and we ride the flood, helpless, swept away by a power we can't control, unable to peer through the rain or to imagine what lies ahead until the tires find pavement and we drive on, shaken, and pull into a House of Pancakes on Biscayne Boulevard for a last breakfast together.

It's my last day in Miami, the last morning, the last hour, and all we can do is sit at a window booth watching the rain sweep the street, drinking coffee and poking without appetite at cold pancakes. We're a dozen blocks north of the *Miami Herald* building where I no longer work. We came here after a movie on our first date, we're back again on our last morning together. Mariela dressed for work, me in jeans and a work shirt, ready for a three-day drive to Nebraska. Drained from one last night together, fresh out of ways to say good-bye. Even now, with no makeup after a sleepless night, she is one beautiful woman, my Cuban lover, tantalizing in a crisp white blouse and a short green skirt. I reach too far across the table and brush her left nipple with the backs of my fingers. She pushes my hand away.

"Don't," she says, looking out the window, away from me. "That rain is terrible. Maybe you should wait and see if it clears. The turnpike's gonna be dangerous."

"I have too far to go."

"Yeah, I guess. You have to promise me you'll be careful."

"I'll be careful. I don't want to go."

"I know."

"It's not too late. You could pack your things. We can leave today, drive straight to Canada, find a justice of the peace, get married on the way. I can go to work for the *Toronto Star*. Hemingway worked for the *Toronto Star*."

"Jacko . . ."

"I know."

"I can't do it."

"I know."

We've been working this groove for a month now, since I stayed off work sick one day and went down to check the mail on a hot Miami afternoon and found the letter, knowing what it would say before I opened it: "Greetings . . . You have been ordered to report for induction . . ." It was a letter you didn't have to read, but I called Mariela and read it to her anyway. We had three weeks left. Three weeks to inhale sex, as though you could fill your lungs with it and store it forever. We made love on lazy Sunday evenings, our skin still hot from a day at the beach. We made love on the carpet when I was burning up with fever and she came to take care of me. We made love as though the act could make time stop, and the earth kept turning anyway, and now we are out of time.

"I hope they don't send you to Vietnam."

"I hope they do send me to Vietnam. Anything else is hypocritical. If you're going to go, you go. If you're not, you go to Canada or you go to prison."

"Oh, Jacko, don't say that."

"It's true. If I'm going to be in, I want to go to Vietnam. Least that way I'll have something to write about later. I'll be Norman Mailer for this war. *The Naked and the Dead.*"

"Please don't say that. Please don't say that. I won't be able to stand it if they send you to Vietnam."

"Then come to Canada with me."

"Jacko . . ."

"I know. You can't."

I can't either. I've thought about it, but I can't turn my back on my country. I'm an American boy, grew up in the heartland, tried to make it as an officer in the United States Marine Corps, washed out with bad knees. Now they are drafting me. I hate the war and Nixon and Agnew and the generals in the Pentagon who are so obsessed with body counts they can't see they are losing this war, that it is a war that can't be won, a war that should never have been fought. I hate everything about it, but I am an American boy. I remember what JFK said: "Ask not what your country can do for you . . ." I hear FDR, too, saying: "Today, December 7, 1941, is a day that will live in infamy." I spent two years of university getting pumped up before track meets by humming the Marine Corps hymn under my breath. I hear "The Star-Spangled Banner" and I get goose bumps and want to raise the flag over Iwo Jima. It's been like this since I was old enough to lift a toy gun and say, "Bang-bang, you're dead." In two years of antiwar marches I have not been able to set myself apart from that boy, the one who ran circles around the living room with his arms flung out like the wings of a B-17, shouting, "Bombs over Tokyo!" until Pop picked me up under one strong arm and toted me off to bed, still yelling, "Bombs over Tokyo!"

There is more. The *Miami Herald* is a luxurious dream, a great newspaper in a corrupt and steamy city where the stories fall from the palm trees like ripe coconuts. I have just turned twenty-three and I'm a reporter for the *Miami Herald* and the *Herald* is one of the best newspapers in America. When I walk into the *Herald* building in the morning I walk with a swagger—notebook tucked into back pocket, tie loosened, assignments waiting in a pigeonhole upstairs. *Miami Herald* reporter. Future foreign correspondent. Lover of the beautiful Mariela. When she comes to visit me at work and we stroll through the newsroom, heads turn, a hundred pairs of eyes follow her long legs. I walk taller, Mariela clinging to my arm. Vanity and pride in this job and this woman. If I leave the *Herald,* if I leave Miami, if I leave Mariela and leave my family and leave my country, who will I be?

There is more. The pathetic Tom Clagg, who was dating Mariela when I met her, squiring her around for more than a year and settling for a good-night peck on the cheek, is still hanging around her like a hungry spaniel. Mariela is a sucker for the lost, and he is so hopeless she can't bring herself to toss him out of her life. I wonder what will happen if I'm on the other side of the world in Vietnam and Clagg is at her door with his little bouquets of flowers, his need stronger than love.

There is no cure, there will be no reprieve. We have spent long, sad afternoons sitting in a Coconut Grove coffeehouse, playing the Peter, Paul, and Mary version of "Leavin' on a Jet Plane" over and over. The "Greetings" letter is in the glove box of the car. The *Herald* has already hired a reporter to replace me. He comes in so I can show him around on my beat before I leave, a captain fresh out of the Marine Corps, a graduate of the same officer-training program I was in at Quantico back in the summer of '67 when I still believed in the war. He is waiting to take my desk; sometimes when I come in to write a story he's already at my typewriter. I feel it all slipping away: my job, Miami, Mariela.

My buddy and roommate Rich Wallace, the Peyote Coyote, says good-bye and forgives me for the time I stalled his Austin-Healy Sprite convertible in a cloudburst on I-95 and couldn't get the top up. I have a last talk with the city editor at the *Herald*. I will be discharged in November 1971 and my job will be waiting, he says. It's the law. To me 1971 is a future so distant we will all be creaky and old, shopping for false teeth, doddering along the beach looking for lost coins. I nod and promise to be back in the same spot in two years, ready for a fresh assignment. Somehow I know it will never happen.

It's time to go. The waitress brings our checks and I start to pay but Mariela says no, she'll buy. We splash through the rain to my old white Plymouth and drive the flooded streets and kiss, one last frantic kiss good-bye at the door of her office. Then she is out of the car and gone, the flash of one long, tanned leg under her tight green skirt the last thing I see. I sit there in the Plymouth for ten minutes alone trying to remember how to put the goddamned thing in "go." Toy with the goofy push-button transmission on the dash, hit "drive," and the car rolls obediently through the rain, finding its way to the turnpike on automatic pilot.

The rain is two inches deep on the turnpike, cars hydroplaning off the road, visibility down to about as far as you can toss a slab of concrete, engines stalled by the slosh of water from underneath. When an eighteen-wheeler blows by it's like driving underwater in the wash from his tires. I stop a half-dozen times, waiting to see if the rain will clear, sitting in turnpike rest stops reading newspapers I have already read three times, feeling sorry for myself because it will be a very long while before my byline appears in a newspaper again. I call Mariela twice, shoving change into pay phones, but there is nothing to say. I hate the rain and I hate the draft and I hate this war that is tearing us apart. I hate it all and I miss you and with luck I will get leave and we will see each other at Christmas. Or maybe I'll donate a couple of legs to help make Vietnam safe for fat South Vietnamese colonels with Swiss bank accounts, and then I'll come back to Miami and you can push my wheelchair in the sun.

I don't say that. I don't believe I can die in Vietnam. I despise the war but I don't fear the war. I am no braver than the next guy—I fear night and the unseen, nerve endings raw with watching, sniffing, listening, the enemy that tightens around you like a boa constrictor. The pungee stick, the hand grenade wired to a tree branch, the mortar probe, the ambush, the firefight, death that comes with a sucking chest wound. I still don't fear the war because we all know the simple math of it— how the U.S. has five soldiers in-country for every one actually in the bush, how the massive service and supply and public relations effort dwarfs the actual fighting, how slim the chances you will find yourself hunkered down in a firefight on a moonless night, peeing your pants in fear, emptying clip after clip from a smoking M-16 at a phantom enemy.

We are young, and the young are immortal. I will come back to the *Herald,* back to Miami. Back to Mariela. I tell myself this but I don't believe it, driving all that day, Halloween 1969, crawling through the rain on the turnpike. I make it as far as Orlando just after dark, give up and check into a cheap motel and fall asleep on a saggy bed listening to the rain leak through the roof and drip onto the carpet near the window, worn out and numb and running on empty.

■ ■ ■

Next day the rain eases. I get up early and push it, heading north at a steady 85 miles an hour as far as the southern suburbs of Atlanta, where it's still raining enough to cause a fifty-car pileup in the southbound lane on I-75. Rain, death, twisted metal, sirens, ambulances, jackknifed trucks, cars crushed almost flat, some on fire. Those who can move climb out of their cars and stumble around bleeding in the downpour, their screams seen not heard as northbound drivers gape. Georgia state police in rain gear bellowing at the traffic to keep moving, keep moving, get on out of here. My hands shake, knees turn weak. It's a bad accident but still just an accident, it could happen anywhere and anytime—but the weather and the carnage match the mood. Woodstock is history, Altamont looms. This is Nixon's country now, a snarling place where the Republicans and the rednecks are in charge. My country, love it or leave it.

Once out of the Atlanta traffic I pull into a truck stop, nausea rising, head into the men's room to splash cold water on my face and neck, fighting the urge to retch. On the side of one of the stalls someone has scrawled, "Wanted—nigger to ride on top of my 18-wheeler and watch for low bridges."

In Fort Lauderdale in the hot summer of 1969 I was sent to cover a "riot." A disturbance in the ghetto, more like it, but there were reports of snipers and the streetlights were blacked out. I followed a tank down a dark street, a radio reporter beside me and a double wing of National Guard soldiers fanning out on either side, safeties off their rifles, nervous and scared and trigger-happy, ready to shoot anything that moved. Screams from a building at the end of the street: "You white motherfuckers are gonna die! C'mon, you honkie cocksuckers! Show me your white face, I'm gonna put a bullet between your eyes!" I worked for the *Beacon-Journal* in Akron in the summer of '68 when a man named Fred "Ahmed" Evans parked a Cadillac in the middle of a street in Cleveland and waited until the cops showed up to tow it. Then he and his followers started picking off police officers with rifles, touching off a destructive riot. You never knew. The screamer at the end of the street could be having a little fun with whitey, or he could have a bead on your chest, ready to squeeze the trigger on a high-powered scope-sighted rifle.

We stayed close to the tank, crouched low, trying to scribble notes in the dark while on the move. Someone hit a light switch on the ground floor of a tenement building off to the left and one entire wing of National Guard troops, half a platoon, tore at the building. They hammered through the glass door with their rifle butts and six or seven soldiers stormed inside. They came back out shoving a slender shirtless black man in blue jeans ahead of them. The man was barefoot and when he stepped on the broken glass at his front door he screamed in pain and leaped into the air, and the soldiers clubbed him to the ground with their rifle butts. The radio reporter and I watched, stunned, as he was handcuffed and dragged away. We were about to join the sweep on down the street when we heard someone crying inside. We found a young mother and two little girls, one a baby, the other three years old, hiding in the closet near the front door. We asked her what happened when the soldiers burst in on them.

"I don't know. We was in here in the dark, and the baby was cryin', and my husband went to get a bottle to keep her quiet, and when he put on the light to see what he was doin' in the kitchen, all of a sudden they just come through the door with their rifles and took him away. He didn't do nothin'. He was just fixin' a bottle." We saw where the baby's glass bottle had smashed on the floor in the kitchen, where he had spilled the milk when the soldiers grabbed him.

I wrote the story for the *Herald*. A few days later I was called to testify at the man's pretrial hearing. He was charged with inciting a riot, resisting arrest, assaulting a peace officer. I testified, the judge threw out the charges. In the hall outside the courtroom the man's wife cried and hugged me, and their little girl hugged my leg, and the man, a skinny guy with a big Afro, shook my hand and thanked me.

Something was always colliding in Miami: black against white, white against Latino. Anti-Castro Cubans plotted invasion and revolution, elderly Jews who had survived the concentration camps lived out their lives in dilapidated South Beach apartments dreaming of their grandchildren in Brooklyn, developers elbowed one another in the face to see who would build the next strip mall, sullen blacks wondered when they were going to get a piece of the pie. It was crazy, and I loved it. Loved the sound of it, loved the way you could come out of a chilly air-conditioned building at midnight into the warm, damp air fragrant with something tempting and mysterious. Hot, sexy, corrupt, sultry, half-Latin, dangerous, seductive Miami. I loved it as soon as I got out of the car at 2 A.M. on the night in May when I made it to town after the long drive from Nebraska and went straight to the *Herald* building— magnificent at the end of a twin row of palm trees in the light of a full moon—even before I looked for a motel. I stepped out of the car and inhaled the lush air and said to myself, "Yes, this is my place, I belong here."

I turned up to report for work the next day and a desperate assistant city editor barely introduced himself before telling me to grab a notebook and get out on the street: a Dade County sheriff's deputy had been shotgunned in the stomach by a heroin dealer three blocks from the *Herald* building. All the other reporters were out on stories so I had to take it, the editor shouting directions at me as I sprinted to the elevator. I beat the ambulance to the scene by thirty seconds, got there in time to see a young man in a deputy's uniform writhing on the hood of his cruiser and screaming for help, trying to hold his guts in. Before I could get out of the car a merciful wave of ambulances, sheriff's deputies, Miami police officers, and medical technicians came pouring in, so many that no one noticed me standing at the edge of the mob trying to figure out what a real reporter would do in this situation.

I phoned in the first report: deputy shotgunned in the stomach while trying to arrest a heroin dealer. Time, place, apparent condition of victim, no comment from Dade County Sheriff's Department deputies on the scene. Just the facts, ma'am. Then I puked into the bushes behind the phone booth. At the hospital later I tried to find something to say to the deputy's sobbing wife, but there were no words for what had happened. I was there thirty minutes, alone in the waiting room with her until another *Herald* reporter showed up, a husky good old boy from Georgia. He took one look at me, green and stricken, and put a hand on my shoulder.

"You don't look so good, son," he said. "You did all right. I'll take over now. Why don't y'all go on home and have yourself a little drink. I find a bourbon and soda or two always puts me right. You'll get used to it, more or less."

I thanked him and stumbled out as he sat down and said some gentle words to the deputy's terrified wife, somehow knowing things to say that would not sound arrogant or invasive or callous. The deputy lived. The good old boy wrote the story and wrote it far better than I would have, and it ran on the front page of the *Herald* next day under our joint bylines. Life as a reporter in Miami, lesson one.

Big things were happening that summer, but the *Herald* had star reporters who flew off to Chappaquiddick when Ted Kennedy drove off the bridge, to Los Angeles when Charles Manson went on a murderous rampage, to Utah when the air force managed to nerve-gas a few thousand sheep, to Cape Kennedy when Neil Armstrong landed on the moon. I was assigned to the Dade County Sheriff's Department the day of the moon landing, so I wrote a sidebar on the deputies watching the moon landing on stolen TV sets. Next time I went to work, they wouldn't talk to me: the story had landed them in hot water because they weren't supposed to touch the stuff in the stolen property room. Next day I was on the rewrite desk, fielding endless calls from people who insisted the moon landing had actually been filmed in a remote part of Nevada or Arizona.

That was Miami in the summer of 1969. Stories that left me shaking and weeping. Sweet interludes with Mariela. Weeks of boredom covering the Pompano Beach city council budget hearings, moments when the craziness and violence of South Florida would sweep everything away and leave me sitting at my typewriter, chain-smoking Marlboros and trying to write about an airline pilot who may or may not have beaten his wife to death with a ball-peen hammer—the bougainvillea vines climbing the walls around the home where the pilot had lived with his wife, the hammer, the mystery intruder who supposedly killed her when the pilot stepped out for a hamburger. So in love with my own prose that I almost missed the bitter heart of it, how some man had taken a hammer and beaten a woman to death.

I would get a cup of coffee and a candy bar and a pack of cigarettes from the vending machines at the *Herald,* sit down at one of the old upright manual typewriters in the racket of the newsroom, bang out the story as fast as I could roll new takes into the typewriter carriage, finish it, type "30" at the bottom and stub out the last cigarette at the same instant, and race through with a black pencil, correcting my mistakes. Hand it to the assistant city editor, wait for questions, dash to the car, and take Old Cutler Road south to where Mariela lived, avoiding the traffic and the fast food joints along South Dixie Highway.

Windows open in the old white Plymouth. Half-bald tires going whuff-whuff-whuff over sticky tar in the pavement cracks, the sun like a rotten tangerine slipping down behind the mangrove swamps, banyan trees along the road hanging so low they trailed moss over the car. Dodging slow-crawling land crabs, dozens of them on the asphalt, hearing the whump and crunch when I wasn't quick enough and a crab shell went flat. All those things out there dying and decaying had nothing to do with me, racing under the shadows of the banyan trees at sunset, more alive than at any time before or since, pushing the Plymouth almost fast enough to outrun the smell of death.

There are things that can't catch you. The Selective Service is not one of them. I could outrun the smell of death and swamp gas on Old Cutler Road, but I couldn't outrun the draft. I went to Miami as an intern in the spring of 1969, but when the *Herald* offered a permanent job I didn't even think about tearing myself away from Miami and Mariela. I decided to stay instead of returning to the University of Nebraska to complete the last semester I needed for my degree, figuring I could take the courses at the University of Miami. As soon as I decided not to go back to enroll for the fall term, I lost my student deferment. I was reclassified 1-A and ordered to report for a draft physical in Miami. I had the letter sitting on the dash of my car when I picked up a hitchhiker headed north on I-95 from Fort Lauderdale, a French-Canadian from Montreal. "Man, you don't wanna go in the army!" he said. "That's bad news. Come with me. I'm going to a rock concert at this place called Woodstock in New York, and then I'm going home to Montreal. In Montreal we got the most beautiful women in the world, and they love American guys. You'll have a blast, man, you'll love Montreal!"

It was the first time I heard of Woodstock, but I wasn't interested. "No way. I already have the most beautiful woman in the world, and I hate snow. I'll never live where it's cold."

I reported for my physical on a glum, cloudy Saturday morning with my Marine Corps discharge in hand. An officer looked at it and drawled, "Son, you were discharged from an officer-training program. We're draftin' you as a private. Step over there now and take your physical."

So I took it. Stand in this line, that line, eye test, hearing test, turn your head and cough. A doctor listened to my creaky knees and my explanation of the Marine Corps discharge. I didn't really know what was wrong. I was a scholarship athlete at Nebraska, and during my last couple of seasons as a high jumper each knee had to be drained a half-dozen times. The knee on my takeoff leg was almost always stiff and sore after thousands of jumps over a dozen years. Any heavy physical activity and the knees puffed up like balloons; that was all I knew.

Had I kept records every time the knee was drained at Nebraska I might have stood a chance. With no proof of knee problems other than my word, the doctor nodded and gave me an appointment to see a specialist in Fort Lauderdale. By the time I got as far as the doctor's office a week later, I knew I was going to be drafted. The walls of his waiting room and his office were covered with photos of his World War II destroyer. He tapped my knees a couple of times, listened for about a minute to my catalogue of problems, and decided I was fine fodder for the draft. After that, there was nothing to do but wait for my "Greetings" to arrive in the mail.

Two months later the whole draft system would shift to the lottery. My number, when the lottery was drawn in January, was high enough to have kept me out of the draft, had I returned to school at Nebraska for one more semester. If I had kept records every time my knees were drained, I would never have been drafted. If I'd had my draft board registration transferred to Miami to stall for time until the lottery came into effect, I might have escaped. If, if, if . . .

No time for irony now. Driving much too fast, trying to make up for the lost day in the rain in Florida. If that massive pileup on I-75 had been in the northbound lane I would have hit it at 85 miles per hour, stacked up in that sizzling pile of metal and death with everyone else. Slow down, concentrate on the road.

Georgia flashes by—red clay, piney woods dark and smoky, a shadowy tunnel of trees. Wondering what Mariela is doing, wondering when I'll see her again. Wondering if I'll see her again. Near the Tennessee border the skies clear. The hills around Chattanooga are gold and red and yellow, colors exploding into the smoky distance, the air crisp and cool, the sky the deep blue you see in the water off the Florida Keys. During the Civil War this would have been a beautiful place to die. Tennessee is sweet country—hills, leaves, rivers like smoked glass way down below running white where they spill through rocky gorges under bridges that are a filigree of old iron. I will bring Mariela here, show her a place doesn't have to be tropical to be beautiful, how you can slip through the seasons and get different frames on life, something other than heat and palms and ocean.

At a roadside restaurant just over the state line in Tennessee a man helps a woman into her coat, a gesture that looks odd after half a year in Miami. I watch them, feel a bite in the air, dig my old jacket out of the trunk. Back on the road, the one radio station out of Nashville that is not playing country spins three or four songs from *Abbey Road*. The day the album first came out, a Miami FM station played the whole thing, both sides without stopping, while Mariela and I drove aimlessly from Miami Beach to the city and back across the causeway

again, just for the sheer pleasure of driving and listening to
the Beatles. The passenger seat empty now, the place where
Mariela used to ride just a hollow in an old car being pushed
way too hard.

I make Kentucky before dusk and sail past Louisville, bluegrass and thoroughbred farms where leggy horses graze,
thinking how much my old man the horseman would love this,
how he should have come here to make his fortune training
Kentucky thoroughbreds instead of Nebraska plugs, working
them in these blue-green pastures where the white fences look
as though they are painted fresh every morning.

Sometime after dark I cross the border into Ohio and stop
for the night at a little motel in the southwestern corner of the
state, take a shower in a narrow rusty stall under a tap that
dribbles like an old man pissing through the pain, find an almost empty diner where I can get something to eat. A tired
waitress brings a greasy menu. I order a chicken-fried steak
and a Coke. She says "Uh-huh," yells something at the cook.
A TV set flickers high on one wall, carrying the evening news.
Blah-blah in the Delta, bombing campaign stepped up, local
sergeant killed in action. This evening's news like all the rest
until the face of Spiro Agnew, dumb and pugnacious and
bullyboy mean, looms in fuzzy black and white. The owner of
the diner—a greasy man with an apron that has not been
changed or washed since the Korean War—strolls over and
cranks the volume up. Seems he doesn't want to miss a word
from Spiro, patron saint of the dumb and belligerent.

I believed in it once. We all did. Not Agnew, or that shifty-eyed
liar Nixon—but the rest of it, absolutely and without question. "Ask not what your country can do for you . . ." A fierce,
selfless ideology. Once more unto the breach, dear friends,
once more, for a fine young president and his fine young country. I grew up with it. My father, who turned forty-eight the
day I was born in 1946, was a doughboy in World War I, en-

listed out of Oklahoma, where he was driving eighteen-horse teams hauling barrels of oil out of the oil fields. In France they took a horseman and made him a truck driver. He missed combat but distinguished himself by turning a truck over in full view of General John J. Pershing, commander of the American Expeditionary Force (and another Nebraska boy) while racing back for a regimental review. He also learned to wind puttees over his socks, to shoot craps, drink beer, and talk to Frenchwomen in Gay Paree. *"Mademoiselle, voulez-vous promenade dans le boulevard ce soir avec moi s'il-vous-plait?"* He served with a balloon company, driving a truck for a balloonist who went up to spy on the German lines, the balloon attached to the truck with a winch and cable. One day in 1918 the cable broke. Maybe it was hit by a German sniper with a Mauser, maybe it just gave way. The balloon drifted over German territory and the soldier in the balloon was never seen again.

My father came home singing "Mademoiselle from Arm-and-tears, hasn't been kissed in forty years." Summers, weekends, holidays, anytime I wasn't in school he'd wake me at 5 A.M. to milk the cows by singing the doughboy's version of reveille: "You sonofabitch, you're stuck in a ditch, you're in the army now." He also taught me the full rifle drill by the time I was ten, practicing with my .22 in the back yard. Right shoulder arms, left shoulder arms, port arms. He could make the rifle flash and spin, the barrel gleaming in the sun as he went through the routine. He told me the story again and again, about his buddy up in the observation balloon floating away into the sun, the flash of his binoculars a target for German riflemen in the trenches. I thought it was tragic and wonderful.

My uncle Jimmy Wilson, my mother's younger brother, served as an antiaircraft gunner on the battleship *Tennessee* and was at Pearl Harbor on December 7, 1941. Two weeks after the attack my mother got a smudged, oily postcard with the message: "OK—Jimmy." Jimmy went all the way through the war as a gunner on the *Tennessee* and won a medal at the end for downing kamikazes as the Japanese turned desperate. Back home he would not march in the parades or even talk about the war. I met him only once, when I was still very young. He was going bald. I thought all heroes should look like Audie Murphy or John Wayne and I found it strange that a hero who could shoot down all those kamikazes could also lose his hair.

Jimmy was not there to shoot down the kamikaze that hit the destroyer *Hazelwood* off Okinawa in April 1945, with the end of the war four months away. My cousin Edwin Johnson died on the *Hazelwood,* doing fire control when the suicide plane hit. Edwin was killed instantly, although the *Hazelwood* made it back to port, and Edwin's parents got his last letter a few hours after they received the telegram from the war department telling them he was dead. When I was born eighteen months later, my mother remembered Edwin. His name became my middle name.

Another cousin parachuted into Normandy on D-day and posed on the eve of battle in the famous photo of Dwight Eisenhower talking to the paratroopers. Another went ashore at Guadalcanal as a muscular 200-pound Marine and came off the island weighing 160. His brother island-hopped across the Pacific, landing to landing. One battle-hardened vet after another would come to visit us out in Nebraska; evenings after dinner they would sit around on the back porch, swatting mosquitoes, eating watermelon, telling war stories.

I saw them all as heroes, but the one who made me want to be a soldier was my adopted brother, Red. Red was seventeen when he joined the navy right at the end of World War II and served all the way through Korea. After he mustered out of the navy he joined the Army National Guard in Casper, Wyoming. He was a sergeant in a tank unit when I was a boy, and when we drove up to see his unit march in the Fourth of July parade in Casper, Red would always do the same thing: marching with his platoon, eyes forward, counting cadence, he would lift the fingers of his right hand off the butt of his rifle for just a moment as they went by, saying hello to his little brother. That was what I wanted, so fiercely I could almost taste it: to march in starched combat fatigues, with my combat boots spit-shined and my rifle gleaming in the sun. After the war, my war, a war even greater than World War II, I would come home and parade down Broadway in Scottsbluff with my tank unit, pretty girls and little old ladies waving and blowing kisses and thanking me for saving the world from the communists.

We didn't have a television set until I was fourteen, so evenings at home I'd sit listening to Gene Autry or the Cisco Kid on the radio, poring over copies of the *Junior Encyclopedia Britannica,* staring at the color drawings of Americans in uniform from the French and Indian Wars through Korea. Sometimes I wanted to be a tank commander. Other times I wanted to be a grunt, marching through the mud, dug down in a foxhole at Monte Cassino. Or a fighter pilot in a furious dogfight in the skies. Or a gunner on a battleship like the *Tennessee,* throwing ack-ack at the skies as the Zeros dove and strafed. I got my first failing mark in eighth grade for a book report on my favorite subject which began: "World War II. A time of death and destruction." The teacher flunked me for an incomplete sentence. I started writing complete sentences but retained my obsession with war and with books about war. In high school I read a collection of Ernie Pyle's pieces on World War II; William L. Shirer's *Rise and Fall of the Third Reich;* Ernest Hemingway's journalism from the Spanish civil war, *A Farewell to Arms,* and *For Whom the Bell Tolls;* James Jones's *From Here to Eternity* and *The Thin Red Line.* The graphic description of a dying soldier in *The Thin Red Line*—crawling up an embankment screaming and trying to hold in his intestines—haunted my dreams. I wanted to be that soldier, crawling to glory, dying a glorious death for a glorious cause.

The chicken-fried steak takes forever. Spiro is in full rhetorical flight. I want to climb through the TV screen to get at him, throttle him in mid-sentence. The owner of the diner leans forward, hanging on Spiro's every word. This is his truth, this gassy bile from the bowels of Middle America. Now he's watching me, zeroed in on the long hair, the jeans, the fact that I'm not egging Spiro on the way he is.

"This is the only man in America," he says, "who knows what he's talking about. Spiro Agnew. Wasn't for him, this country would be down the toilet already." Agnew hammers away on Vietnam and the cowards who hate the war—limp-wristed, placard-carrying, draft card–burning weenies. This from a crook whose idea of the American way is to steal what you can while the stealing is good. The owner of the diner laps it up like a mangy dog licking bacon grease: "You tell 'em, Spiro! You tell them fucking peaceniks! We oughta put 'em all in jail, you ask me!"

He stares. Daring me to respond. "This is America," he says. "Love it or leave it, that's what I say. Love it or leave it."

Temper, road weariness, leaving Mariela, the looming induction into the army, Agnew's coarse features and lips like a small-mouth bass, this nasty little man. It's too much. Like my father, I can go from dead quiet to the eve of destruction in a heartbeat. I know how it will happen: First throw the heavy glass of Coke and ice, a four-seam fastball right through the TV screen. Smash what's left of the TV over this twisted little creep, then drop him with a left hook. That is what my father would do, thoroughly and without hesitation.

Something kicks in like a tranquillizer dart and I put the glass down a heartbeat short of general mayhem, throw a couple of quarters down to pay for the Coke, and storm out without waiting for my chicken-fried steak. I leave half the remaining rubber on my rear tires peeling out of the parking lot, drive aimlessly up and down the highway looking for somewhere else to eat, find nothing, go to bed hungry. There is a pay phone in the motel office. I try to call Mariela but the phone rings in an empty house. There is nothing left to do except go back to the room and lie there and try to go to sleep with an empty stomach, the white lines of a thousand miles of highway still scrolling through my mind.

I roll out of bed in Ohio the next day, eager to make it as far as Lincoln before nightfall. No dinner the night before, one more thing to blame on Spiro Agnew. Find a little mom-and-pop diner twenty miles down the road and have a triple-barreled breakfast on a sunny fall morning, the sweet gray-haired couple that run the place fussing and kidding about how much food I'm packing away. "I swear, young fella, you must be hollow inside." This is the flip side of America, good people who like everyone they meet, open and sunny and ready to help a stranger with anything he might need. This is my America, the America I believe in. If I told these people how I felt about the war, they would probably disagree—but they would listen to what I had to say and they would think about it. And millions of people just like these two *had* turned against the war. They didn't demonstrate and they didn't burn flags, but they knew right from wrong.

Back on the highway, through most of Ohio, Indiana, Illinois, Iowa. A straight run along Interstate 80, Nebraska on my mind, America the beautiful outside the window—fallow fields after the harvest, pretty little rivers, the rolling hills of Iowa. I cross the Missouri River at Omaha and pull into Lincoln early in the evening, back on campus, where it all started.

■   ■   ■

Twin journeys, across the heartland and back in time. Remembering: A flaming Buddhist monk who turned himself into a funeral pyre in Saigon. Photos of the bodies of Vietnamese president Ngo Dinh Diem and his brother Ngo Dinh Nhu lying on the back of an armored personnel carrier in pools of blood like black water in the photos in *Time.* I remember Big Minh, and helicopters. Green Berets visiting hamlets, and who can stand up to the Green Berets? Marines storming ashore in 1965, and who can stand up to the Marines? Vietnam ticked its way into our consciousness a death at a time, a clock that is too loud in a quiet room.

In 1859 the French naval commander Charles Rigault de Genouilly wrote home to explain why the flower of the French military had failed so dismally in its first attempt at the glorious conquest of Vietnam, the nation he called "Indochine." Rigault's troops had been defeated by heat, insects, snakes, bizarre tropical diseases—and guerrillas. "Everything here," he wrote, "tends to ruin." Was there anyone in the State Department in 1964 who had read Rigault de Genouilly? In the Pentagon? Anyone who might have understood, had they come across that century-old dispatch? Surely some had read Graham Greene, who wrote *The Quiet American* in Saigon in 1953. Greene saw it all in his character Pyle, the quiet American, saw exactly what would happen to America in Vietnam a decade before it began. The idealist Pyle, smug in his certainties, sowing incidental death and destruction everywhere he goes, always with the noblest intentions. Did they not see Pyle when they looked in the mirror?

In October 1963—a month before John F. Kennedy was assassinated—the journalist I. F. Stone put the case against the war in his biweekly newsletter. Stone described how Ho Chi Minh had risked everything to reach a moderate agreement with the French in 1946, accepting what was supposed to be limited independence. How the French promises were broken, beginning a bloody war that would cost France $5 billion, along with the blood of her best young professional soldiers. Because Ho and his guerrillas fought with the American OSS (the forerunner of the CIA) against the Japanese in World War II, Ho thought America would back him against the French. Ho gave the U.S. too much credit. America supported the colonialist French instead, pushing Ho Chi Minh closer to the Chinese, the traditional enemies of the Vietnamese people. After eight years and the disaster at Dien Bien Phu, the French were defeated. Stone saw America stepping into the same quagmire. He issued a clear warning. "Another of those opportunities is now being lost," he wrote. "The international situation makes this a favorable moment to negotiate an end to the war with China and North Vietnam."

The Pentagon and the State Department ignored Stone's warning. Men like Dean Rusk, Robert McNamara, and McGeorge Bundy pushed America to the brink of war. Lyndon Johnson, afraid to be seen as soft on communism, went along. By the time of the Tonkin Gulf Resolution in 1964 we were all thoroughly familiar with Vietnam, even out in the Nebraska panhandle. America was going to war to halt the spread of international communism, and by God we were going to do our part. Like everyone else, we supported LBJ when the fraudulent incident involving a Vietnamese gunboat and an American destroyer in the Tonkin Gulf was used as a pretext for war. We had a naive faith that our president knew what was best for America and that he would never lie to us.

As 1965 turned to 1966, the war became a living thing, escalating from week to week. I hesitated between a basketball appointment to the Air Force Academy and a track scholarship to the University of Nebraska, decided on Nebraska at the last minute because I thought I couldn't handle the science and math at the Air Force Academy. Friends back home in Scottsbluff enlisted and shipped out for Southeast Asia.

American ground troops took over more and more of the war from the reluctant, corrupt, and inept South Vietnamese army. General William Westmoreland sent Americans out on huge search-and-destroy missions. American troops fought a

pitched battle against North Vietnamese regulars in the Ia
Drang Valley. The casualty rates mounted. I cut out a series
of pictures from *Life* magazine, Marines fighting their way
through the jungle, and taped them above the desk where I
studied Wordsworth and Keats and fidgeted, sure I was missing something important in Southeast Asia, afraid the war
would be over before I graduated and got into the fight. Finally, I decided to enlist in Marine Corps officer training. I
wanted to be a soldier, the Marines were the toughest, and the
Marine Corps recruiters who came to campus looked the
sharpest in their dress uniforms. With a track scholarship and
a job on the student newspaper and a full course load, I had no
time for ROTC, but with the Marines you signed up and con-
centrated on your schoolwork during the school year and
spent part of your summer vacations doing two six-week
training courses at Quantico, Virginia. After graduation you
went through another twelve weeks of training and then you
were a Marine lieutenant, ready to lead a platoon into combat.

In the scorching summer of 1967 we came piling off buses
from the Washington airport sometime after midnight,
dumped in this hellhole that was Camp Upshur, fifteen miles
from Quantico, surrounded instantly by screaming drill sergeants shouting incomprehensible commands: "Heyaaahhh,
harrrrggg!!! Abbaaayoouuuuh haaaaich! AAAARRRGHH
HAAAYET!" We stood motionless, uncomprehending until
they thrust their faces three inches from ours and asked, with
perfect diction: "What's the matter, college boy? You mother-
fucking maggots don't understand English? They don't teach
English at Pussy U? The only language you know how to talk
is maggot, college boy, is that it? Now I said, 'Heyaaah,
HAARRRGG!' motherfucker! Now you better goddam
heyaahhh haarrgghhh and double-time it or I'm gonna have
your asshole on my corn flakes for breakfast! HEYAAGH
HARRGHH!" It was chaos and madness, heat and sleep depri-

vation. Drill sergeants at your elbow day and night from the moment at 4 A.M. when they threw galvanized tin garbage cans onto the cement floors of the barracks and screamed, "You got five minutes to shit, shave, shower, and be lined up outside!" until the moment twenty hours later when they finally relented and let you have four hours of restless sleep.

Virginia in July is hot and steamy, Camp Upshur nothing but Quonset huts and parade grounds and trees, all of it shimmering in the heat. "A little bit of Veeyet-Nayum, rat cheer in the U.S. of A.," was how one cracker sergeant described it. If enlisted basic in the Marine Corps was hell, this was worse. We were worked and harassed and kicked when we fell out just like the enlisted trainees, but our physical hell was interrupted by courses on map reading, military law, how to help your men care for problems such as foot fungus and frostbite. If you tried to doze off, the sergeants were always there, ready to stand on your desk with their combat boots if they had to, threatening to kick your face in if you fell asleep.

Because it was officer training, we had twice the normal complement of platoon sergeants. You were never left in peace. They'd walk up and down the middle of the tables in the mess hall, and if you ate too slowly they'd kick your tray into your lap with the polished toe of one combat boot, and then scream at you for making a mess.

Still, we all giggled when a thick-necked sergeant pinned a terrified recruit up against the barracks wall. "You think I'm a motherfucker, don't you, boy?" the sergeant screamed in the boy's face.

"No, sergeant!"

"Don't you lie to me, boy! You think I'm a motherfucker!"

"No, sergeant!"

"Fuck, I hate liars! Tell me the truth, maggot! You think I'm a motherfucker!"

"Well, yeah. You are kind of a motherfucker, sergeant."

"You goddamned right I'm a motherfucker! And I'm a travelin' motherfucker, boy—and your mother is next!"

The Marines would send us through a double row of doctors holding vaccine needles who gave us six shots in each arm, then march us out into the 100-degree heat to hold our rifles at arm's length until we screamed in pain or fainted. When a fat trainee fell out on a training run, three sergeants surrounded him and kicked him in the stomach until he puked. It didn't matter. We picked him up and carried him through the rest of the run. We felt like Marines. Gung-ho and Semper Fi, the Halls of Montezuma and the Shores of Tripoli, Iwo Jima and I'm-gonna-grease-me-some-gooks and wait till them Viet Cong in the 'Nam get a handful of us, they'll wish they never heard of Ho Chi Minh. We sang as we marched:

> Mama, mama, can't you see
> What the Corps has done to me
> Made me lean and made me strong
> Made me so I can do no wrong.
> Sound off! One! Two!
> Sound off! Three! Four!
> Bring it on down! One, two, three, four . . .
> One-two—THREE FOUR!

And then my knees blew up like grapefruit. I woke one morning with so much fluid on both knees that I could slap it around like a bowl of Jell-O. The sergeants sent me to a navy corpsman, who sent me to a doctor, who sent me to another doctor. I told the doctors I'd be OK if the knees were drained, but they had no time for such procedures during boot camp. They sent me to a colonel, who told me I was a washout and they were sending me home because the Corps was not a place for the unfit. But because I was an athlete and he thought I'd make a good Marine officer, he was willing to give me a second chance: I'd be asked to have the knees examined by a civilian doctor. If the knees could be surgically corrected, and if I could prove I was totally healthy, they might take me back into the Corps.

It was the beginning of August 1967. I went into Washington, D.C., on weekend leave with another NPQ (Not Physically Qualified) recruit, a kid from Oklahoma who was also waiting to be processed out. We got drunk in the afternoon, playing "Duke of Earl" over and over on the jukebox in a dingy bar, and carried on to a strip bar where the women danced in pasties and G-strings and we got drunker, so drunk we could barely stand. There we hooked up with a couple of hard cases in fatigues, Marine corporals who had just returned from a year in the bush in Vietnam.

We slid into the back seat of their car and they drove to a black neighborhood looking for whores, finally met up with a slender black kid about our age who said he would take us to a place where they had every kind of woman we could imagine, black and white, Swedish or Vietnamese, whatever we wanted. He took us up the backstairs of a dingy building and asked the regular Marines to put their money in an envelope for safekeeping, and they were dumb enough to do it while we watched, pissed off because we didn't have enough money for hookers. We waited ten minutes, twenty minutes. Finally one of the Marines grabbed the envelope, tore it open, and discovered that it was stuffed with torn strips of newspaper.

The Marines didn't hesitate. They stormed down the stairs, dove into the car, and took off, determined to find the kid who'd made off with their money and kill him. They each had a .45 pistol they had carted back from Vietnam, and every time they saw a black kid on the sidewalk they would pull up next to him, point their guns at him, and threaten to blow his head off. Then they'd tear off again, hitting speeds up to seventy-five miles an hour on the city streets, pulling U-turns, going the wrong way up one-way streets. We watched the whole thing unfold with the detachment of the thoroughly drunk and took turns getting out to vomit whenever they stopped the car. When we asked them to drop us off near our hotel, they told us to shut up or they'd blow our heads off.

When they announced they were going to roll queers in Lafayette Park, we decided to walk back to our hotel. This time they let us go. Somehow we made it back, pulled up the last two strips of floor in a room sleeping eighteen similarly disqualified recruits from Quantico, and fell into a dead drunk stupor. Next day we all raced up the steps of the Washington Monument, and I won, bad knees, hangover, and all. We came down and flopped on the grass, sweaty and giddy from the climb, and watched a girl about sixteen years old run down the long grass slope that led up to the monument. She could really run—long, powerful strides, graceful as a gazelle, running for the pure joy of running. I felt happy watching her, certain I would never forget her, my heart still pounding from the sprint up the steps. Happy to be alive, happy we had survived the insanity of the night before.

After the first disappointment when my knees blew up, I was not unhappy to be out of the Marine Corps. That night with the two enlisted Marines confirmed what I had already begun to suspect. The Corps was not for me. I could not imagine myself in command of these wild combat veterans, and I had reservations about the war that were growing deeper every moment. Between the day when I enlisted in Marine officer training and the day I washed out at Quantico, too much had changed. By the late summer of 1967, I knew enough about the war to know that it was at least possible that America was making a tragic mistake in Vietnam. Most of my friends were already opposed to the war. I was not quite ready to admit that my country could be wrong, but once I was free of the Marines, I began to think seriously about the war. After that it was only a matter of time until I joined the hundreds of thousands of young Americans who were already working for peace.

■ ■ ■

It's strange to be back in Lincoln on an Indian summer day in early November 1969, a draft notice in the glove box of the car. I came here as a gawky farm kid in 1965 and left as a committed antiwar journalist in May 1969, and both these characters now seem like strangers. Now the campus looks less like Nebraska and more like Coconut Grove. Long hair, beards, and bell-bottoms everywhere, the girls in tie-dyed tops or long, flowing dresses—bras definitely out. You smell the sweet scent of marijuana all over campus. Two buddies from my years on the *Daily Nebraskan,* Dan Ladely and John Schmidt, are sharing the top floor of an old house. I crash with them for a couple of days, listening to Otis Redding and Procol Harum, drinking red wine, telling stories about Miami, getting caught up on events at the university.

If I am a reluctant and heartsick draftee now, it is because of the things that happened here, at this university in the heartland, and the people who finally made me see that the war was wrong.

I flew home from Quantico in early August 1967, staring out the window the whole flight, thinking about the Marines and the war in Vietnam, knowing that in a month I would be back on campus, where opposition to the American involvement in Southeast Asia was growing almost by the hour. I couldn't wait to get back to the university. There were changes blowing in the wind, and as the managing editor of the *Daily Nebraskan,* I would be in the middle of everything that was happening on campus. Meanwhile, I went back to work on the construction crew and spent a month laying asphalt on the streets of Scottsbluff in the blazing sun. We worked on the street that ran through the red-light district. My partner on the asphalt

machine was a star football player; we joked with the prosti-
tutes who tried to coax him in for a quickie on our lunch hour,
offering to do it for half-price because he was so good-looking.
"Damn," one of them would say as he peeled off his shirt,
"that boy so pretty, we should be paying *him* to fuck!"

We put in twelve-hour days and tried to avoid political arguments with the full-time construction workers, whose hard-
hat attitudes mirrored what Nixon was saying in Washington.
As we sat in the shade eating our sandwiches on a hot afternoon at the end of August, one of them spat in the dust and
summed up his attitude toward the Vietnam War: "What I
don't understand is why we fuck around over there. I'd drop
the big one on Hanoi tomorrow, that's what I'd do. Nuke
the little yellow sumbitches. Ain't no point getting American
boys killed when you can nuke the bastards, end it just like
that." There was no point in arguing. I changed the subject to
women, and pretty soon he brought up some little honey in
town he was going to see. "T'night I'm gonna take her for a
drive," he said, "get me some poontang out in the boon-
docks." I laughed with the rest of them but my mind was at the
other end of the state, back on campus.

When we try to untangle the circumstances that led to the
great events in our lives, we find chains of cause and effect
leading off in bizarre directions. Like students across America,
those of us on the Lincoln campus eventually would have
come to oppose the war anyway, but a strange set of circumstances planted seeds of doubt in us as early as 1965. The philosophy department at Nebraska in the early 1960s boasted
among its professors one O. K. Bouwsma; during the 1940s
and 1950s, Bouwsma had studied at Cambridge University
with Ludwig Wittgenstein, one of the pivotal thinkers of the
twentieth century. Bouwsma's presence in Lincoln attracted
two brilliant graduate students, Carl Davidson and Al Spangler, who happened also to be among the national leaders of the

antiwar movement and the left-wing Students for a Democratic Society. When Davidson and Spangler arrived on campus in the fall of 1965, they learned that Bouwsma had left the previous spring for the University of Texas. Instead of following him to Texas, however, they stayed at Nebraska to give a conservative campus its first exposure to the ideas of the New Left. Wittgenstein himself, I think, might have savored the irony of what followed at a football-obsessed state university in the American heartland.

Every week there was a Hyde Park forum in the student union. Davidson and Spangler made this their soapbox, haranguing students dressed in the conservative uniform of the season—the women in stockings and skirts that reached below the knee, the men in slacks, yellow shirts, burgundy sweaters, and heavy wingtip shoes. For the most part, the students gathered to make fun of these wild-eyed, long-haired crazies with their stacks of philosophy books, their torn jeans and goofy ideas. I agreed with Davidson and Spangler on many issues, especially the effort to integrate the racially divided South, but I wrote a piece for the student newspaper saying that if they wanted people to take them seriously, they should get a haircut. When they talked about Vietnam, I had the urge to shout them down. This was unpatriotic, subversive stuff, and I was not prepared to listen.

Spangler and Davidson, however, began winning converts. In the spring of 1966, a small group of antiwar demonstrators tried to hold a candlelight vigil in the rain outside Love Library on campus. We stared at them, the peacenik weirdos, thinking they were probably commies, because you would have to be a commie to oppose a war against communism. One was a tall, thin, balding man in his fifties, probably a professor. He had black-rimmed glasses, and he could hardly see through the rain. He was trying to shelter his candle and keep it burning while a group of young jocks in letter jackets taunted him. I saw his face, and it stayed with me. He seemed noble; his quiet dignity planted a seed, a shred of doubt. Was it possible he could be right?

I had friends among those who were won over to the antiwar cause as early as 1966. Among them were my first beatnik acquaintance and future roommate, Larry Grossman, and Mick Lowe, another young journalist, who was among the first in my crowd to turn against the war. For the most part, I watched from the sidelines, busily hurrying from class to track workouts to my job on the student newspaper. I knew what was going on around the country, because with the track team I traveled to campuses such as Wisconsin and Arizona State, where the antiwar movement was already prominent. But even at Nebraska, demonstrations against the war got bigger every year. Many of the short-haired kids who taunted the demonstrators and laughed at Davidson and Spangler in 1965 were growing their hair and carrying their own candles by 1967. The debate over the war was fierce—the Hyde Park forums at the student union where Davidson and Spangler delivered their fiery speeches were sometimes disrupted by pushing and shoving matches between prowar and antiwar students. We argued the war in the student union, in the off-campus bars, on the way to classes, during class, with our friends and lovers on weekends.

By the spring of my freshman year, I was already bored with the humdrum courses in journalism school. Literature was infinitely more exciting than writing mock newspaper stories; I decided to take a double major, and threw myself into English literature courses with real passion. We studied Keats and Shelley and Shakespeare, but we also looked at modern poetry, including the war poems of Wilfred Owen and Randall Jarrell. If Owen's bitter irony hinted that it might not have been sweet and proper to die for one's country in the War to End All Wars, and if Jarrell could write something as deft and angry as "The Ballad of the Ball-Turret Gunner" about World War II, then how much less sweet and proper was a war as ugly and pointless as the conflict in Vietnam? I read Jarrell's short poem over and over, wincing anew each time the ball-turret gunner was washed out of his turret with a hose. There were dimensions to war that the recruiting sergeants, the Pentagon planners, and the jingoistic presidential speechwriters neatly avoided. Literature teaches you to see; as the war spiraled out of control, there was plenty to see. As long as I had the commitment to the Marine Corps, I managed to keep back my own doubts. Once I had my discharge, I was free to think for myself. If you wanted to believe in the war, the one thing you could not do was think.

By the time I returned after the Marine escapade for my junior year, the campus was a political hotbed, with arguments, debates, marches, speeches, rallies everywhere. My own political world revolved around the *Daily Nebraskan,* which we called "the Rag." The newspaper staff had its share of Young Republicans, but it also had an antiwar gang led by Mick Lowe and news editor Cheryl Tritt, who would take over as editor that spring. I wavered while Tritt and Lowe pressed their point of view. It was almost certain that I would follow Tritt as editor of the paper, and they wanted me on their side. Everywhere I turned that fall, it seemed there was someone else trying to convince me the war was wrong—including my mother, who was furious when I joined the Marines. "What do you think," she asked almost every time I talked with her, "those Viet Cong are going to come over here in their sampans and invade San Francisco?"

One day in October, Mick Lowe helped me finish proof-reading the next day's edition of the *Daily Nebraskan* and I drove him home. Mick was by far the most radical student in our group, an antiwar activist who took part in every demonstration, wrote antiwar columns, and tried to persuade me to turn against the war. On this night, he was determined I was going to listen. We sat in the car talking until long after midnight. Mick knew his stuff. We went through the history of it, especially the way John Foster Dulles, the secretary of state under Eisenhower, had worked to deny Ho Chi Minh the free elections he was promised after the Viet Minh defeated the French in the 1950s. We talked about the corrupt South Vietnamese leaders, and the fact that while eighteen-year-old Americans were being drafted to fight and die in Vietnam, the South Vietnamese were not yet drafting their own eighteen-year-olds. We talked about how the so-called strategic hamlets, designed to win "hearts and minds," were little more than concentration camps. We talked about international communism, and Mick emphasized that the pragmatic Ho Chi Minh was a Vietnamese nationalist first, a communist second.

"Hey, Jack, did you have a Career Day when you were a senior at Scottsbluff, the way we did here at Lincoln Southeast?"

"Yeah, we did."

"And did you get visits from all four branches of the service, wanting all the guys to enlist and telling you what a wonderful, invincible, ultramodern fighting machine we had, and how we were the most powerful nation on earth?"

"Sure."

"Well, just answer me one thing: how is it that we're being fought to a standstill by a bunch of guys in black pajamas wearing sandals made out of old jeep tires? It just doesn't add up, but we both know that much is true. Why?"

I had no answer. Mick paused to light another Camel.

"Because we're being shipped halfway 'round the world to go shoot some poor sonofabitch standing in a rice paddy about a hundred yards from his wife and kids, that's why. They fight better because they're fighting for their own homes. And what the hell are we fighting for? It's a bullshit war, Jack. I don't know about you, but I won't help fight it, period."

It was a step I could not imagine taking, but Mick finally wore me down on the war itself. By the time he got out of the car that night, I was firmly in the antiwar camp. I would oppose the war, do what I could to end it through marches and editorials and arguments in the student union, but if I was drafted, I had no doubt that I would serve. Fortunately, we still had a couple of years of college left before we had to worry about the draft, and surely the war would be over by then—especially if we all joined forces and worked hard to bring it to an end.

It was a strange season in America. Middle-class kids were in the streets, chanting their opposition to an American president in language that would have been unthinkable even a year before: "Hey! Hey! LBJ! How many kids did you kill today?" Johnson, a president we had once admired, was now seen as a monster. All across America, young people were mobilizing to stop the war. We thought we could force Johnson to make peace and bring the boys home instead of pouring more lives into the quagmire. We were a brilliant generation, the baby boomers born after World War II, brainy and idealistic and committed to the vision of our dead hero, John F. Kennedy, conveniently forgetting that Kennedy got the United States into Vietnam in the first place. We were going to make the world a better place, and we were going to begin by forcing our government to put an end to an immoral and disastrous war.

While we mobilized to stop the war, the State Department and the Pentagon kept insisting that America could see the light at the end of the tunnel. But in January 1968, the Viet Cong and North Vietnamese launched the Tet offensive with seventy thousand troops. They were able to mount coordinated attacks throughout South Vietnam, to occupy part of the American embassy in Saigon, and to shock the world. The Viet Cong suffered such heavy losses that their ability to fight would be seriously hampered for the remainder of the war, but the impact on American politics was almost worth the sacrifice. Two months later, Lyndon Johnson announced that he would not seek or accept the Democratic Party nomination to run for another term in 1968, his vision of a Great Society destroyed by a pointless war on the other side of the world. Four days after Johnson's speech, Martin Luther King, Jr., was murdered in Memphis. On May 10, 1968, peace talks finally began in Paris, but more Americans would die in Vietnam after the talks began than in the three years before the two sides got to the table. In early June, Bobby Kennedy was murdered in Los Angeles. While I watched in impotent fury from my desk in the newsroom of the *Detroit Free Press,* Mayor Richard Daley's police rioted in Chicago, and Hubert Humphrey defeated the antiwar candidate, Eugene McCarthy, for the Democratic nomination.

In the fall of 1968 I took over as the openly antiwar editor of the *Daily Nebraskan.* Humphrey waited too long to cut himself loose from the war policies of Lyndon Johnson. We watched the election the first week of November in despair. Nixon and Henry Kissinger took over the war. In Nixon's first year in office, ten thousand Americans died in Vietnam, and Lieutenant William Calley and Sergeant David Mitchell were indicted for the massacre of South Vietnamese civilians at My Lai.

By the time I got my draft notice, American ground troops had been in Vietnam four and a half years. We had dropped more bombs on Vietnam than we dropped on Germany in World War II. The war went on.

■   ■   ■

On the way out of Lincoln I pick up a long-haired hitchhiker on the outskirts of the city. He's a thirty-year-old Australian with granny glasses and long, curly hair, an engineer by training who has worked all over the world. When I mention that I'm on my way into the army, he has a story to tell.

"My great-grandfather was a Yank," he says. "Deserted from the Union army during the Civil War and went to Canada. Then he decided he wasn't far enough from all that insanity, so he got on a boat in Vancouver and sailed to Melbourne.

I'd be a Yank myself if it wasn't for the Civil War, most likely. You should think about it yourself, mate. I know some Aussies who've been killed in Vietnam. Nasty place, pointless war. No reason to get yourself killed in a war they can't win, y'know?"

I drop him off at Ogallala, where he's catching the new stretch of Interstate 76 that forks off southwest to Denver. Ogallala is where the country does a shape-shift going west, Nebraska a lot like Indiana or Illinois or Iowa until you reach this old cow town where the road bends northwest to Cheyenne. The trees thin out, the air turns dry, you hit the first of the badlands, and the vault of blue sky overhead is suddenly higher by a dozen miles than the smoggy sky back east. You enter God's country with a little gasp and a prayer, thinking this is just where God would kick back if he had time, up at the top of one of those hills in a big old ranch house with a herd of white-faced Herefords spread out below and sunsets like this one: a runny three-egg omelet red with Tabasco sauce cracked over the ragged line of bluffs in the distance.

It's home. No matter what else, I will be home for the first time since Thanksgiving 1968, back in a place that moves me like no other spot in the universe. I drive the last stretch in growing darkness with the speedometer locked on 90, in a hurry now, past fallow beet fields, past the feedlots out back of the sugar factory where Pop and I hauled thousands of tons of alfalfa, summer and winter. I hit the edge of town, brake hard, and crawl along East Overland behind slow-moving pickups, taking it all in. The streets wide and smooth, people on the sidewalks nodding and saying hello as they pass, a traffic jam four cars backed up at a traffic light. Cross the railroad tracks, make the right onto West Overland, ease on down six blocks to our tiny white house on the corner with the porch light on, Mom waiting at the door, Pop and my sisters behind her. Chili on the stove and pie in the oven and by gosh, Jack boy, it's good to see you.

*

I suppose you can grow up in a place and leave it and never think about it again, comb it out of your system the way we used to comb alfalfa out of our hair. Not Scottsbluff. Not for me. It is harsh and dry and wild and beautiful and strange, and I love it like no other place on earth. It's in me like blood or breath, perhaps because you rub up so close to life and death in country like this.

I was thirteen on an icy Christmas Eve in 1959 when Pop called me out because our big old Holstein cow was about to calve. We tried to help her for three hours, gave up and called the vet. By the time he rolled up in his pickup it was near midnight and we were close to losing cow and calf. With the vet giving instructions, I started our old tractor and backed it into the corral. We wrapped a big soft rope around the calf's front legs and tied it to the rear hitch on the tractor. I put it in gear, easing off the clutch. The big tires began to turn, biting deep into the frozen manure. My legs were shaking with cold. I was terrified my foot would slip off the frozen metal clutch pedal, the clutch would slip, and the tractor would tear the calf apart. Pop kept motioning with one big hand, "Go on, go on . . . take 'er easy, now, easy . . . go on, give 'er a little gas . . ." Easing the tractor an inch at a time, the rope taut, the calf's head clear with the vet guiding it. The calf free at last, steaming in the cold, the big old cow bellowing in joy or pain, the calf wrapped in blankets to spend the night on our kitchen floor, sleeping in front of the heater while I stumbled to bed, too tired to say how good it felt.

Three years later, my first summer working out from home, my friend Johnny Vorse and I earning a dollar an hour as cowhands and all-around flunkies on a 1,600-acre ranch owned by a banker who didn't know livestock or machinery or much of anything except how to cuss at us, which he did long and often. The sour smell the hot wind carried down from the high bluffs that day said there was a Hereford up there with cancer eye, a disease that would start with a dripping eye and if a vet didn't catch it soon enough it would rot out a cow's head so you could smell her for miles. We rode up a mile or more into the hills and found the cow dead, half her head missing. We went back for the big tractor and two shovels, tied our shirts around our faces so we could take the smell, wrapped a log chain around her hind legs, dragged her a quarter mile downhill, and towed her off the edge into a deep gully. We worked most of the afternoon to bury the smell under hard clay, scraped up enough dirt to cover her, fell back worn out in the buffalo grass and stayed there flat on our backs for an hour, watching the high clouds drift.

"So that's death," Johnny said after a while.

"Yep," I said. "I guess it is."

We rounded up the rest of the herd on foot because the banker was too cheap to board one of Pop's horses and got them headed back to the corrals where a vet could check them for cancer eye. The sun was going down, the high bluffs painted rose with the sunset, the shadows long and cool, a hundred head of cattle easing down the slope ahead of us. A messy death, hot, dirty work under a sun that would strip your skin, a sunset that could make you ache from the sheer beauty of it. A place that was not going to let you go, no matter how far you wandered.

Back when they called this part of the world the Great American Desert, Scotts Bluff was a towering landmark for the wagons rolling west along the Oregon Trail on the south side of the Platte, which cut right through the bluffs, or the Mormon Trail on the north side, which followed a gentler, less steep path along the edge of what was our farm. Even from a distance you can see the lines in the rock that show how the bluffs were formed, in layer after layer over millions of years— a story told by a writer with infinite patience, chiseling his yarn out of the hills with wind and water and time. Scotts Bluff rises eight hundred feet almost straight up from the valley floor. On a clear day (and most days are clear out here) you can hike to the top of the bluff and catch your breath on one of the outcrops with a view all the way to Laramie Peak in the Rockies, a hundred miles to the west. The town is called Scottsbluff but the county is Scotts Bluff, and the bluff itself is a national monument—or the bluffs, because it is really one large bluff with other bluffs all around on either side of what was once the Oregon Trail. The bluff and the town and the county are all named after Hiram Scott, a fur trapper who had the misfortune to get himself wounded by an Indian arrow and was left here by William Sublette's party in 1828. Scott crawled to a spring at the base of the bluff and died. Sublette and his men found his skeleton the following spring on their next trip west. Scott's wife got his pay and he got a kind of immortality—but I imagine if you asked him, he would just as soon have taken his pay packet back to the wife and let them call the bluff after someone else.

It is high and dry up here, near four thousand feet above sea level, hot in the summer and sometimes bitterly cold in the winter, with nothing to stop the winds that blow across the plains, sometimes throwing up towering clouds of brown dust that seeps through windows, stops traffic, chokes off breath. Up in the ranch country, you're taught to pick up a bale of hay by turning it toward you so you'll have it as a shield in case there's a rattlesnake underneath. Closer to the river, the farmers who grow sugar beets and corn and beans and alfalfa on the irrigated land are rousted out of bed at 3 A.M. by the ditch rider, to be told that a head of water is coming their way and that they'll have to work eighteen or twenty hours a day for three or four days to divert the precious water to their crops, digging ditches in hip boots, hands down in the alkaline water until their skin cracks, siphoning endless tubes out of the narrow ditches and down the corn rows. And count themselves lucky they aren't out in the fields all day with the Mexican migrant workers, hoeing weeds and thinning beets, stooped into a permanent boomerang by labor that pulls a man down into the soil.

■ ■ ■

Home. Pop's easy chair up close to the furnace so he can fry his back while his feet freeze. Leaner and meaner and crazier than ever, seventy-three years old now and still working fourteen-hour days seven days a week training his horses. My mother gone straight from raising us to caring for a neighbor's kids, with more time now for her Chekhov and Tolstoy and Balzac and scratchy opera recordings on the old turntable, a woman ground down by decades of poverty, finding her salvation in books and children.

They're a strange couple, Jack Carney Todd and Maxine Marguerite Morgan. He quit school after second grade and had to move his lips when he read, running his finger under every line. She made it through tenth grade before her mother died and left her an orphan with two younger brothers to care for—but she never stopped reading and learning. He comes back from the corrals and tracks horse manure through the house, and she looks up from reading Chekhov and screams at him as she has every day for forty years to take his boots off outside, and he goes right on through to the bathroom at the back pretending he doesn't hear, stomps through the house again on his way out, kisses her on the neck and grabs a feel and goes back to the horses. When he's gone, she mops up his footprints and returns to her book.

He was on the downhill slope as a boxer when he picked her up in 1929, a thirty-one-year-old veteran of more ring wars than he could remember, riding a motorcycle with a side-car over the bridge between Scottsbluff and Gering, offering a ride to a pretty young pedestrian. She was nineteen, the daughter of a marriage that got her mother booted out of the house of Squier Jones, one of the wealthiest ranchers in Wyoming.

Velma Jones had married a no-good bronc rider named Frank Morgan, who left her with two kids—Maxine and her younger brother Kenny. Another marriage to a salesman who died young left Velma with another son, Jimmy Wilson. Velma was always frail, so much of the work of looking after Kenny and Jimmy fell to Maxine, even though she had a crippled left arm from a tumble into a fireplace at the age of three.

Pop came to Nebraska as a fourteen-year-old with five brothers and three sisters, the boys sent ahead from southeast Missouri to drive a hundred head of cattle across two states in 1912, while the women followed behind in wagons with the family patriarch, old W. T. Todd, a powerful, athletic man who could still hold a broomstick in both hands and jump over it when he was seventy years old. With four older brothers, Pop came out of the crib fighting and never really stopped—the Todd brothers always ready to fight at the blink of a crossed eye. They settled first in the sandhills ranch country up in northern Nebraska, and every Fourth of July the Todd brothers would go in to fight the town of Ainsworth. People would come from miles around to see the brawl, the Todd boys against all comers, Pop fighting the first of a lifetime of battles as a scrawny fourteen-year-old. If you asked him then or at any age how it was going he would say, "I'm a-fightin' 'em," and he was.

They were married in Denver in the summer of 1929, made a go of it on a homestead west of Scottsbluff through the early years of the depression. When his brothers started working in the defense plants in Oregon at the beginning of World War II, they sold the homestead and headed west. In a bar in Wyoming, Pop met a man with shares in a copper mine in Nevada to sell, handed him the proceeds from the sale of the homestead and never saw him again. Six months later, sick of the rain in Portland, he spotted a tree frog one morning and made Maxine start packing to go back to Nebraska. "Max," he said, "when it's so wet the frogs are takin' to the trees, it's time to go home."

Back in Nebraska, after seventeen years of an infertile marriage, I was born on his forty-eighth birthday. Eighteen months after that, he was driving the tractor pulling the harrow through the fields too fast because he wanted to make it to a barn dance that night, Maxine riding the harrow until he took a turn too quickly, flipped her off, and broke her leg—the second time she had suffered that particular accident, both times because he was in a hurry. She was in bed with the broken leg in a cast, and he was supposed to be watching me and wasn't. I got in the corral with a four-hundred-pound boar hog who tore my head open, probably with his tusks, split the skull in front, and almost ripped one eyelid off. Pop found me bleeding in the corral, carried me into the house, dropped me on the bed beside her, and said, "Max, I reckon the boy's dead." She screamed and grabbed, felt a heartbeat, called the doctor, who sewed me up good as new except for the split in my forehead which would never go away. She never forgave him for that, although I never understood whether she was angry because of the broken leg, because he let the hog get me, or because he told her I was dead, although it was probably a bit of all three.

There were other things she might have held against him. Until I was four we lived in a basement house, a one-story home set down in the ground so that only the windows peeked out. He drove her almost crazy, putting a ramp up to the edge of the roof where it hung down to the ground so he could race his motorcycle up and jump it over the house, a man past fifty years old still jumping motorcycles, chasing women, riding wild horses, and dealing with any difference of opinion by knocking out the man who disagreed with him, which tended to reduce her circle of friends. But after me there were three sisters, and he did what he could to take care of us—meaning that he worked, as he put it, from "cain't to cain't. So dark a man cain't see when he starts, so dark he cain't see when he's done."

What land we had left started as a three-hundred-acre farm down between the edge of town and the North Platte River. He sold it off piece by piece because, hard as he worked, he was too preoccupied with horses and boxers and women to make a go of it in the ruthless business of farming. Instead he trucked hay for a living at four dollars a ton and trained horses for the love of it, and I was seven the first time I drove the truck in the hayfields, twelve when I started working full days— every weekend, every holiday, every birthday. Every day all summer unless it rained, Sundays included. Thanksgiving, Christmas Day, New Year's Day, our shared birthday. On my twelfth birthday we were supposed to be shoveling manure out of the corrals all day and I rebelled, fought him in a running battle all that day and into the evening, found myself working in the headlights of the truck until near midnight, scooping horse manure like I was told. Winters we forked loose hay that sent cascades of snow sliding down our necks, in summer we heaved seventy-pound bales all day long when it was 100 degrees up in the sandhills and the stubborn deer flies made little cuts on your face that stung when the sweat ran into the cuts. We went home at night stumbling tired with cows to milk and pigs to feed, to bed on summer evenings with the light still fading outside, not yet light next morning when I'd hear him growl: "Let's go, Jack boy. We got hay to move. Up and at 'em." If I didn't move fast enough to suit him he'd grab one foot and yank me out onto the hard wooden planks of the floor.

We used to kid about how tough he was, but it was a thing to behold. He would get impatient waiting for me to bring a hammer and drive a bolt into the tractor with his bare fist, and I would come back to find him cussing and licking the blood off his knuckles. When I was ten, he roped a mule and dallied the rope around a post. He caught three fingers of his left hand in the rope, and when the mule took off the rope sawed two of the fingers clean off and left the other dangling. He hauled the mule in, got the rope off its neck, picked up the severed fingers, drove himself to the hospital, and dropped the fingers on the receptionist's desk.

"Do you reckon you got anybody here can sew these back on?" he asked.

She fainted. The fingers stayed off.

■ ■ ■

I'm standing in the doorway now, just home from Miami, bending to give my mother a hug, seeing how stooped and gray and frail she is. Pop starts on me.

"Say, you gotta get a GI haircut before you go into the army, son. You can't go in to be a fightin' man when you look like a girl."

"Why would I get a haircut when they're going to shave my damned head anyway?" Knowing that if I push it, big as I am, he will cut me to pieces with those fists. Seventy-two years old and he can still throw punches from all directions in ways you can't stop. He has never hit me. He doesn't have to, because I've seen what he can do, and I know how quickly an argument with him can end with big, strong men lying unconscious on the ground.

As usual, we do some yelling instead of punching and sit down to dinner, tempests in our family like dirt devils on the prairie. They blow up quick and disappear quick. We shift to safer ground, the one thing we share—a passion for boxing and admiration for Muhammad Ali. Long before Ali won his title as Cassius Clay, Pop was saying he would be the greatest fighter who ever lived. Unlike most white Americans he never wavered, not when Clay became Ali, not when Ali refused to be inducted in 1967, not now. We don't see eye to eye on the war, but we agree on Ali. It's a start.

Chili and cornbread and carrot salad and a corn casserole

all out on the table, apple pie in the oven. I am full of myself, bragging about the *Herald* and Mariela. We are all talking at once, trying to forget that I have a November 13 date with the Selective Service. As usual, Pop has a dozen questions I can't answer: How many presses do they have at the *Herald*? (I don't know.) Is Miami a port for Atlantic shipping? (I think so but I'm not sure.) When they built all those bridges out to the Florida Keys, how did they sink the supports in the ocean? (I don't know.) Are the big skyscrapers in Miami built to stand up to a hurricane? (I don't know.) Is there anything about Miami I do know?

My mother hates the war almost as much as I do. We wait to talk about it until he has finished dinner and is back in his easy chair, ten feet away but too deaf to hear what we are saying.

"You know, I think I'd almost rather have you in Canada than over there fighting this stupid war," she says.

"I know. I thought about it. I don't think I could stand the thought of being cut off from my country forever and ever."

"Well, it's better than you getting killed, isn't it? Or shot up so bad you spend the rest of your life in a wheelchair?"

"Mom, that's not gonna happen."

"You don't know that."

"They have to end this war. They can't keep fighting it. The whole country is against it. Nixon might bring everyone home before I get through basic."

I don't believe that, but I have to say it. Sitting in that kitchen where the linoleum is still cracked, where the single bare bulb in the kitchen still hangs from a cord heavy with electrician's tape, where the swaybacked ceiling looks like it might collapse over the dinner table, where the wind blows through the cracks in winter. She is almost sixty now and worn out, having raised four children in this tiny house, usually with no more than twenty dollars a week for grocery money, often with much less. I will never know how she got us through the winter when I was twelve, when Pop spent six months in the veterans' hospital in Cheyenne after falling off a hay truck and at the end of the winter we had nothing left to eat except corn-bread with milk and butter from the one cow I had to milk morning and night.

We have been hurled into the world on the force of her dreams. Having come this far, she will concede nothing to a nasty war in a far-off place. There is nothing I can say that matters. When I leave the kitchen she is still sitting at the table, lips pursed, chin resting in her palm, thinking.

Sonny comes busting through the door late the next after-noon, just in time for dinner. Like he always did, like it hasn't been more than three years since we've seen each other, like we just walked home from school two hours before. Says he was driving by and saw my car with the Florida plates and hit the brakes. Comes in grinning that let's-get-into-some-trouble-to-night grin, still nearly eight inches shorter than me but heavier than he used to be by ten pounds of muscle—that and a tight khaki T-shirt the only sign he has been anywhere near Uncle Sam's army. He's been out just long enough to make it home from Fort Dix in time to catch me on the way in. He sits down and helps himself to meatloaf and scalloped potatoes and car-rot and pineapple salad, the two of us hugging and backslap-ping and talking with our mouths full. Apart from Mariela, there is no one on the planet I would rather see.

Mom keeps a weather eye on Sonny. I was four years old first time we hooked up, the way kids do, his parents just moved into the first of the new houses they built where our farm used to be, the two of us out in the field chasing grass-hoppers when we decided to be best friends for life. I invited Sonny into the kitchen where Mom was unpacking groceries from the co-op. He scrambled up onto the table and ripped open a box of corn flakes and started shoving the dry cereal into his mouth, and I thought it was the funniest thing I'd ever seen until Mom told me to get that kid out of the house and tell him he was never allowed in our kitchen again. That rule lasted about a day, but she always kept her eye on him anyway, just in case he decided to hop up on the table and attack the groceries.

Me, I'd find Sonny hard to forget even if I wanted to. I have a scar on my right forearm where I ran into the back of a pickup truck trying to catch a pass from Sonny while we were playing touch football on the street. A scar at the hairline on my forehead where Sonny threw a dirt clod at me and found out too late there was a rock inside, a fact we established after I finished pounding on him and went to the hospital for stitches. No scar at all where we tried to leave one, when I decided in fourth grade that I was in love with a girl named Vicki Ruplinger. We went fishing down by the Platte River and Sonny helped me carve her initials on my left arm with a dull pocketknife, a job that took most of the afternoon. The "V" was easy, the "R" hurt like hell. Both scabs healed and disappeared before my mother noticed what I had done to myself. No scar either from the time we were fishing at the gravel pit and the gravel along the shore caved out from under me and I fell in, a panicky, fully dressed ten-year-old, and Sonny stayed cool enough to pull me out with his fishing rod.

We hunted crawfish together along the banks of the Platte. We wrecked red ant hills just to see how long it would take the ants to build them back up again. We played marbles in the dirt along the street they would call Avenue F after they paved it, "potsies" where you drew a circle and tried to drive the marbles out of the circle with your shooter, "chasies" where you tossed a marble out and tried to hit it from five or ten feet away. We threw rocks at everything, especially stray cats, birds, streetlights, and little sisters. We played basketball and football and baseball, Sonny better at everything until I got too big for him to handle.

When I was sixteen and six foot five and could finally throw harder than he could, I put Sonny in the hospital playing sandlot baseball. I was pitching and fielded a ground ball and whirled to throw to second base. Sonny was sliding in and the throw caught him in the kidneys. When he could finally move I had to help carry him home. When he started urinating blood the next day, his parents took him to the hospital. It didn't matter. We forgave each other for everything. We took my .22 rifle and his .410 shotgun and blasted at everything that moved in the woods which ran from the edge of our old farm another mile down to the river. Sonny, following along behind me one day when we were thirteen or fourteen, blew a magpie out of a tree five feet above my head with the shotgun. Blood, guts, and feathers rained down on me. I ripped the shotgun out of his hands and pummeled him until he was as bloody as I was, then we got up and laughed over the whole thing, the pair of us covered with blood and feathers and bird guts.

When I wasn't out on the hay truck with Pop, we made up Robin Hood games and fired real arrows at the sheriff's men, cleverly disguised as bales of hay. We let a big, shambling neighborhood kid named Ron Bales follow us everywhere and play Friar Tuck while Sonny was always Robin and I was Little John, and we would have quarterstaff fights with long wooden poles. We played World War II, building snow forts in winter, dirt forts in summer where the new housing was going up. Ron always had to play the Nazi, Sonny and I were the GIs who blasted him out of his bunker on D-day. Ron never complained when we got a little rough. He was so big and strong he could have crushed either of us, but he was easygoing and patient and never lashed out except when we attacked the red ant hills. Ron said it was mean to pour kerosene down an anthill and light it on fire, especially when we put firecrackers in there, too.

We graduated from playing marbles in the dirt and throwing rocks at the streetlights to dragging Main chasing girls, but

we stayed friends. We were together the night they fried Starkweather in Lincoln in the summer of '59, a bunch of us hanging out with some older kids a few streets away, everybody
crazy because we knew Starkweather was going to die. Some
kid who had been indoors listening to the radio came out to
say that when they fried Starkweather at the state pen, it took
so much current the lights dimmed in that part of Lincoln. We
raced through the streets, played kick the can and necked with
girls where we hid in the darkness under the hedges, high and
crazy because we were young and alive and the killer with the
Coke-bottle eyes was dead.

When I went away to the university Sonny stayed home, did
a year at the junior college in Scottsbluff, finally gave up on
school in 1967. That cost him his college deferment, and he
was drafted and sent to Vietnam. Sonny doesn't talk about the
army much now except to say that he hated it. When he got
back from Vietnam the chickenshit at Fort Dix nearly drove
him crazy, bitter noncoms and officers who hadn't been in
combat riding his ass for no reason at all. He nearly got into a
fight with one noncom at Fort Dix, went AWOL for a week,
ended up going back to finish his hitch. That much he'll talk
about, but if I push him about Vietnam, he clams up altogether.

My last night in Scottsbluff I head down to Sonny's after dinner. We have a couple of beers upstairs with his parents, take a
six-pack down to his bedroom in the basement. There are me-
mentos of Vietnam everywhere. Pictures of Sonny with his
unit or in Saigon. A North Vietnamese helmet and pistol belt
without the pistol. A bayonet. Sonny's old combat boots. I flop
on his bed and open another beer and we sit there yakking
about the Cornhusker football team and a girl Sonny liked in
high school, speculating about where the army is likely to send
me. Everything is cool, we're about two beers into the six-

pack. We're quiet for a minute, and then Sonny looks at me with the expression of a man who has just run into his own ghost in a dark alley.

"You can't go," he says. "You just can't go."

"What?"

"You can't go into the army. I mean it. You can't go. You gotta go to Canada."

"Sonny, man—I can't do that. I told you. I thought about it every way there is and I've got no choice. I've got to go do my hitch."

Sonny shakes his head, staring at the floor.

"Look, I can't let you get drafted. I'll drive you to Canada myself. We can take off right now. You can't go through that shit. I took enough of it for both of us. We have to get you out."

"Thanks for worrying about me, man, but I did Marine Corps officer training. I know about the bullshit. I can take it. The army can't be as bad as the Marines."

"I'm not talking about chickenshit sergeants. I'm talking about Vietnam. You got no idea how bad it is there. You don't know how fucked up you're going to be if you make it back."

"You went, and you don't seem all that messed up."

He looks at me slow and steady, and I know what a dumb thing I just said.

"You can't go."

"I gotta go, man. I promised Mariela. And I can't do that to my folks. God, look how old they are. It would kill them if I went to Canada."

"It's gonna be worse for them if you go to 'Nam and get shot up. I had a piece of shrapnel go right through me, almost took my nuts off. I'm lucky to be sitting here right now. And that wasn't even the worst part."

He sits there rocking back and forth, arms wrapped around his ribs like he's trying to hold himself in.

"Look," he says. "I'm gonna show you some pictures. Nobody has seen this stuff except the guys who were there, but you have to see it because you gotta understand what you're getting into."

I put a hand on his shoulder again and try to steady him, but he doesn't want to be steadied. He pulls his old army foot-locker over to the foot of the bed, opens the lock, pulls out two or three big stacks of photos, and sits down on the bed next to me. When we were kids we sat in this same room and thumbed through his father's collection of men's magazines from the '50s, all of them full of pictures of women with pneumatic breasts (the nipples always artfully concealed) and stories like "I Was a Nazi Love-Slave," illustrated with a drawing of a beautiful woman tied to a post, her dress ripped half off, a cruel Nazi colonel about to ravish her. What we are looking at now is obscene in a way those corny old magazines could never be.

For the next three hours, Sonny does everything he can to persuade me to go to Canada. He doesn't say much, just a word or two to explain where a picture was taken, who was in it. The first photos are very ordinary, young soldiers stripped down to the waist, standing outside tents, playing cards, drinking beer, lying on their bunks. There are at least a hundred photos taken all around the helicopter base where Sonny served as a perimeter guard—shots of him and his buddies smoking cigarettes and playing poker, *Playboy* pinups on the wall in the background, all of them grinning like they were away at Boy Scout camp for the summer.

Sonny pulls out a shot of some of the helicopters, then one of the guard towers, another of him with a German shepherd. "See these dogs, they're supposed to warn you if anything is coming. I was in-country a week, I did my first shift on night guard duty. Scared shitless, you know. Like it's just you and your rifle and the dog and it's dark as hell and you know you're not going to make it till morning. The sun comes up and we find the guy on the next tower, him and his dog, both of 'em with their throats slit. We didn't hear a fucking thing, but they're both dead. That poor damned dog never even got a chance to bark."

Sonny had to go back on guard duty after that. Night after night, week after week. Waiting for sapper attacks, holding a .12-gauge shotgun to hit an enemy at close range in case the Viet Cong broke through the perimeter and were on top of you before you saw them. Waiting for night when they would sneak in, moving into the wind so the dog wouldn't pick up their scent, killing you quiet. The Viet Cong never got any of the dogs or the guards again while Sonny was there. They didn't have to.

He keeps leafing through the photos. Guys in his unit strung out on patrol in one photo, and you can almost smell the boredom and sweat and fear. Another shot: three body bags, dead GIs killed in a sapper attack. More photos: soldiers smoking potent Vietnamese dope, using the barrel of an M-16 as a handy pipe. "Guys were wired all the time," Sonny says. "Speed and weed. The speed hops you up so you hear everything, the weed cools you out so you don't jump right out of your skin. Beer, scotch, tequila, some kind of killer hooch the Vietnamese make. Anything, just so you stay fucked up."

Sonny was out on patrol one afternoon and his platoon fell out for a break. He went off fifty yards into the jungle to take a shit in peace. He had his pants down around his ankles when a small man in black pajamas came around a bend in the path a dozen feet away, AK-47 dangling at his side. Sonny brought his M-16 up and panic-fired the entire clip on full automatic, all twenty rounds. M-16s on full automatic have a tendency to climb, so he fired the first shot over the head of the V.C. and the rest of the clip into the trees and was left holding an empty rifle with the muzzle pointed at the sky. The Viet Cong was a kid—sixteen, maybe seventeen years old. He pointed his AK-47 at Sonny's chest, aimed—and for no reason at all just melted away into the jungle without firing a shot. The rest of Sonny's squad came crashing through the bush a minute or two later, but the kid was long gone.

The mortar attacks were bad, the suicidal sapper attacks were worse. Viet Cong sappers carrying satchel charges to blow up the helicopters attacked the wire at night, night after night. It should have been impossible for them to get through but they got through anyway. There was coiled razor wire around the perimeter, and there were Claymore mines rigged with tripwires low to the ground, and GIs with radios, shotguns, rifles with infrared night scopes, spotlights and flares and M-60 machine guns and all the rest of the hardware supplied by the richest nation on earth, and still the Viet Cong slipped through, sometimes in twos and threes, sometimes swarming the wire in company-sized attacks. A few got as far as the helicopters and the big birds went off like fireworks on the Fourth of July, making targets of the GIs silhouetted against the burning choppers. When the Viet Cong came in strength there were massed attacks on the razor wire, Claymores exploding, pitched battles at close range with the Viet Cong screaming and the guards firing blindly into the darkness with their .12-gauge shotguns and M-16s, never knowing whether they hit anyone until they found the bodies on the wire next morning.

That's how we come to the worst of it, photos taken the morning after one of the assaults on the wire. Dead GIs zipped into body bags, Viet Cong in their black pajamas still draped over the wire, some with chunks of their bodies blown away by the shotguns. Soldiers with dead eyes stare into the camera, grinning, necklaces made of Viet Cong ears around their necks.

Sonny is not in any of the photos. I don't know if he took them or if they were taken by someone else in his unit or if Sonny was even present when they were taken. We're not talking a whole lot now, just staring at the pictures. There is no passing judgment on the GIs in the snapshots. They were in a nasty war ten thousand miles from home, their buddies dying around them for no reason they could understand. They had no one but one another. They killed in furious combat and then, half crazy with fear and blood and triumph, took their trophies. They were operating in a country where every smiling kid on a bicycle might be carrying a grenade or a satchel charge, where every mama-san might be a Viet Cong.

No wonder the guys who were there went a little crazy: One day you're hanging out with your buddies in the parking lot of the A&W trying to pick up girls. Four months later you're killing a man with a shotgun in the dark, cutting off his ears, grinning for a buddy with a Kodak. You do your tour, fly home to The World, find it nothing like the world you left behind, go back to the A&W, try to pretend everything is the same—and the first thing you learn is that no one wants to hear the stories you don't want to tell.

There's nothing I can say to Sonny that won't sound cheap and dumb. He packs the photos back into the footlocker, padlocks it without saying a word. We pop open the last two beers, sit there looking at our feet.

"Y'know, the only way I can go to sleep, I have to turn on every light in the room and leave the radio on. Even then, most nights I just lay there."

"Maybe you should see if they'll give you a little help. You know, help you get back into the world."

"Shit. I can't go talk to some shrink, some asshole's gonna tell me to feel good about myself. I know what's there and I know what's here and, man, you just can't go from there to here. One way or another, you have to stay out of the army."

"I can't, Sonny. I just can't do it."

"You can't go, man. You just can't."

"I have to."

We sit there quiet for a while, finish the beer, make plans for Sonny to drive me to the bus station the next afternoon for the trip to the induction center in Denver. I walk home, crawl into bed, lie there staring at the ceiling, thinking about the memories Sonny takes to bed every night. Grinning GIs and body bags, the smell of blood and cordite, the chatter of AK-47s, moans of the dying, the coolness of damp clay when your face is pressed into the dirt and the earth shakes from the concussion of mortar rounds, shrapnel screaming through the night.

At 4 A.M. I hear Pop get up right on time, stomp around getting dressed, make a racket before heading out to do his chores. I'm too wired to sleep, too tired to help him with the livestock. I pull the blankets up to my chin, shivering with cold, wait till sunup to crawl out of bed. Mom has coffee on, pancakes, fried eggs, bacon, orange juice. She asks me if everything is OK with Sonny.

"Yeah, Mom. He's just fine."

Part II

IN THE WINTER OF ALTAMONT

THE TRAILWAYS BUS from Scottsbluff to Denver is more like a station wagon than a bus. Six or seven of us aboard, the others headed for draft physicals. I'm the only draftee. Not wanting to talk, busy saying good-bye to the bluff, the badlands, the Wildcat Hills. Thin late autumn sunlight over rough country, dark before we reach Cheyenne, hunkered down in the back seat of the van staring out the window. Remembering high school basketball trips over this same road on the way to play Cheyenne Central, and summers laying asphalt on the highway between Scottsbluff and the Wildcat Hills. Long days in the heat then, off at six or seven in the evening, make the forty-four-mile drive to Kimball to visit a girlfriend, back after midnight, up at five for another twelve-hour day laying roads. Working all day, making out half the night, so tired on the job I fell asleep reeling cable out the back of a pickup truck one hot afternoon, tumbled out of the truck onto soft earth and stayed put, dreaming sweet dreams until a foreman came along to kick me awake.

Scottsbluff to Kimball, Kimball to Cheyenne, Cheyenne to Denver. Nebraska to Wyoming to Colorado. I know one of the guys on the bus from high school. We room together at a big old hotel in Denver where the Selective Service picks up the tab, grab some dinner and get far too drunk in a strip bar across the street. A blonde stripper joins us at our table. Four or five drinks later, alternating tequila shots and beer, and she's in our room. An hour later two Denver vice squad detectives are banging on the door, beginning a chaotic escapade with the detectives threatening to lock us up because we won't lie and swear we paid her. It ends with them escorting the two of us directly from the Denver jail to Selective Service headquarters at eight the next morning after a sleepless night, massive hangovers just beginning to kick in. But they aren't going to 4-F you for a hangover, not even if your eyeballs jump out of your head and do a jitterbug on your skull.

Inside this big, gloomy building in downtown Denver they are already doing what the military does best, which is to make you stand in line for no reason before they shuffle you somewhere else and then decide it's all a foul-up and send you back where you started. Papers to fill out, eye tests, another physical. "Turn your head and cough. Next! Turn your head and cough. Next!" We all look pale and sickly, standing there shivering in our white jockey shorts, waiting for bored doctors to squeeze our balls. Meat on the rack.

Amazing how long it takes to get drafted. By noon it has started to snow outside in downtown Denver, a sparse November snowfall. My head is throbbing. I keep going to the water fountain, but no matter how much water I drink it isn't enough to counter the booze from the night before. A little man with a jackhammer is trying to bust out of my skull, but this is not a place where you can walk up to someone and say you need a couple of aspirin. I can't help but feel the numb horror of it all, even through the hangover. All these young men and old boys shuffling along on autopilot, sheep to the slaughter.

At this point the only way out is to do what Muhammad Ali did—to refuse to step forward to take the oath. When they tell you to step up, you stay put and keep your mouth shut and let them do the rest. That's your only choice, because the physicals are a joke. If you don't foam at the mouth, if you have four limbs more or less attached to your body and you can see ten feet in front of you, you are going. We all try to look as sickly as we can, hoping some kindly doc will discover we have congestive heart failure or syphilis or polio or beriberi and send us home, but at this point if you can walk and breathe, you're a soldier. There is one exception: a tall, skinny hippie kid about nineteen years old, hair halfway down his back and patched jeans and that special light in his eyes that says, "I just dropped two tabs of Sunshine acid and I'm tripping my brains out and I don't give a fuck what happens to me." He says he was hurt in a motorcycle accident. He has a long purple scar as thick as a snake which begins at the back of his neck, curves down over his hip, and disappears somewhere inside his thigh. He strips down while two or three doctors examine the scar. They ask exactly what the injuries are and when the accident happened, and he explains how he wiped out on a Harley running too fast on a dirt road west of Boulder, and they send him home classified 4-F. Not physically qualified for duty in the U.S. military. We all stare. It's a miracle, Lazarus rising from the dead. He wanders over to us, giggling, high as a Chinese kite, a free man, his shirt still off so we can admire this talisman, his passport to civilization. A motorcycle wreck is a terrible thing, but that scar has real beauty, like a prairie sunset or a loaf of fresh-baked bread or Brigitte Bardot's lips. We all want one just like it. We watch him leave, cursing the awful luck that kept us from the sort of accident that shatters bone and rips flesh and leaves a lovely deep purple 4-F scar curling like a diamondback rattler from the nape of your neck all the way to your crotch.

In mid-afternoon we are called into a big room and forced to stand at attention, shoulder to shoulder. Backs straight, eyes forward, men and boys. We are to be evaluated for the U.S. Marine Corps, beef on the hoof. The proud Corps is supposed to be an all-volunteer unit—Semper Fi and Montezuma's balls and the whores of Tripoli and all that—but as the Vietnam War drags on it becomes more and more difficult to find young men who are brave enough or stupid enough to join the Marines, so the Corps has been forced to take draftees. One experience with the Corps was enough for me. I'm twenty-three now and I smoke like a '56 Chevy in need of a ring job. If officer training at Quantico was like being dead, I can't imagine what Marine basic for enlisted men is like. I hunch my shoulders and pull in my chest, do my best to look like a geek who has never done a pushup in his life. The Marine sergeants march up and down the line and pick out a dozen muscular nineteen-year-olds with low foreheads and thick shoulders. Dumb and strong, perfect Marine material. The Dirty Dozen are marched off to a separate induction. They will end up at the Marine base in San Diego while we are bound for the army at Fort Lewis, Washington, an hour or so south of Seattle, within sight of beautiful Mount Rainier.

Fort Lewis is also, although this will not occur to any of us for some time, within easy hitchhiking distance of the Canadian border and the beautiful Canadian city of Vancouver.

Within an hour we are sworn in. Standing there waiting to step forward, I think one last time about refusing to take the step, following Ali's example. But Ali knew what he was going to do and had lawyers waiting. This is not the kind of thing you do on an impulse. When the time comes and they order us to step up I take a deep breath, wait a beat or two as the others move forward in unison, finally move up as a sergeant's glare warns of the consequences. "Raise your right hand and repeat after me . . ." It is the second time in three years I have taken an oath of loyalty to the U.S. military. The first time I wanted nothing more than to lead a platoon of Marines through the jungle. This time I mumble along with the rest, but I don't believe a word of it. My oath, if I have pledged it, belongs to Mariela in Miami, not to the U.S. Army.

Before we are put on buses to Stapleton Airport for the flight to Seattle, there's time to call home to tell my mother we're bound for Fort Lewis, and then time to call Mariela in Miami. It's an awful call, standing there at a pay phone in that big, cold building in Denver watching it snow, feeling guilty as hell about the stripper, even if I was so drunk I could hardly remember my own name when the detectives came kicking at the door. Mariela is crying. I stare out at the snow beginning to collect on the streets of Denver, the darkening November afternoon. I couldn't cry if I wanted to. I just feel empty, numb, and hung over. So desolate it's like being dead without the body bag.

"I love you, Jacko," she says.

"I love you, too." It's the only time I say it to her when I don't mean it. To be in love, you have to feel alive.

I doze a little on the plane to Seattle. One night sitting up with Sonny looking at the pornography of Vietnam, next night split between a stripper and the Denver jail. I haven't really slept in sixty hours and I'm too tired to care what happens to me. In Seattle there's another long wait before buses take us to Fort Lewis, somewhere outside Tacoma. We arrive sometime after midnight. In the Marines they jumped us as soon as we got off the bus, a dozen sergeants screaming contradictory orders. We did pushups that night until our arms were ready to fall off and hit our beds dead with exhaustion for a four-hour sleep. The army just sends us off to bed. We don't want to be here, and it seems they don't much want us either.

We get five hours' sleep, wake numb with exhaustion. It's dark outside, a heavy, liquid night, but the lights are on in this large, echoing room. Brilliant lights, lights for an inquisition. Men running everywhere, shouting, the thud of heavy combat boots on concrete floors. It's Quantico, Camp Upshur, 1967, Marine Corps, sergeants on our case, have to move. Move. Wake and move.

I sit on the edge of the top bunk. Guys in their skivvies running around, shivering, sliding into blue jeans and sweaters and running shoes, the picture all wrong. Not Quantico but where? When? What is going on here? Dream?

Beefy drill sergeant with his face in my face.

"What is it, you long, tall drink of water? You a fucking princess, you don't have to get up with the rest of the world? I said you got two minutes to shit-shave-shower and line up outside! Now move-move-move-move-MOVE!"

Dazed, pulling on jeans like the rest, slow dawn of a reality chilly as the rain outside. November. 1969. Drafted. Army. Fort Lewis. Jesus H. Fucking Christ. Sweet Jesus. Not this again. I can't take it. No way.

Fall into clothes, fall outside, line up by platoons. Hundreds of men and boys, still in civvies on this first morning of basic, forming up as far as you can see in any direction, distant platoons fading into the mist. Some with hair down to their shoulders or longer. Black guys with tall Afros. Hippies with wet curls dripping in the rain. Here and there bell-bottom trousers. Blue jeans, some ripped. One guy in sandals. All of us wandering about, no idea how to get into formation, sergeants bellowing. I stand there like the rest until I hear enough, then do what we would have done in the Marine Corps. Tallest guy goes to the right, front rank. Get myself up there, holler at drifting civilians to form a rank to my left. You there, dress right. Yes, that means look at me, put your right arm out, touch the left shoulder of the guy on your right to get proper spacing, get in line before we have to do pushups in the rain.

Rain falling that is not rain. More like mist. Cold mist. Our faces wet with it. No hats, not even a barracks cap. Streetlights on all over the base, still inky dark outside the cones of light, no idea what this place might look like when the sun is shining, if the sun ever shines here. Barracks and streetlights and sidewalks and the rhythmic thwick-thwick-thwick of combat boots on wet gravel as other platoons double-time through the mist, rifles held at port arms, looking like real soldiers. Not like us: freaks, insurance salesmen, petty thieves, journalists, drug dealers. Drummers and dreamers and derelicts, gawking at the troops.

March to breakfast. Left-right-left, more or less. Watery eggs, burnt toast, soggy potatoes, bacon black as the night outside. Choke down a few bites, bowels tight with nerves. Back outside, march to a warehouse. Issued fatigues: baggy, meant to fit an alien army somewhere in outer space. We look ridiculous, especially next to the drill sergeants with their starched fatigues and spit shines. Boots good but stiff and uncomfortable. Drop civvies into bags, pull on army gear. Army socks, army underwear, army T-shirts, army fatigue pants, shirts, good warm field jacket. Double-time to the barber shop. Wade through long piles of hair to the chair, lose a three-month growth in less than sixty seconds, stumble back outside and try to recognize one another, blinking in the rain. Is that guy over there the one with the long blond ringlets? Funny, now he looks like a rapist. Hey, what happened to the 'fro, bro? You're shaved lean and mean now. The brothers look better with shaved heads, white boys become pointy-headed goofs.

It's November 14, 1969. At Cape Kennedy a Saturn rocket sits on the launch pad oozing liquid oxygen, preparing to send Pete Conrad and his *Apollo 12* crew on the second manned flight to the moon. South of the Cape in Miami, *Herald* reporters and editors will be working at breakneck speed, monitoring every minute of the flight. Around the country, organizers are putting together another national moratorium aimed at ending the Vietnam War. Hundreds of thousands of antiwar demonstrators will come out across the country the next day, November 15—250,000 in Washington, D.C., alone. Most of them quiet middle-class people who simply want to see an end to the killing and dying. In Vietnam the war goes on.

Here we march in the rain to a medical center where we are
pushed and prodded and vaccinated against what seems like a
hundred different tropical diseases. We are weighed and mea-
sured. Somewhere along the line I've shrunk an inch. I've been
a half inch over six foot five since I was sixteen, six foot seven
when it suited the purposes of a basketball coach. To the army
I'm a half inch over six foot four and a skinny 178 pounds.
On my identity card, a document so ugly it could be used to
frighten small children, I have a pointy head emphasized by
the absence of hair. ("This here," I can almost hear Governor
George Wallace saying, "is your basic pointy-headed intellectual, enemy of the white race and the great state of Alabama.")
Eyes closed tight in the picture, because there are some things
you can't bear to look at.

We are issued dog tags so they have something to check before they put you in a body bag. Assuming there's enough of
you left to scrape into a body bag. Assuming your dog tags
aren't blown to bits with the rest of you. Assuming there's anyone left to look for the pieces. We march back and forth in the
rain. We stand at attention next to some nameless building
while the sergeants disappear for half an hour and come back
and march us somewhere else. Also the wrong place. Another
half-hour wait at attention in the rain. Back to the beginning,
start over.

"Shape up or ship out!" the sergeants scream. Well, then,
we'll ship out.

Every platoon has a fool. It's a long-standing army tradition:
the Roman legions that marched into Gaul had to have their
quota of idiots. Ours is a bigger fool than most. His name is
Fillmore, he comes from Idaho, he has a sloping forehead and
buck teeth, and he does not belong in the army. The first day
they issue identical shaving kits to all of us and march us to
our permanent barracks, where we find lockers and bunks and
settle in. Everybody except Fillmore. Fillmore wanders from

bunk to bunk. Our platoon sergeant enters the barracks, a big, burly black sergeant who says we're to call him Sergeant James. Someone barks "Atten-SHUN!"

Fillmore wanders.

"Atten-SHUN!"

Fillmore wanders.

Sergeant James jumps in front of him. Fillmore drifts to a halt. James bellows, "Private, what do you say when a sergeant enters this barracks?"

Fillmore hesitates. "Hi, Sarge?"

We explode in guffaws and giggles. It's the tag line from the old Jim Nabors TV series, *Gomer Pyle*. Except that Fillmore doesn't mean to be funny. He doesn't mean to be anything at all. For laughing, we have to drop and do twenty-five pushups. Most of us aren't capable of doing more than ten. We fall on our chins, giggling. For that we do more pushups.

Sergeant James tells Fillmore to find his bunk and his locker. Fillmore circles the room slowly. Once. Twice. Three times. Opens a locker here, a locker there. Finally he stops in front of a locker and stands there, vaguely at attention.

"Is that your locker?"

"Yeah, Sarge."

"How do you know?"

Fillmore shrugs, reaches in, pulls out the shaving kit.

"Because this is in it?"

We explode, laughing until we cry. There are fifty identical lockers in this room and every locker has a shaving kit just like the one Fillmore is holding. We do more pushups, wondering what kind of army is so desperate it would draft poor Fillmore.

That evening five hundred of us with newly shaved heads and new fatigues sit at desks in a large lecture hall, filling out an endless stream of paperwork dealing with next of kin, birth dates, civilian jobs, grandmother's maiden name, known communist affiliations. An officer steps up to a microphone and announces that our proud astronauts are on their way to the moon, that the launch of *Apollo 12* has gone off without a hitch. Our joy is without limit.

We put our civvies in a box and address the box for shipment home. Write on the box: "Dear Mom. Here are my clothes. Hope to see you soon. Your son, Jack."

■ ■ ■

Day after day the rain falls like the end of time. It closes off the horizon, tightens the circle, blurs everything around the edges so the world seems to end a hundred yards away, as far as you can see. It's you and your rain slicker and your boots and your rifle and trying to keep your cigarettes dry, and maybe it's the guy next to you and the drill sergeant if you can hear him. We listen to the rain beating on the barracks roof at night, wake to it in the morning, march through it, do pushups in the mud, police up soggy cigarette butts and crumpled cigarette packs off the parade ground every morning, lie in the wet trying to fire M-14s through the drizzle at targets that disappear in a haze of cold hard rain. If there's a world out there, it's beyond the place where the targets vanish into the mist. It's easier to believe there is nowhere else, easier to imagine the world ends at the tree line. If there is no other place, then this place is less bad than it might be—so there is no other world, no other time. Time and the universe shrink to the next step and the step after that, following on the heels of the man in front. When it's quiet, when the shooting stops, when the sergeants fall silent, when you lie shivering in bed at night, you hear this: DripdripdripDRIPdrip. DripdripdripDRIPDRIPdrip. Drip. Dripdrip.

The astronauts of *Apollo 12* go to the moon and come back. November sloshes into December, colder but just as wet. Somehow we hear about the concert at Altamont in California, the Hells Angels stabbing a man to death in front of the stage while the Rolling Stones perform, the official death of the Woodstock Generation. If there ever was a Woodstock Generation, if any of it was ever more than record company propaganda. Whatever, it is gone now, lost to Mayor Daley and the Chicago cops, to Nixon and Kissinger and the Pentagon, to bad drugs and killer bikers. It's the winter of Altamont, but we have no time to mourn. It rains, we march. It rains, we shoot. It rains, we do pushups. It rains, we clean our boots and fold and refold the socks in our footlockers. It rains, we write letters home.

There is an army rule: every other window in the barracks has to be left wide open. We freeze at night under thin blankets on bunks that are too narrow for some, too short by six inches for me. We all have colds and hacking coughs that never go away. I lie awake shivering, or doze and dream about Mariela. Mariela here, on this narrow, hard bed. Mariela waiting at the far corner of the continent, three thousand miles away. Mariela on the beach.

Friday evenings we march two miles for haircuts at the PX. We have to pay seventy-five cents each time to get our heads shaved all over again, but after the haircuts we're allowed to have a beer or two if we can choke them down fast enough. After the haircuts and beer the drill sergeants make us run back to the barracks and keep us doing pushups and situps until at least a dozen guys puke. Every week the same thing: haircuts, beer, run, pushups, puke. Sunday mornings they leave us alone and we call our girlfriends or our mothers and talk about how fine everything is. How the sergeants are fine and the weather is fine and Fort Lewis is fine and the guys are fine and we are all just so fine we are about to bust.

Most of us are going to go to Vietnam. Some of us are going to die, although you cannot find one man on the entire base who thinks it will be him. The Bouncing Bettys that blow your balls off, the six rounds from an AK-47 that stitch your rib cage, the mortar shrapnel that rips your intestines out and leaves you lying there in the broiling sun, still conscious, watching the ants crawl over your insides while you scream for your mama. Those things are meant for Hitchcock in D Company, not me. The guy in the next bunk, the next platoon, the next batallion, the next fort, the next war. We fire our rifles and march and cough our lungs out and shiver through the night, and sometimes when the sun peeks through we see Mount Rainier and we want to walk to the top of the mountain and sit there in the glistening snow and meditate until the war is over, until the mountain wears down to a sorry little hill, until the end of time.

One day I find time to knock off a letter to my friend Larry Grossman, now in Washington, D.C., studying Vietnamese at the State Department:

> Your letter wafted into this hellhole this week like a gentle wind from civilization blowing over my Army-tarnished soul. Your description of the peace march was beautiful. I could hear it and see it and feel it. Truth and beauty and beauty and truth and some things wrong but all very right in the end.
>
> This is the grayest, most stoic place you can imagine. Hundreds of barracks, dull green or dull pink in color, all precisely identical in structure. . . . Identical streets, rifle ranges, physical training fields. No women, no Cokes, no candy bars, few cigarettes, very, very little conversation. A lot of mopping barracks, spit-shining shoes, left-left, left right left, yes drill sergeant, no drill sergeant.
>
> Yesterday we went through the tear gas chamber—*sans* mask. The most awful feeling you can imagine. If you can avoid it, never tangle with tear gas. It turns you into a desperate, gagging, crying, slobbering animal. After the chamber we went out on the course and had gas turned on us as we crawled under wires. It is amazing the way your mind

works. You are hurting, gagging, gasping, but you stop and move very carefully, rolling over on your back, getting the mask out, putting it on, clearing it, all in seven or eight seconds, thinking don't run, stay down, warn the rest, keep your rifle clear, get your helmet back on. Then the breath of fresh, clean air after the mask is clear, like a gift from heaven. I remembered two words from a Wilfred Owen poem— "gas! gas!" Wish I remembered the rest.

I hope you can try to imagine what it's like here at least long enough to appreciate how really fine it is not to have to do this. I could list the things I'd give my right arm for—an hour with *The Sun Also Rises,* a good talk in Casey's, another night in bed with Mariela, a chance to cover a fast-breaking story, write an editorial, talk to Bachittar Singh or Larry Grossman or Ricky Mann for an hour. Value those books. They're beautiful, baby. If only I had a briefcase with the *New York Times* magazine in it instead of a pack with my wet-weather gear and an ammunition pouch full of M-14 shells.

The temperature most days hovers a few degrees above freezing, just enough to keep it from snowing. Snow would be better than rain. Within twenty minutes after we leave the barracks every morning we are wet through. Any concentration we have on those targets in the rain-smeared distance evaporates even before we cram the shells into the magazines for the rifles, twenty to a magazine. The army won't even give us proper rifles. Even the air force has been training with M-16s for at least six months. If we're going to die in Vietnam we're going to die fighting with M-16s—but here we're stuck with these big old clunky M-14s, heavy with their wooden stocks. Our fingers are too cold to manipulate the cartridges, so we ball our fists and hammer them in, skinning our knuckles. After that we don't care enough to hit the targets. All we want is to find a way to get dry and warm, to get enough shelter to light a cigarette under someone's helmet, to puff the damned thing a few times before it gets too soggy to smoke. A guy with a reliable lighter gets his cigarette going, then we light the rest of our smokes, one off the other. That's called a chicken-fuck light for some reason, although I have seen plenty of chickens fuck, and chicken fucking doesn't have anything to do with the way we light cigarettes.

Sometimes during cigarette breaks the drill sergeants, in need of a little amusement, make us hold the smokes in our mouths and stand at attention, hands at our sides while we inhale and exhale on command. "Inhale! Exhale! Inhale! Exhale! Inhale! . . ." And hold it, hold it, hold it, standing there with a gutful of smoke until we're ready to puke. We should quit, but smoking and jerking off are about the only two things we have that the army can't take away. Funny they don't think to make us masturbate on cadence.

"AWRIGHT, EVERYBODY THINKIN' ABOUT JANE FONDA? OK, get 'em out and start strokin', every swingin' dick of you! On my command! UP down UP down UP down UP down . . ."

Like any bunch of healthy young men in a situation that is less than life-threatening, we enjoy one another's company. We laugh, joke, curse the army, talk endlessly about women and the elaborate things we will do to them on leave.

"Y'know," one of the Texans drawls, "when ah was in the eighth grade, ah thought if yer dick was big enough, you could stack three women on top of each other and fuck 'em all at once, just go in the pussy of one and out her ass and into the next one, see? Hump 'em all straight down, take the three best-lookin' girls in town and just pile 'em up and fuck 'em all. Then ah fucked this pussy and ah found out y'go right up to her navel like, not out her ass. That was a real bummer. Don't matter how big you are, you can't even do two women at once." He looks positively stricken, like he's remembering the worst day of his life. Everybody in the barracks laughing until they choke, saying only a slack-jawed puke from Texas would think something that stupid. But you see some guys scratching their heads, wondering.

About three weeks into basic I phone Mariela from the long line of pay phones outside the mess hall. She says she told Tom Clagg to get out of her life the night before, told him they can't have dinner anymore even if it is innocent and no necking. All that because she's in love with me, because we're going to spend our lives together. I say maybe we should get married at Christmas leave. She doesn't say no. I say we could get married the day after Christmas, have five or six days for a honeymoon in Key West before I have to get back to Fort Lewis. She says that would be nice, she'll talk to her parents, we'll figure out the details when I get to Miami. She says we'll get married and she'll find a place in Coconut Grove, and when I get out of the army and come back to Miami to work at the *Herald* she'll have a place for us, small but cozy, where we can start our life together.

Knowing Mariela is waiting makes the rain a little warmer, the sergeants a little funnier, Fillmore a little smarter, Vietnam a little farther away. It rains and we march, and as we march I run my tongue from her little toe to the nape of her neck and back down again, in a warm room in Key West where the salt breeze stirs lace curtains over the bed.

■ ■ ■

On the rare days when the cold rain doesn't fall, Fort Lewis is so beautiful we forget everything else. Forget the monotony of basic, forget the stupidity of the brute sergeants, forget that it will rain again tomorrow and the day after tomorrow. Before dawn on these few sunny days we shower, dress, choke down a few bites of breakfast, and burst out into warm winter sunshine. Birds singing, the sun gleaming off our rifles and the snow on Mount Rainier in the distance, light-dazzled soldiers released from the prison of the rain.

No matter what else goes on, no matter how much the officers and other noncoms get on our case, no matter how much we hate them and talk big about fragging them if we ever get to 'Nam, we make an exception for Sergeant James, the big-shouldered platoon sergeant who looks like a slightly roly-poly football star. Sergeant James is tough but he's fair. He's a hard-ass, but he's a cool hard-ass. If we have to be in a firefight, we want it to be with Sergeant James. If Sergeant James says get down on your knees and clean toilets with a toothbrush, we get down on our knees and clean toilets with a toothbrush, because Sergeant James doesn't mess with you for no reason like some of the sergeants, because Sergeant James can turn a morning march into a Mardi Gras parade. On clear days he marches us out toward Mount Rainier, snow-capped in blue haze in the distance, the lilt in his voice carrying us along as he counts cadence like a jazz trumpeter doing a riff:

"Yo lay-ef rye-ut lay-ef, gimme yo lay-ef rye-ut lay-ef!

"Gimme yo LEF yo rye yo LEF yo rye yo LEF RYE LAY-EF!"

Or he will sing in that high tenor voice, straight from the back row of a get-down Baptist gospel choir:

"Well I know a girl in Buffalo Hills . . ."

And we echo back: "I know a girl in Buffalo Hills!

She won't do it but her buffalo will!"

He shifts to a cadence that is more jazz monologue than military march: "COL-UMM LEF', HARCH! Yo' LEF'! . . . Yo' LEF! . . . Yo' LEF, rye-ee LEF! . . . Fill-MORE! Goddammit, Fillmore, if you don't find your lef' foot, boy, I swear I'm gonna paint it red! Sweet mother-humpin' Jesus, didn't your mama teach you LEF' from RIGHT? Your lef' foot is the one on the LEF' side of your fuckin' HAY-ED, Fillmore, I hearda men with two lef' feet but I swear Fillmore got THREE! Fillmore's DICK a left foot just like the other two. Good thing Fill-more a white man or he be trippin' over that one too, my sweet Jesus, the DEFECTIVE MERCHANDISE they give me in this army, shee-it, we couldn't lick ENGland in a fair fight, and everybody know ENGland a DEE-feated NATION! NOW! Gimme yo LEF yo rye yo LEF yo rye yo LEF RYE-EE LAY-EF! Fill-MORE! GODDAMMIT, Fill-MORE, GET YOUR HEAD OUTA YOUR ASS BEFORE I PUT MY BOOT IN IT! Yo' LEF! Yo' LEF!" James walking step for step with Fillmore, all but moving the poor kid's legs for him and Fillmore still stum-bling, turning left on a right face, right on a left face, the whole platoon falling apart around Fillmore until Sergeant James himself laughs and shakes his head and goes back to singing:

> Upon her head, she wore a yellow ribbon,
> She wore it for her baby who was far, far away . . .

And we answer back:

> Far away . . . far away
> She wore it for her baby who was far, far away.

On these sweet mornings we will follow Sergeant James to the summit of Mount Rainier and across the Pacific if we have to. We will belly-crawl through the jungle until we have hunted down every last Viet Cong and made all Southeast Asia safe for Christ and Conoco. Too bad Sergeant James doesn't run the whole U.S. Army. It might almost be tolerable.

Most of it is pointless and infuriating, like the tear gas. We don't react very well to the gas, but we don't do anything very well. We don't march well. We don't keep our dress shoes pol-ished. We look lousy in formation. We flunk bayonet drill. We can't shoot straight. We lie in the mud missing targets. We curse the rain, the cold, the Pacific coast, the state of Washington, the sergeants, the officers, the Viet Cong, the Joint Chiefs, the Pentagon, the Selective Service, J. Edgar Hoover, Henry Kissinger, Richard Nixon, Spiro Agnew, Ho Chi Minh, and the entire cast of *Laugh-In*—everybody except our girls back home, who are probably out with some National Guard weekend warrior with a well-connected daddy while we wallow in the mud, missing everything we aim to hit.

I know how to shoot. I've been shooting my whole life. But here I'm as bad as the rest, even though the medics say I have 20–10 vision in both eyes and the lieutenant says I qualify for sniper school, where you can learn to crawl around Vietnam with a souped-up rifle, testing windage and humidity and distance in order to take out a North Vietnamese officer a mile away, then hope you can escape before his men hunt you down, cut your balls off, stuff them in your mouth, and hang your naked carcass from a tree. Thanks but no thanks. Anyway, I'm shivering so much I can't even hit the 75-meter targets.

Our aim on the firing range is so awful the battalion commander, a full colonel, comes around to talk to us. We have set some kind of record for the worst marksmanship in the history of Fort Lewis, or maybe it's the worst in the history of the army, or the worst in the history of warfare. He's not unsympathetic. Conditions on the firing range are awful and he knows it. He says he knows that some of us don't believe in what we are doing—but that rifle is all we have, the only thing in some situations that can keep us alive, and we had better goddamned bear down and learn how to shoot or we are going to get ourselves killed and our buddies along with us.

It doesn't help. We go back to the range the next day and try a little harder, but if we were standing on the slopes of Mount Rainier we could fire a thousand rounds and miss the mountain. The Viet Cong are safe. Shadows in black pajamas, they are at least the equal of tough Marine Corps units and elite Green Berets. A platoon of drafted hippies, plump bank clerks, and real-world rejects, we are more a menace to one another than to enemies foreign or domestic.

The risk we pose to one another is real. Fillmore is in our squad. He's usually between me and the squad leader on the rifle range. We do everything for him: load his clips with bullets, twenty to a clip, load the clips in the rifle, show him how to point, aim, and squeeze. Fillmore never hits a target, but at least he keeps his rifle pointed in the right direction most of the time—until the morning when he turns and points his rifle at the belly of another recruit standing near him.

"Fillmore!" He hears me shout, so he swivels his M-14 with a full clip so the muzzle is planted in my navel, Fillmore pulling frantically at the trigger. "What's wrong with this thing?" he's saying. "It won't shoot!"

I scream and grab the muzzle. A sergeant yells and dives for Fillmore. Fillmore turns the muzzle into the sergeant's belly, still pulling the trigger. The sergeant twists the rifle out of his hands. I'm shouting, the sergeant is shouting, everyone is shouting and pushing poor Fillmore, who has no idea what is wrong. He's still trying to tell us his rifle won't shoot, he doesn't know why we're picking on him. I feel like I'm going to puke. The rifle didn't fire because Fillmore had the safety on or he would have blown out my insides. The sergeant is shaking and yelling at Fillmore, I'm shaking and yelling at Fillmore.

"Fillmore, you stupid, dumb, hopeless fuck! You coulda killed somebody!"

The kid stands there, mouth open, blinking from one of us to another, his eyes blank. Until this moment I felt sorry for Fillmore. Now I want to kill him. I see all the stupidity of the army in his sloped forehead and buck teeth and spaced-out eyes. Shoving the muzzle of an M-14 in my belly. Pulling the trigger. For fuck's sake. The sergeant orders Fillmore to get away from the rifles and to sit out the rest of the day. It's absurd. Fillmore would be dangerous in the Boy Scouts, never mind in the army with live weapons in his hands. No one wants to be throwing a hand grenade next to Fillmore, helping Fillmore learn how to fire a mortar. The sergeant gets Fillmore squared away, comes back and asks if I'm OK. I nod, ask if he's OK. I feel for him. I'm just trying to get out of here alive, which is bad enough. He's supposed to be training us to fight, which is impossible.

It's the end of 1969. The whole country is going nuts. The way things are, it would be an appropriate death, stitched from belt to neckline with bullets from an M-14 fired by an idiot. Bleeding to death in the mud at Fort Lewis during basic training, an ocean away from the Viet Cong and the grave danger they pose to the most powerful nation on earth.

I turn into the latrine when we get back to barracks and find myself staring at this huge, mud-spattered soldier in the mirror. He looks dangerous and possibly crazy, a gaunt, rifle-toting giant, a creature to be reckoned with and avoided if possible, a man capable of mayhem. It takes a second or two before I realize I'm staring at my own reflection. I have a cold and a fever. My eyes blaze like the eyes of someone about to go over the edge. I take my helmet off and wash away some of the mud, which helps a little. The vision in the mirror is almost as disturbing as Fillmore's rifle. I sit on the edge of the sink and light a cigarette and watch some of the other guys straggle in— muddy, angry, and exhausted. Half of them look as bad as I do or worse.

Upstairs I strip off the damp boots and wet fatigues and towel off and put on dry clothes and try to get warm, which is impossible as long as the windows are open all over the barracks. I'm still sitting there shivering when mail call comes. There are a couple of letters from my mother, as usual, nothing from Mariela (as usual because Mariela says she's too embarrassed to write to a writer), and one letter from *Newsweek* in New York which someone at the *Miami Herald* was kind enough to forward to Fort Lewis. I tear it open. It's from the managing editor, Hal Bruno. In the spring I'd been one of twenty finalists for the sixteen internships at the *Washington Post*. I was disappointed when I didn't make the cut, but *Post* publisher Katharine Graham owned *Newsweek* as well, and someone at the *Post* told Bruno he should recruit me to do rewrite for *Newsweek*. Without benefit of an interview, Bruno offered me a job in *Newsweek's* New York office. I had to turn him down because I had already accepted an offer from the *Miami Herald,* but Bruno promised to get back to me. "I imagine by now you've had enough of that Florida sunshine," he says, "so I want you to know we have a job waiting for you at *Newsweek* in grimy old New York." If I weren't sitting on a footlocker at Fort Lewis, even Mariela couldn't keep me away from New York. I read what he has to say a half-dozen times, wad the letter into a tight little ball, and sit there squeezing it, wanting to hit something.

Fillmore comes in then and walks right across the carefully waxed and buffed floor in the center of the barracks, the place you are never, ever, supposed to walk except in your socks, leaving great, muddy tracks from his combat boots. I shout at him to move or take off his boots. Pretty soon the whole platoon is yelling at Fillmore to get his dumb ass out of the middle of the floor and to take off his fucking muddy combat boots. Fillmore stares at us, blinks a couple of times like he did on the rifle range, and keeps walking, leaving a thick, muddy track with every step.

■　　■　　■

Apart from poor Fillmore and a half-dozen Texas rednecks who don't much cotton to sharing bunk space with the men they call "Nee-groes," the guys in first platoon are all right. There are five or six of us from Nebraska, maybe eight or ten blacks from the West Coast, a couple of Mexican-Americans, three or four guys from Washington State, and one sorry excuse for an Englishman who volunteered because he wanted to go fight communists. About three days into basic he realizes what a terrible mistake he made and starts to caterwaul about how much he wants to go home to Merry Old England. We have no sympathy: a man who would deliberately put himself into this mess when he could be chasing lovely young things on Carnaby Street is just too pathetic for words.

Our platoon is different because, for some reason, we are older and better educated than the average recruit. The rough rule of thumb in the military is the smarter the man, the poorer the soldier. When you're young and dumb, you do what you're told. Company C is at half strength, with two fifty-man platoons instead of four, one hundred men instead of two hundred. Most of the men in our platoon are in their early to mid-twenties. Second platoon is made up mostly of eighteen- and nineteen-year-olds who are either more gung-ho or more cowed by the military, and the difference is obvious from the beginning.

While second platoon gears up to fight, first platoon is disappearing right before our eyes. By the second week of basic they are already leaving, slipping out one or two at a time. By December 22, the day we depart Fort Lewis for Christmas leave, our platoon of fifty men has shrunk to thirty-six: fourteen recruits either have been sent home or have gone over the hill, Absent Without Leave. On our little corner of this huge base, it seems like the U.S. Army is melting away. Two deserters from my platoon are caught and brought back and are cutting wood in the base stockade. Because I can drive a truck, I get detailed to take a shipment into the stockade and spot them running a big two-handed saw. We have time for a quick conversation before the sergeants intervene; their plan was to go to San Francisco and live underground, but they were picked up hitchhiking outside Seattle and brought back to base. They were lucky because they were caught inside thirty days, which means their punishment will be a couple of weeks cutting wood in the stockade. Up to thirty days you are merely AWOL; after thirty days you're a deserter, and deserters face up to five years in prison, doing hard time in a place like Fort Leavenworth or the Presidio.

We all know the consequences, and still the army loses more than a dozen men from our platoon in six weeks. Men find a way out, sneaking off the base at night, hitching a ride into Seattle, disappearing one or two at a time. We never seem to hear about it in advance; we just wake up in the morning and find an empty bunk. The company commander comes in with two MPs and they go through the guy's stuff and then huddle with the drill sergeants, talking in low voices so we won't hear. We cross our fingers, hoping the poor bastard got away. It's like the movie *The Great Escape,* where Steve McQueen keeps breaking out and the Germans keep bringing him back.

The army doesn't seem to know what to do with us. Army basic in 1969 is haphazard, sloppy, lacking all conviction. From the first day it feels like the mighty U.S. Army is coming undone. One day we'll be worked to the point of exhaustion doing pushups in the rain, then we'll have no physical training at all for a week. For two or three days the sergeants will be brutally tough, then it seems they can't be bothered. We will be told we are going on a dreaded night-firing exercise, and then someone upstairs will change his mind and we'll spend the night in our barracks, writing letters and smoking cigarettes and wondering whether anyone in this man's army has the foggiest idea what they're doing. The drill sergeants, most of them Vietnam vets, don't seem to believe in any of it. The lieutenants have no clue how to inspire or discipline their troops. The company, battalion, and base commanders have a massive morale problem on their hands. The confusion and inertia probably go all the way up to the Joint Chiefs in Washington, who have to know by now that they are backed into an impossible corner in Southeast Asia, no matter what bullshit they put out for public consumption. At our level, in the mud of Fort Lewis in basic training in 1969, it almost seems the army has given up.

Even with morale as low as it can go, this is the most powerful army the world has ever seen. There are 120,000 men at Fort Lewis alone in December 1969, more than in the entire Canadian Armed Forces. Artillery booms in the distance day and night, thousands of other recruits at various stages in their training march past in all directions. We'll be strung out along the road on a long march when someone yells, "Hit the ditch!" and we dive off the road and lie there as a column of monster tanks shoots past at forty miles an hour, their big guns trolling back and forth. We feel the ground shake. We imagine the terror of a peasant army forced to do battle with machines like this. Little men in black pajamas who believe in what they are doing, they are making war against jets, napalm, helicopter gunships, B-52s, and tanks the size of bungalows, armed only with AK-47s, mortars, satchel charges, and pungee sticks. If they are willing to fight these machines with what they have, then they are going to win this war—and it won't matter how many thousand-pound bombs we drop on Hanoi.

Two weeks into basic I get a message to report to the platoon commander's office. He's a nervous, skinny little lieutenant who seems as uneasy as I feel, standing at attention, waiting to see what he wants.

"You remember me?"

"Uh—you're the platoon commander, sir."

"No, I mean from somewhere else."

"No, sir."

"Well, I applied for a job on the *Daily Nebraskan* once and you didn't hire me. Guess you were too busy writing all that antiwar bullshit."

Small world. Turns out that because we once met in another life, he wants to ask for my opinion. Morale is terrible. We aren't performing well in any aspect of our training. Men are going AWOL right and left. He wants to know what he can do to turn things around.

"You could end the war."

"I wish I could."

"Well, maybe you can cut down on some of the bullshit. Not the sergeants so much, they have a job to do—but some of these corporals hanging around are real assholes."

The corporals like to play sadistic little power games. One in particular is going to get a beating if we ever catch him off base, because one day during our first week in basic he made us get down on our hands and knees in the rain to spend three hours picking all the black rocks from the gravel beds outside the barracks.

We're also not getting enough to eat. There's an obese kid in our platoon, and the rule is that no one can eat until we all hand-walk our way across a horizontal ladder suspended eight feet above the ground outside the mess hall. He can never make it, so we stand there waiting, smelling the food inside and dizzy with hunger while he falls off the second rung again and again. By the time the sergeants let a couple of us help him, the guys at the back of the line only have time to choke down a few bites of chow. The barracks are freezing at night and we all have colds because of that dumb rule about leaving the windows open in all kinds of weather. And our training is inadequate, because we can't be expected to do five hundred pushups one day and then spend the next week without physical training of any kind apart from marching back and forth in the rain like the lost platoon.

There are no major complaints. Anything we might encounter in Vietnam will be infinitely worse than this. But when you are trying to improve morale for a bunch of reluctant, unhappy draftees who hate the war we're being trained to fight, there are a few basic things that could be done. The lieutenant nods, listens, thanks me for my time.

Nothing changes. The company commander, a thick-necked spit-and-polish fool named Captain Benning, calls me in a couple of days later and chews me out for feeding my peacenik bullshit to his lieutenant, says he knows just how to handle fucking pussies like me, that he doesn't care if I'm a newspaperman in civilian life, in here I'm a private and I'll shut up and follow orders or he'll have my hippie ass. I spend two full days on KP duty, peeling potatoes from four in the morning until eight in the evening with a few breaks for cigarettes and meals.

The rain falls. We march. Guys go AWOL.

■   ■   ■

The worst thing about the army is not the rain or the long hours or the drill sergeants or the physical exhaustion or even the fear that you might get your ass shot in Vietnam. The worst thing is the complete lack of privacy, living in a big, drafty room with fifty other men night and day with no place of your own, nowhere you don't wake in the night to the sounds of snoring, farting, coughing men. You can be going through all kinds of brutal stuff—the Vietnam terrors, Dear John letters from home, news that your mother has cancer—and you have to endure it all with fifty shaven-headed strangers watching your every move.

A couple of weeks into basic I draw supply guard duty, which means missing four hours of sleep to sit up alone in the supply room with a loaded M-14, watching over the company's stash of rifles and hand grenades and ammunition, keeping it all safe from a raid by the Black Panthers or the Weathermen or Little Old Ladies in Tennis Shoes Against the War. Pulling supply guard means you go on duty at 10 P.M. and then grab a quick four hours' sleep after you're relieved at 2 A.M.—or the guard coming off duty wakes you at two in the morning and you sit there until six slapping yourself to stay awake before joining the rest of the platoon for a full day of drills.

After that first night on the two-to-six dawn patrol, I volunteer for supply guard duty every night and pull it two or three times a week, volunteering because the supply room is a haven where I feel I'm getting away from the army, trading the sleep deprivation for a few hours to myself. We aren't allowed to keep books in our footlockers during basic, but someone has left a half-dozen good books in the supply room, all of them well worn and covered with notes written in pencil in a small, neat hand: Henry David Thoreau, Teilhard de Chardin, Andrei Sakharov, Albert Camus's *The Plague*, Ken Kesey's *One Flew Over the Cuckoo's Nest*, Bernard Fall's famous study of the French disaster at Dien Bien Phu, *Hell in a Very Small Place*. The most heavily underlined of all the books is Thoreau's essay on civil disobedience.

The second or third time I pull supply guard duty I meet the phantom reader. The name stenciled on his fatigue jacket is "Powers." He is a pacifist with a hair-trigger temper, a tough guy who quotes Thoreau and Sakharov on the need for political dissidence. He has a black belt in karate, but he's trying to get a conscientious objector discharge from the army. He's a six-foot-three, 225-pound mass of solid muscle, a former seminary student who will knock you on your can, then deliver a lecture on pacifism while you're down. In the space of a night, Powers becomes my best friend in the army.

Powers was drafted three months before me, went AWOL during basic, and returned after twenty-nine days to seek a conscientious objector discharge from the military. The way the courts have interpreted the law on conscientious objectors, a Catholic can't be considered a C.O. because the Catholic

Church itself is not pacifist, but Powers has succeeded in convincing everyone in the chain of command at Fort Lewis that he should be discharged as a conscientious objector. Now he is waiting for a final decision from Washington on his case. Meanwhile he has to serve, but he cannot be forced to carry a rifle or to participate in bayonet drills. Somehow he has convinced the army that his special status extends to his hair, which has begun to grow long and curly. He's attached to our platoon and he does come along on marches, which is good because Powers is bigger, stronger, and more physically fit than almost anyone else on the base. He'll begin a march carrying nothing at all and finish it toting two packs and a rifle for weaker men who are about to fall out.

Almost every night when I'm on supply guard duty, Powers drops by at some point. He doesn't seem to need more than three or four hours' sleep, so we sit there night after night, talking about Thoreau and Sakharov and Camus and arguing about the war. We agree that it's stupid, callous, destructive, murderous, probably illegal, and certainly immoral. We disagree only about our own responsibility for bringing it to an end. Powers argues that if I believe it is criminal for the U.S. to go on killing people, then I have a moral obligation to refuse to fight: "Man, you're part of the machine or you're out. You can't have it both ways. You want to be a nice little soldier boy for a couple of years, do your time, then go back to Miami and join a couple of peace marches for your conscience? Work for George McGovern or Gene McCarthy in '72 and hope they straighten out this mess? Is that it? That's chickenshit, man. If we're all like you, then those bastards can go right on dropping napalm on babies for a hundred years, because nothing's going to change."

"Hey, you're in the army, too. You got your draft notice and you didn't do a damned thing."

"I know—but I saw the light, brother. Read Thoreau. Read

Tolstoy. Think about Gandhi. You gotta draw the line somewhere. Walk away. Tell 'em you wanna go C.O. too. If nothing
else, we get a thousand guys doing that, we jam up the bureau-
cracy. If you don't have the guts to fight 'em here, then just
walk away. Live underground, join the movement, make 'em
waste money hunting you until this is over. Maybe it's not as
good as going to prison, but it's better than being part of the
machine. I heard Pierre Trudeau might even change the rules
so deserters can go to Canada. You can be in Vancouver in
three hours."

"I can't do it, man. I thought about it for two years, but I
can't do it. I'm an American and I don't want to be anything
else."

Powers knows that I have applied for assignment to the
army's journalism school and that I will probably get it—that
I'll end up writing press releases somewhere. That bothers him
too.

"What if you were going infantry? What if they were asking
you to go over there and grease gooks? What if you were going
to get your balls blown off?"

"Hey, I tried to get over there as a Marine Corps lieutenant,
man. Marine lieutenants have the highest casualty rate in Vietnam. It wouldn't make any difference. I'm in the army now
and I'm staying in."

"Your whole problem is you're hung up on this Cuban
woman. If you weren't in love, you'd be in Canada already.
You're doing the wrong thing and you know it, just because
she's afraid of a little snow."

I tell him that isn't true, but I don't know anymore. I'm finding it harder and harder to explain to myself what I'm doing
here, even if Mariela is waiting in Miami. Trouble is, there is
no course now that is really the right one. If you make the sacrifice, if you go to Canada or refuse induction or file for a C.O.
discharge, you hurt your family and your friends and your

own future. Years of protests against the war haven't changed a thing; there is no reason to think that any individual sacrifice will help. If you do your hitch and go back to your job, you make it easier for the people who are waging the war to get away with it. If you end up in combat and you are wounded or killed, you die for no reason at all. If you're wealthy or connected, you can avoid it all by wangling a 4-F deferment or an assignment in the National Guard—but you will know what you have done, and you will have to live with your conscience.

Powers is my conscience, following me everywhere. With the company strung out on a long night march, he lopes along beside me carrying someone else's pack, quoting Thoreau and Jerry Rubin. With his long, curly hair and without a rifle or helmet, Powers is like a hippie in fatigues following us around, flashing the peace sign, subverting everything the army is trying to pound into our heads. Some of the Texans call him a hippie faggot commie when he isn't around, but none of them dare say it to his face because they know Powers can and will kick their teeth in, conscientious objector or not.

There are others who think like we do, although they don't say much. There must be others, or we wouldn't have guys going AWOL at every opportunity. Those who are really thinking of going over the hill keep their mouths shut. Some of those who aren't ready to desert try to find other ways to escape. One morning a tall recruit from Seattle falls down on the parade ground and starts screaming that he's having an acid flashback from taking LSD. He's carried away kicking and screaming, but the next day he's back in the ranks. The acid flashback routine is already old hat to the army. They're hip to that one, and they're hip to the kiss-the-drill sergeant routine, and if you try obsessive, around-the-clock masturbation they just yawn and tell you to put it back in your pants before somebody shoots it off. In an army that has drafted Fillmore, deviant behavior is to be expected. If you have sex with vegetables and call your rifle "Mommy," you are just about ready for combat.

■ ■ ■

A month into basic training, I try to go AWOL.

It starts on a Sunday morning in the barracks when two or three sergeants attached to our company decide they're going to get in a little sadism instead of going to church. They force our entire platoon to spend most of the morning in what they call the "Chinese thinking position"—holding ourselves up on our toes and elbows on the hard barracks floor without letting our knees or stomachs touch the ground. It doesn't sound bad until you try it. After two minutes your elbows and back are in agony and your entire body is quivering from the effort of holding yourself up—and the taller you are, the harder it is. The sergeants strut around, bellowing and cursing, laughing at our pain.

It's a beautiful, sunny day and second platoon has the morning off. We can hear them shouting and horsing around through the weekly Sunday morning touch football game while we go through hours of harassment. I'm supposed to call Mariela, but by now she will have gone to the beach. A drill sergeant plants his combat boot in the small of my back and pushes me down to the floor while I try to hold the position. "What's the problem, you long tall drink of water?" he asks. "Can't take the pain, you pussy? You're gonna make a great target in 'Nam, you skinny piece of shit. I figure you're dead in a week." If I go for him they'll beat me senseless and I'll end up in the stockade for assaulting a sergeant. If I don't I'll be a coward in my own eyes. I bite my lip and push myself back up into the thinking position and hold it.

By the time the sergeants finish playing games, the only thing I can think about is getting out. I already know that a friend named Dave Banville is planning to desert Sunday night. Banville is twenty-five, the oldest guy in the platoon. He served a full two-year hitch in the army—including a year in Vietnam—and was happily married with a good job in Seattle before he missed too many reserve meetings. The penalty was immediate and brutal: Banville was drafted and sent back to basic to start all over again. Now he's bitter and he wants out. He says that his wife is going to wait for him on the highway after lights out and drive him straight to Vancouver.

I do some thinking while I'm down in the Chinese thinking position with the sergeant's combat boot planted in the small of my back. As soon as the sergeants leave us alone, I tell Banville I want to come along. He's glad to have the company. He says we'll wait until after lights out and then tiptoe out of the barracks carrying our combat boots, and as soon as we're outside we'll put our boots on and take off, carrying whatever we can stuff in our pockets. If we're caught leaving the barracks we'll just say we can't sleep and we're going for a smoke. Soldiers come in and out all night long anyway, going to and from perimeter guard duty or supply guard duty or having a cigarette or stumbling to the latrine downstairs for a pee. Because we're on the extreme corner of Fort Lewis nearest the highway, it should be easy. Once we're out of the barracks we'll have to crawl past the perimeter guards, but after that it'll be a breeze.

No thought, no sober period of reflection here. Just damn the drill sergeants and go. I try to call Mariela but she's still at the beach. I try to tell Powers after mess but can't find him. Before we hit our bunks I go through my footlocker, grab my letters and my toothbrush and a couple of extra pairs of underwear and socks and stuff all of it in the pockets of my fatigues, then lie there fully dressed pretending to sleep. Thirty minutes after lights out, Banville taps me on the shoulder.

It's raining outside, the endless cold, steady drizzle of Fort Lewis in December. We run as far as the supply room, which is next to the muddy parade ground, and stand under the dripping eaves to gather ourselves. I want to make a run for it. It's about a quarter mile across the parade ground, the distance I ran in high school on a state-record mile relay team. Banville doesn't think he can make it, so we decide to do the army crawl, elbows and knees the way they taught us on the obstacle course, through a quarter mile of mud.

Halfway across we see the two perimeter guards, a couple of muscular idiots from second platoon, going by on their rounds. We hunker down, pulling our slickers over our heads. They're busy talking about the soldier's favorite topic—pussy, and how much of it they're going to get during Christmas leave. Finally, muddy and soaked, we make it as far as the highway, dash across the road, throw ourselves into the barrow pit on the far side, and wait. Banville's wife is nowhere to be seen. We flatten out in the ditch when other cars go by, but they don't even slow down. We wait until it's well past midnight and we're drenched through. When she still doesn't appear, we start to panic. What if we're caught out here? We can't claim we're just out for a smoke, not this far from the barracks, not when we've been out here two hours and we're soaked to the gills. We have no choice. We crawl back through the mud, run along in the shadow of the buildings as far as our barracks. Outside the door we take off our muddy boots so we won't leave tracks.

We creep up the stairs and back to our bunks, the sound of a half-dozen snoring recruits masking the noise as we slide over the floor in our socks. We slip the boots under our bunks and are about to peel off the muddy fatigues when we hear the lieutenant downstairs beginning his nightly round of inspection. We dive into bed in our muddy clothes, pull the blankets up to our chins, turn to the wall and feign sleep. The lieutenant comes around slowly, taking a good look. My heart is pounding so loud I'm sure he can hear it. The flashlight plays over the wall next to my bunk and moves on. Surely there are traces of mud, rain tracked in, something. The lieutenant moves methodically down the far wall, checking the sleeping soldiers across the way. When he's gone I hear Banville sigh from the other side of the barracks.

We get lucky again the next day. It's laundry day, so we roll our muddy fatigues in our muddy sheets and dump the anonymous bundles on the gigantic pile bound for the laundry, the traces of our attempt to go AWOL gone in the wash. It turns out that Banville's wife waited for us until 3 A.M.—at the wrong corner of the fort, miles from the highway where we were lying on our bellies in the mud.

I feel relief more than anything. I almost did a very stupid thing, allowing a sadistic sergeant to get to me, making a decision that could change my whole life because I was pissed off and wanted to hit somebody. Obviously I'm destined to stay in the army. Within a couple of weeks I'll be in Miami with Mariela. Nothing else will matter. The two-year hitch will pass. I'll go back to work at the *Herald*.

I should know better. These are times when the ground under your feet tends to buckle and shift, when things that are sure today are gone by morning.

Fillmore is finally sent home. We all feel sorry for the kid, but he doesn't belong in a place where people play with guns. The rest of us aren't becoming soldiers exactly, but we're doing a little better. It's a thing you can hate and love at the same time. You love that you can get through it, that it's a hard thing you endure. You share it with others who are enduring it too, and the bad part makes the good parts better: Mount Rainier in the morning, Sergeant James counting cadence, a cigarette with a buddy on guard duty. We start to pull together, to trust one another. We get tougher. Training with pugil sticks—cudgels with heavy pads at either end—one of the burly Texas rednecks and I get carried away and have to be pulled apart. We've been arguing about the Cornhusker and Longhorn football teams, and now we want to kill each other. The sergeants love it.

After that one abortive attempt to desert I tune Powers out, try to forget about the things I believe in and to concentrate on being a soldier. There are days when it's 1967 all over again, when I'm back in the Marines and all I want is to go to Vietnam and fight communists for democracy, when I feel like a big, strong, swaggering dude with a rifle and I can almost see myself wading through a rice paddy looking to grease somebody.

On a rainy afternoon ten days before Christmas we go for bayonet training. Before we can try it ourselves we get a demonstration from Sergeant Cruz, a tough Puerto Rican who terrifies us during physical training, and Sergeant Dixon, a black noncom built like an All-Pro athlete. They begin at opposite ends of a platform about fifty feet apart and go at each other from there—attaching bayonets to the muzzle of their rifles, glaring and charging, rifles spinning and bayonets flashing until they are face to face with the tips of the bayonets poised at each other's throats. It's a dazzling display, because if one of them goofed or stumbled, the other would be impaled. It brings out the blood lust in all of us.

We spend the rest of the afternoon screaming "Kill!" driving the bayonets into the dummies. "Stick it in his bellybutton and pull UP!" the sergeants yell. "Tear his guts out! If you cannot free your weapon after he is dead, fire one round and your weapon will come free!" (But if you had one round, we want to ask, wouldn't you just shoot him dead in the first place?) By the time we're finished we feel like bad dudes, mean mothers, killers who could leave a guy trying to stuff his intestines into his belly and not even look back. We swagger on the way to the barracks, listening to Sergeant James do his thing, singing along like real soldiers, loud and lusty and clear:

> Oh how I want to go
> Back where the roses grow

But they won't let me go
Home . . .

We're halfway to the barracks when we hear the bells of the
base chapel tolling the old Christmas carol: "Peace on earth
and mercy mild / God and sinners reconcil'd." The bells ring
through the damp air, their message pure and clear over the
sound of our marching boots ringing on wet gravel. Peace on
earth, bayonets and church bells. I feel like I've been slapped.
Screaming "Kill!" and then hearing "peace on earth" from the
chapel. What are we supposed to do? Get down on our knees
and pray to God for a chance to stick a bayonet in a man's bellybutton and pull "UP"? I feel sick, disgusted with myself as
much as anything. The young guys, the men who believe in the
war, you can't blame them. But I know better. I know the brass
in the Pentagon would find it perfectly moral and acceptable
to go to chapel and sing Christmas carols and pray for the
strength to kill some poor Vietnamese peasant, but it's wrong,
and their version of muscular Christianity does not make it
right. We march two more miles back to the barracks, plenty
of time to think about the village they had to destroy in order
to save. The Tet offensive. How the French started talking
about the light at the end of the tunnel in 1954, and it's almost
1970 and we still haven't found the light. Sonny's pictures. A
necklace made of human ears. Dead Viet Cong in black pajamas draped over the razor wire. All the images we have been
watching in living color on the evening news, the rows of body
bags, napalm bursting on the tree line, a young girl screaming
as she runs naked down a road, fleeing a war that will follow
her without pity. Church bells and bayonets. Peace on earth
and rip his guts out. Stick it in his bellybutton, pull UP, fire
one round to free your bayonet from his guts, look for someone else to kill. The old Christmas carol is lovely to hear, but
I'm afraid "mercy mild" is a quality that has been strained
from our blood this cold December.

It's been a long day. The strap from the M-14 cuts into my shoulder. As the tallest man in the platoon I'm always on the right of the front rank when we march. Everyone has to dress off me, I have to keep to cadence without missing a step. Now I lose track, drift out of step, hitch to get back, lose it again. Pretty soon the whole platoon is stumbling. Sergeant James calls a halt.

"WHAT is the MATTER with you, Private Todd? Did you forget how to walk? Did you lose your motherfuckin' lef' foot, or do you not know which one it is? We been doin' this shit five weeks now. If you don't know your lef' foot from your motherfuckin' right foot by now, you don't belong in this man's army! Get your ass to the back of my platoon, Private, and when we get back you are doin' pushups until you're ready for Social Security!"

There's no point arguing. The sergeant is right. I am messing up his platoon—and I don't belong in this man's army. We have gotten crosswise, the army and me, and this whole sick drama has taken on a dangerous edge. I have never forgiven the company commander for calling me in and reaming my ass because the lieutenant from back home wanted some advice on platoon morale, and now I've begun to play a little game. The captain is a thick-necked, tight-assed sonofabitch, as good a symbol as any of the kind of mentality that got us into Vietnam in the first place. When he comes around to inspect the company late at night, I sit up in the supply room, draw a bead on his head with the M-14, and follow him as he crosses from one barracks to another. Take a deep breath, get a spot weld on the stock the way Red taught me, breathe out all the way, and hold it. Aim just below his ear. Hold it and squeeze. Don't pull the trigger. Squeeze. A little more pressure and a little more, and if you do it right the rifle goes off all by itself. Steady, steady. A little more and his head will explode like a grapefruit.

We stay on the safe side of death and prison, the captain and

I, but this is how fraggings happen on the other side of the world. An officer screws up often enough, gets enough guys killed, you roll a smoke grenade into his tent, a little warning. He screws up again, you go with a fragmentation grenade. No fingerprints, no traces. They just pour him into a body bag.

■　　■　　■

We talk on the phone a couple of times a week, but Mariela writes only one letter. I keep pleading for something, anything. A line. She keeps saying she's embarrassed to write to me. I say it doesn't matter, just a postcard with her name on it would be good enough. She's the most camera-shy beautiful woman I have ever known, so I don't even have a picture—but finally I get a letter. It's two thirds of a page long, written in blue ink on white, lined paper, and the last four words are "I love you, Jacko." The letter is now my most precious possession. I read it a half-dozen times a day, carry it everywhere. She is everything to me, this shy, intelligent, kindhearted, beautiful young woman waiting in Miami. The only thing I want out of any of this—the only thing—is to get back to Miami and to see her when I wake in the morning, those kind, dark eyes looking at me across the pillow. On the last Sunday morning before Christmas, I call her right after breakfast, expecting gentle words, comfort, sweet talk about the five days left until Christmas leave.

It isn't to be.

It started one steamy night that summer, the night we first made love. It had taken me two months to persuade her to surrender her virginity, but it finally happened in her bed late on a Saturday night when her parents were out of town. Next morning I felt like the king triumphant, conqueror of the untouchable Mariela. Lying in her bed, smelling coffee in the kitchen. Digging the symbolism of the white sheets, white bedspread, white walls, everything in her bedroom a virginal white.

Mariela brought strong Cuban coffee and pastries on a silver tray, service fit for a conqueror. She sat on the edge of the bed, sipping coffee, watching me eat. I awaited her compliments, her expressions of unbridled delight in my prowess as a lover. I dropped a couple of hints but she didn't respond.

Finally she sighed. "So that was sex, huh?" she said. "So what's the big deal?" Crushed, humiliated and disgraced, I made up some urgent errand and fled without finishing my coffee.

That week I had a few drinks with an old friend from Nebraska who was also a reporter at the *Herald* and the best writer I knew. I told him about my plight. He had a reputation as a lady's man. I asked if he had any suggestions. His advice was pithy and direct. I followed it. Mariela was happy, I was happy. Surf, sex, sun. Until the draft intervened, we lived a few beautiful months on the edge of paradise.

Now, on this sunny December morning a few days short of Christmas, I stand in the long row of outdoor phone booths, tell the operator I want to make a collect call to a number in Miami, wait impatiently. Mariela answers, accepts the call.

"Hello, baby."

"You shit. You sonofabitch. You bastard. How could you?"

"How could I what?"

"You told everybody what I like in bed. You told your friend we were doing it, and you told him what I like."

"What?"

"Don't you try to lie to me, you sonofabitch. I know what you did. One of your buddies was in a bar the other night, and he saw Tom Clagg and started giving him a hard time. You know what he said? He told Tom he should have done it to me the way you did, and then I'd love Tom the way I love you."

"Oh, no. Mariela, I didn't . . ."

"Don't you deny it. You shit. You sonofabitch. Tom came right here from the bar Thursday night and told me everything, how you've been bragging all over town about the things we do in bed. It's over. I never want to see you again. Don't you come here for Christmas, you bastard, because I won't be here."

"Mariela, I never bragged anywhere."

"I don't want to hear it. You go around talking about our sex life, you're not the kind of man I want to marry. I didn't want anybody in the world to know we were doing it, and then you go and tell him everything! Everything! And he says that to Tom in a bar, right in front of everybody! You shit!"

"Mariela, the only reason I told him was because . . ."

"Shut up! I don't want to hear your excuses. I said it's over. You're a shit and I will never speak to you again! Good-bye!"

And she hangs up. I stand there staring at the receiver, thinking this can't be real. Other soldiers waiting for the phones, laughing and joking with their wives and sweethearts, making last-minute plans for Christmas. And here I am dangling at the end of the world, holding a phone that has gone dead.

I call the operator back, make another collect call. The phone rings five times, six times. "I'm sorry, sir," the operator says, "there's no answer. Would you like to try again later?"

I hang up, fish change out of my pocket, dial the number myself. Listen to the phone ring ten times, fifteen times, twenty. Try again. Pick up, Mariela. Please. Pick up. Give me a chance to explain.

No answer. It's over. I put the phone down, stumble away from the booth. Another soldier moves up to make his call. I drift away, stunned, walking aimlessly out toward the parade ground, a place to be alone. Away from the rest, I bend over and try to breathe. It feels like I've been punched in the stomach. No urge to cry, just trouble breathing, the way you feel when you've taken a vicious hit on a football field and you can't get your parts back together.

I can see just how it happened. My buddy is in a bar having a few pops, he sees Clagg, he can't resist. Gets on his case, makes fun of poor, hangdog Clagg with his hopeless, chaste crush on Mariela. Tells him exactly what it is that Mariela likes in the sack. Clagg, beaten in love, knows an opportunity when he sees one. He hightails it to Mariela's house, knowing this is his chance to get her back. What does he have to lose?

And I know her. I know Mariela. Know her fierce pride, her stubborn will, her anger, her intense desire to keep our affair private. She is fiery and uncompromising; that's part of the reason I'm in love with her. Another woman might stay angry for a day, a week, a month. With Mariela, it will take her years to get over it, if she ever does. I'm left to stumble around on the parade ground without a helmet on a sunny Sunday morning, Christmas leave coming up, nowhere to go. If Mariela says it's over, then it's over.

Kenny, our squad leader, sees me acting a little strange and wanders over to see if I'm all right. I can hardly breathe, much less talk, but somehow I manage to tell him that my girlfriend just broke up with me. Kenny is a softspoken Texan who has little in common with the other Texans.

"Jesus, that's tough," he says. "It's happened to a few guys in the platoon, but not like that. That's really tough."

"I don't know what I'm going to do."

"Hell, give her a few hours. Call her back. She'll change her mind if she's in love with you."

"Not this one. She won't. I know her."

"Geez, that's tough, man, right before Christmas leave and all. So what are you going to do for Christmas? Go back to Nebraska?"

I haven't even thought about that one. Everything was so clear when I climbed out of my bunk: five more days of basic, fly to Miami, marry Mariela, go to Key West, back to Fort Lewis, finish my stint in the army, go back to the *Herald*. Now what?

Mercifully, the drill sergeants leave us alone. No Chinese thinking position, no pushups, no firing range. Mercifully, because if a drill sergeant tries to put me in the thinking position today, I am going to hit him first and deal with the consequences later.

Soldiers polish their boots, clean up their footlockers, play poker, sit around the barracks swapping lies and talking about pussy. I sit down and write a long letter to Mariela because I've got to try, post the letter and wander out to the empty parade ground again, trying to think what to do on Christmas leave. Two free weeks and nowhere to go except back to Nebraska, and I don't want to go home and spend two weeks explaining what happened with Mariela. I walk back and forth on the parade ground alone, smoking one Marlboro after another, automatically field-stripping them the way we've been taught so as not to leave butts, trying to think. If Mariela is not there for me, what am I doing here? If I don't believe in this war, why am I in the army? If I really believe the war is illegal and immoral, then why am I willing to fight it?

When we get our leave, there's nothing to hold me. I can walk out with the leave papers in my pocket, no questions asked. Walk out and never look back. But if I go, what will it do to my parents? What about the job at the *Herald*? What if I get caught and thrown in prison? Can I do five years in Leavenworth if I have to, or will I end up hanging myself with my bootlaces? How can I tell my mother? How could I possibly explain this to Pop, the old soldier from World War I? An hour passes. Another. Another hour after that. I try to concentrate, to think about what I have to do, find my mind drifting endlessly to Mariela. Mariela in bed, Mariela on the beach. Mariela in the pancake house. Mariela in my arms the first time we met, her with a broken ankle, me carrying her in my arms to the nurse's station and falling in love with this woman who was biting through her lip in pain.

I don't know what hurts more, the heartbreak over Mariela or the agony of trying to decide what to do now. I know the right thing is to walk away, but it seems impossible. I love this country, and it's the only place I know. I can no more imagine leaving it forever than I can imagine living without my hands. It's not that I live in America or that I am American. We are indistinguishable. You grow up the way I did, you don't know where your country leaves off and you start. I can't take the easy way out, spend a couple of years writing press releases and then go back to the *Herald*. I have to make a moral decision here. I have to be willing to put myself on the line.

I finish one pack of cigarettes and start another, walking back and forth, doing the equivalent of a full day's march, taking a break now and then to sit on the bleachers of the reviewing stand and stare at the distant mountains. With the ties to Mariela and Miami broken, I feel like a hot-air balloon released from its moorings. Floating free, not sure where I'm going. The first thought is that I want to wangle a way into the infantry, go to Vietnam, and die a heroic death so that Mariela will regret forever what she has done. Then I think about going AWOL right now, flying straight to Miami to confront Mariela and sort it out. I know it wouldn't work; the day might come when she will be ready to listen, but this isn't it.

One instant I'm leaning one way, the next moment I've swung in the opposite direction. It's like watching a compass needle waver back and forth, back and forth, until it settles on true north. Then I start to feel it, like a powerful current you don't sense until you're far out in the stream. There is a right thing here. The truth of it flows in one direction, has since the night in '67 when Mick Lowe finally convinced me that the war in Vietnam was fatally wrong. It just took me awhile to understand it.

There is no epiphany. I don't turn at one end of the parade ground and know what to do. The decision comes a step at a time. A slow dawning, like the sun coming up on the prairies. Finally, I know the answer. I crush the last cigarette under my combat boot, refusing to field-strip this last butt. Let somebody else police it up, because I'm not going to be here. I take a deep breath and head back to the barracks, my mind made up. I won't be coming back. I'll wait until Christmas leave, and then I'll say good-bye. To Fort Lewis, to the army, to America. I'll go to Canada or live underground in the U.S. If they want me, they'll have to catch me and drag me back in chains.

Once the decision is made, I realize that I've probably known what I had to do from the day we arrived at Fort Lewis. You don't spend two years fighting to stop a war and then meekly allow yourself to become a cog in the war machine. The war is wrong. To be here is wrong. I have to go. There is no other way. I am going to desert from the United States Army.

■ ■ ■

After mess I find Powers, tell him what happened with Mariela. We go for a long walk, sticking to the shadows, talking low. After looking around carefully to be sure no one can hear us, I tell him my mind is made up: I'm going to desert over Christmas leave. I might try to live underground in the U.S., I might go to Canada, but I'm not coming back. Powers grabs me by the shoulders, looks at me hard.

"Don't do it because you're fucked up over some woman," he says. "That's not right. You'll change your mind in a day. You have to be sure this is the right thing for you, because this is the biggest decision you'll ever make in your life."

"I know. It's partly her, yeah. But it's more like I've been doing the wrong thing because of her. I should have gone to Canada before I was inducted, either that or to prison. But I never thought I could take prison."

"I can dig that. Me either. Jail isn't a place you want to be, not for an hour. Well, if you're sure, man, I can help you. We've got to work out a plan. You can't just take off and see where you end up."

"I can use some help, man. I know that."

Powers is cool, calm, working out what I have to do, making sure I'm not just reacting to Mariela, that this is what I really want to do.

Powers knows Vancouver well. When he was AWOL he stayed for a while in a hotel off Vancouver's skid row. He says it's clean and cheap and safe. Fifteen bucks a week, affordable until I find a job. As soon as we get to Seattle we'll get in touch with the Seattle Committee to Aid War Resisters, find out what they know about deserters in Canada. It might be possible to live legally north of the border—to get a job, live under my own name instead of living underground. Powers has been out of touch here in the army; he doesn't know how the Canadians are applying the rules. Either way, it's better than trying to live underground in the U.S., where after thirty days the FBI will be looking for me.

Powers says I can stay with him over Christmas, then he'll drive me to Canada after the holidays. The trick is to get out of the country before midnight, January 4, when our leave will expire and I'll be due back at Fort Lewis. Powers keeps pushing me, trying to make certain that I know what I'm doing. Both of us talking in whispers, afraid somebody is going to overhear. I get the first taste of that outlaw feeling, shivery and a little scared, not at all like the time with Banville when I was too mad to care.

"You know if you stay you're going to get assigned to army journalism, end up sitting at a desk somewhere writing press releases?"

"Yeah, probably."

"And this is still what you want to do?"

"Absolutely. In a way that would be the most chickenshit thing I could do, to flack for the army. That's almost as bad as dodging the draft in the National Guard."

"You're not going to change your mind tomorrow?"

"Look, I thought you wanted me to go. It took me two years to make up my mind, don't try to turn my head around now."

"I just want you to be sure. This is huge, man. It's not like deciding whether you want to buy a Chevy or a Ford. You just split up with your girl today, man. You oughta give yourself some time."

"I took too much time already. I'm ready to go."

"It's a scary thing you're doing, man. When I was AWOL, I was scared shitless. All this stuff goes through your head—what happens if you get caught, what your folks are going to say. What if they change the law and decide to hang you? You know you might never be able to come back to America?"

"Of course I know! Quit bugging me, man, I'm tense enough. I've gone over this stuff a million times. It's the right thing. Now I've made up my mind, it just feels right. I don't want to be sitting there thirty years from now, thinking this was what I should have done and I didn't have the guts to do it."

"OK, long as you know. It's your ass. I'll drive you to Canada. Matter of fact, if I don't get my C.O. discharge, I might join you up there."

"That would be good. I'd feel better if there were two of us."

The next day it's pouring rain again and we're scheduled to be back on the rifle range. I've had a cold throughout most of basic, but I've never gone on sick call. Now the cold is better, so I say I've got a toothache and I need to see a dentist and they put me on sick call, a day off from the army. The dentist gives me a quick look as soon as I get to his office. I point to a lower molar on the left side which was bothering me six months ago. He nods, taps, clucks, takes an X-ray. I spend the next four hours sitting in his waiting room—reading magazines, staying warm, watching women. The nurses are the first women I've seen since we landed in Seattle and I love everything about them. The smell of their perfume, the sound of their nylons when they walk, their crisp uniforms. It's raining hard outside, and I'm in here watching them. I'm feeling cocky. For once, I've outfoxed the army.

After lunch the dentist calls me back into his chair. He's a huge, amiable Chinese-American from San Francisco who talks incessantly while he works. He fiddles with his instruments, pokes around inside my mouth. A little drilling, a little filling, and I'll have missed a day in the rain on the rifle range. He tells me to open wide, fits something over my tooth. I'm half asleep, lying back in the chair, daydreaming about nurses, trying to scheme a way to spend the rest of the day in the waiting room.

There is no warning at all. He just plants a thick forearm on my chest and yanks. The bastard is pulling my tooth. No Novocain, nothing. Just clamp and yank. I scream and go for his throat with both hands. He pushes harder with his forearm on my chest, leaning all his weight on me. I'm lying flat on my back and the guy outweighs me by fifty pounds. We hang there in a death grip for a minute or more, me trying to throttle him dead, him tugging at my tooth. Then it's over. He holds the bloody tooth aloft, a trophy of battle. He grins.

"You put up a pretty good fight," he laughs, like it's the best joke he's heard all day. My whole body is rigid and quivering, blood pouring from my mouth. I want to kill him but I'm choking on blood and half in shock.

He gives me a hand, heaves me up out of the chair. "Go tell the nurse," he says, "you're one lucky GI! You're on twenty-four hours' light duty!"

Motherfucker. Lucky GI, my ass. Fucking sadist. I stumble out into the hall. There are two nurses standing there. I start to explain: "I'm on twenty-four hours' light . . ."

For some reason, the floor is coming up to meet me. I wake to find four nurses hovering over me. Somehow, they've got me up on a gurney with my boots off. One of them is holding a wet cloth to my head, her breasts tantalizingly close. I remember the missing tooth, the dentist I have to kill. When I start to get up to go after him, she pushes me back down gently. "Take it easy. You need to rest here for an hour. Then you're on twenty-four hours' light duty. No running, no pushups, no rifle training."

I can see her cleavage, smell her perfume. I probe the hole in my mouth with the tip of my tongue. The tooth is definitely gone. A little something to remember the army by. I swallow a couple of painkillers, lie there resting, the painkillers hitting me on an empty stomach like an injection of morphine. The nurses come and go, trailing perfume. Now and then one stops to touch my forehead, cool fingers on hot skin. I feel giddy. All the beautiful nurses. I want to propose to every one. "Excuse me, I just had my tooth pulled. Will you marry me?" Maybe I can come back tomorrow. Have another tooth pulled. See the pretty nurses again.

Somewhere along the line Powers has become a skilled carpenter, so he's been assigned to put up new wooden beams in an empty mess hall. For my twenty-four hours of light duty I'm assigned to help him. Powers has become friendly with one of the drill sergeants, the only one who is a genuine, certified war hero. His name is Sergeant Becker and he spent eight days trapped with his platoon on a hill in Vietnam. At the end it was so bad they were all eating grass, certain they would die on that hill. By the time the weather cleared and the choppers could get in to evacuate them, only a dozen men were left alive. Somehow the experience makes Becker the gentlest, the most sympathetic of all the drill sergeants. He is in charge of the company clerks, who can't type, so Powers starts doing some typing for him. When Becker finds out I can type twice as fast as Powers, he starts pulling me off the rifle range to type. I spend two happy days of basic tapping out army documents while the hunt-and-peck clerks glare at me. Let 'em glare. If typing gets me in out of the rain, then I'll type.

Becker is also in charge of the mess hall project, so he assigns me to help Powers. It's splendid work. It's sunny again and Powers and I are alone most of the day with no one to bother us. I love the clean smell of the wood and the way the beams fit perfectly after Powers makes the cut. I'm incapable of sawing a straight line, but my job is just to lift and heave and hold things in place while Powers hammers. Becker drops in now and then to shoot the breeze, and the three of us have a great time. It's my happiest day in the army, even with that hole in my mouth where my tooth should be.

The next day is my last full day at Fort Lewis. I'm nervous and edgy but my mind is clear. No hesitation at all. I know exactly what I'm going to do and why. But that evening Powers comes around the barracks to say that we have a problem. To get onto the buses that will take us into Seattle, we have to pass an inspection in dress uniform. We've both neglected to polish the brass buttons on our uniforms or to shine our dress shoes. Now we have to be ready to pass inspection or we won't get off the base. The buttons will shine up quickly, but the shoes take weeks of spit-shining to get that even gloss the army wants to see.

"We're fucked," Powers says. "I got the word. They check everybody out with a fine-tooth comb. You don't have your shit together, they send you back to barracks and that's where you stay."

It seems like somebody's idea of a sick joke, all that agonizing over the war and now I won't be able to get out because my shoes aren't shined. I sit on my bunk and start shining the shoes, but it's hopeless. I could stay up all night, they still won't look right.

Fifteen minutes later, Powers is back. The man has limitless gifts. Now he says he's scrounged some kind of magic shoe spray that's going to give us the most dazzling feet in the entire U.S. Army. I'm to meet him in the supply room in fifteen minutes and we'll both polish our shoes. When I get there, Powers is already spraying his shoes. They gleam.

"Look at this shit," he says. "Can you believe it? Those army assholes spend hours and hours shining their shoes, and all you have to do is spray them for two minutes with this. Look at these things shine!"

They are perfect, flawless regulation U.S. Army dress shoes. The product of months of careful spit-shining. Anybody can see that. When we're finished, we have the most beautiful dress shoes in the entire United States Army. We are ready to rock 'n' roll.

Late the next afternoon we're back in barracks getting ready for Christmas leave, giddy and frantic at the prospect of freedom after six weeks of basic. Snapping towels, play-boxing, acting like a bunch of overgrown boys. It's like a high school locker room, virgins bragging about how they plan to fuck so much over the holidays, they won't be able to march when they get back. Some days they drive me nuts, these loud-mouths. Today they make me a little wistful and sad. I'm not going to see these guys again.

Somehow, probably because Powers can't keep his mouth shut, the black soldiers in our platoon know what's up. Three or four come by my bunk one at a time, say good-bye, whisper a few words, offer a high-five and good luck. One, a guy named Skeeter, was threatened with a court-martial the first week of basic for damaging government property. After the army took the clippers to Skeeter's impressive Afro, he finished the job with a razor, shaving his head clean. One of the more sadistic white drill sergeants threatened to have Skeeter court-martialed for that. He claimed that Skeeter's head was government property, so when Skeeter shaved his head he had damaged government property. Skeeter laughed, an act of disrespect which earned him twenty minutes in the Chinese thinking position.

Skeeter has a pretty clear idea of the black man's role in this war. Hispanics and African-Americans who are second-class citizens at home are being sent to the other side of the world to kill Asian boys because a few crazy white men have decided they should. Skeeter might not put it that way, but he understands it all right.

I get Skeeter off in a quiet corner. "Skeeter, man, come to Canada with me. We'll get a place together. You've got less reason to be in this war than I do."

"A black man tryin' to hide out in Canada? They'd throw my black ass in jail in a minute. You white boys, you almost look like Canadians."

"C'mon, Skeeter. From what I hear, Canadians are a lot more tolerant than Americans."

"Nah, I was born and bred in the ghetto, my man. I know a brother went up to Vancouver on vacation once, he said they don't even *have* a ghetto. What am I gonna do, I can't get my barbecue ribs and collard greens? I'd starve to death, man."

"Ah, Skeeter. Don't kid me, man. I bet you hate collard greens. Come with me. We'll find jobs, take care of each other."

"Hey, y'know, I'd like to. I just can't do it. But you get yourself some of them honkie women up in Canada for me, OK?"

"Don't worry about me. You take care of yourself, especially if you get sent to 'Nam, OK? You keep your head down. It ain't your fight."

"I hear you. I hear you. Peace, brother." He gives me a soul handshake and wanders off to finish packing. I watch him walk away thinking, "What's gonna happen to you, Skeeter? What's gonna happen?" I have a bad feeling about Skeeter, a feeling that he's going to Vietnam and he's not coming back. Like he knows it, too, but he can't do anything about it.

We all put on our gleaming shoes and our crisp uniforms and head downstairs to admire ourselves in the mirrors in the latrine. You can hardly breathe in there, so many guys standing at the sinks drowning themselves in English Leather, getting ready for the big moment when they step off the plane to meet their girlfriends, smelling like they spent their last week in the army dunked in a vat of aftershave. Powers and I give each other a quick inspection and a thumbs up: we're beautiful. We'll breeze through the inspection, snappy soldiers in our forest green dress uniforms and spiffy shoes.

Back upstairs, it's time to prepare a parting gesture for the U.S. Army. My footlocker has driven me nuts for six weeks. No matter how hard I try, I can never get things squared away to suit the sergeants, never get my socks, handkerchiefs, underwear, and all the rest of it folded to precise army specifications. At the last minute I decide to take revenge on the footlocker. When we're taken to the PX for one last seventy-five-cent haircut, I buy a dozen chocolate bars. Now I unwrap the candy bars and place them carefully here and there inside the footlocker, which happens to sit right next to the radiator, which is always red-hot to compensate for the open windows. When the MPs figure out I'm gone, they'll have a nice mess of gooey melted chocolate to clean up. Not much as gestures of defiance go, but it's the best I can do on short notice.

Finished with that job, I fold my one letter from Mariela carefully and tuck it in my wallet, go to the supply room to fetch the guitar I bought from Powers for fourteen dollars, pack everything I can stuff into the duffel bag we're allowed to take with us, padlock the footlocker for the last time, and join the rest of the guys—pacing around in our socks so we won't disturb the shine on our dress shoes, smoking and talking, impatient to move out, looking at the empty bunks, stripped of bedding, from which other guys have disappeared.

I feel like I'm breaking up and floating away in different directions. I still look like a soldier, but I'm several hundred miles down the road. And still, part of me wants to be a Marine Corps officer leading troops in Vietnam. Crazy, but you don't just wake up one morning, decide that a war is wrong, and become someone else. If we can't have peace, what I want is a better war. The kind of war when you ask what you can do for your country and march off to battle tyrants and fight for the underdog. Trouble is, this time the tyrants are mostly on our side, and we are definitely not the underdog.

Finally the drill sergeants come by and holler at us to line up outside. We're marched to a vast parking lot where dozens of buses wait to ferry men off the base—buses to the airport over there, buses to downtown Seattle over here. Before Sunday, I thought I would be taking the airport bus, catching a plane to Miami, marrying Mariela. Now the destination is downtown Seattle. Powers and I join one of the lines. At the door of each bus, officers in crisp uniforms are going over every soldier from head to toe, giving each recruit a minute inspection before he's allowed to board the bus and go home for Christmas. Powers and I have nothing to worry about. We're perfect.

I glance down at my feet and my jaw drops. The shoes were perfect when we left the barracks. Now they look like road maps, the gleaming polish cracked in every direction and beginning to peel. Powers's shoes are the same—it's so bad flecks of polish the size of quarters are falling off, leaving a trail of shoe polish behind us. Up ahead, soldiers are being sent back to barracks because of a missing button, an untied shoelace. They'll miss the bus and the flight home, that much we know. After that—what? Are these guys going to miss Christmas leave altogether, with more than half of them headed for Vietnam? Does this mean another midnight belly-crawl across the parade ground if I want to get out?

"You and your bright ideas," I whisper to Powers. "What was that cheap shit you put on our shoes?"

Even Powers, for once, is at a loss for words. "Fuck, I dunno. But I think we're fucked now."

The line snakes along, the officers up front taking their time. They are thorough. There is no way we are going to sneak through. They are going to have a good laugh over our shoes and send us right back to barracks. We are not getting on that bus. There are no more than a half-dozen soldiers ahead of us, waiting to be inspected by a glowering lieutenant. Our fate is sealed. We are going to spend Christmas at Fort Lewis, pulling shit details and watching it rain.

Just then Sergeant Becker comes swinging by, looking insanely happy. Of course he's insanely happy. He's going on leave too, and he doesn't have to pass an inspection to get out. Becker sees us standing there waiting for the bus and wanders over to say hello. "Where you guys going?" he asks.

"Seattle," I say. "But I don't think we're going to pass the inspection."

I point at our shoes. Becker laughs.

"How come you're taking the bus, anyway?" he says. "I'm going to Seattle right now, going to the wildest party you ever seen. C'mon, you two can ride with me."

"Hey!" he shouts at the lieutenant without waiting for us to answer. "These guys are coming with me."

The lieutenant nods. Just like that we're out of the line and tagging along after Becker, weaving our way through the buses and the hundreds of recruits who are still waiting, all of them looking at us, wondering what's going on, figuring we're in some kind of trouble they don't want to know about, being led off by a drill sergeant. I keep waiting for someone to reach out and grab us, for an MP to say we can't leave the base with these disgraceful shoes attached to our feet. No one says a word. We're just a couple of buck privates and a sergeant walking to the parking lot. One minute we're about to go back to barracks, screwed out of our Christmas leave by a shoe-shine. The next minute we're strolling to Becker's car like the coolest swinging dicks in the whole U.S. Army.

As cars go, Becker's is quite the freedom wagon. A big old souped-up '63 Chevy that growls like a dragster when he revs the engine. He even has an eight-track tape player, the first I've seen. I sit up front next to Becker, Powers sprawls in the back seat. The sergeant jams a tape—the second Led Zeppelin album—into the eight-track, reaches into a paper bag on the floor, pops open beers for the three of us, drops the Chevy into gear, and floors it, laying fifty feet of rubber on the way out of the parking lot. We hit the highway to Seattle with the music so loud the car vibrates like one oversized speaker, leaving the army behind at a cool 100 miles per hour, a helter-skelter jail break down a Washington highway with Robert Plant wailing, Powers shrieking like a banshee because we're free, running to the only real light at the end of the meanest tunnel of them all. I hate Led Zeppelin. Always have, always will. But not now, not here. I reach down and crank it up a little louder. Becker grins, pounds on the steering wheel, sings along. He can't sing a lick but he knows all the words.

"You fuckin' guys don't know how lucky you are tonight!" he says. "I'm takin' you to a party like nothin' you've ever seen before. You been locked up in basic, man, it's time you let loose. You want pussy, you want drugs, you want booze, you want music, you wanna dance till your eyes bug out—wait'll you see this place!"

We finish the beers, pop open three more. Becker has the Chevy revved up all the way. The music louder than ever, like a jet engine pumping out of the dash. It feels like the car is going to take off and fly. Nobody is coming after us. We're free.

We sail right into the party at a warehouse in a rundown industrial neighborhood somewhere in Seattle. Powers takes Becker's Chevy to go find his girlfriend at the bus station, Becker and I march in uniform into a scene that is already well out of hand—a thundering wall of sound from speakers six feet tall, maybe three hundred long-haired freaks doing the boogaloo in the middle of a concrete floor while a girl with her top on and her jeans off rides a zonked-out hippie on a beat-up couch off to the side, nobody paying her any attention at all. Cases of beer stacked against a wall, gallon bottles of wine on a table at the back, next to the wine a king-sized punch bowl that is, Becker whispers, laced with Timothy Leary's poison of choice, LSD. Becker plunges right in, dunks a Dixie cup in the punch and swallows it, moves into a slow dance with a slender, long-haired hippie girl he seems to know while I stand on the edge of the party, twirling my hat, feeling like a Martian in army greens and shaved head, the dress shoes still flaking polish.

A little beer is not nearly enough to get you onto the radio wave these people are riding, so what difference could a little cup of acid punch make? You go from abject despair in a bus lineup at Fort Lewis to this in ninety minutes, you have already left the straight way behind, the first step in a trip that has only begun to get seriously twisted. An enormous woman wearing a kaftan the size of a tent drags me out onto the dance floor. Other women slip past, dance for a bit, move on to someone else. Long hair, breasts loose under tie-dyed fabric, no makeup, long-legged healthy West Coast American beauties everywhere, butts and thighs and freckles and wide sweet mouths. After six weeks in the Fort Lewis rain they are sunshine through green trees, and I want them with a longing that is like thirst in the desert. The music so loud talk is impossible, nothing to do but drift with the sound, dance and touch and let go, embarrassed when the touch is too close and I feel my trousers rise at the fly, the need quick and insistent. Drift with the music: Country Joe & the Fish, Janis Joplin, Hendrix, Jefferson Airplane, Crosby, Stills, Nash & Young, some acid stuff I've never heard. In one of the filthy bathrooms at the back a loving couple are making it in a stall while a dozen guys stand in line waiting at the two urinals. The girl, invisible although we can hear her just fine, asks if anyone can pass her a toke. Someone lights a joint and passes it over the door, she and her friend have a toke or two and pass it back out again, their moans climbing in pitch like morning glories on a wall. I stand at a urinal, too wrecked to do anything except think about how much I want Mariela—right then, right there. In the stall, on the floor, on the couch. Knowing there is no way, now or ever.

Powers makes it back around midnight, introduces his girlfriend Barb, a tiny, energetic woman with a lively smile. They drift off. More wine, more beer, more dancing. Somewhere around 2 A.M. the party thins out a little. Exhaustion from basic training kicks in. The couches are full so I roll up my jacket and lie down right there on the concrete floor and fall asleep. I have no idea how much later it is when I wake to find a slender young woman dancing over me, her long skirt up around her waist, legs parted, panties off, open and ready and waiting. I reach for her but the effort is too much, I can't force myself awake even for her. When I wake again, wondering if she was there at all or if it was just a dream, I look across the floor, see her astride someone else, and feel a pang of regret.

Now it's 4 A.M. and a drill sergeant is shaking me awake. Have to shit-shave-shower line up outside, but I can't understand why I'm sleeping on a concrete floor. The sergeant crouches over me, insistent, won't take no for an answer. I'm in some kind of trouble, dazed, wondering what I did and how they found me, aching all over from sleeping on the floor. Try to focus, realize the sergeant is Sergeant Becker. Good guy, Becker. Now it all comes back: the shoes, the buses, Becker grabbing us, the wild ride into Seattle, the party. Powers is there too, and Barb, the three of them trying to persuade me to wake up. It's urgent, I can't understand why. All I want is to go back to sleep. I'm so tired I can sleep anywhere. On the fifty-yard line during the Super Bowl. In the mud at Fort Lewis with Fillmore pointing his M-14 at my head. On a cold concrete floor at a party with a beautiful girl dancing half naked above my head.

Becker needs a favor so strange I have to go to the sink in the men's room and run cold water over my face and neck while he tries to explain. He has a sister who is a paraplegic. She's traveling to San Diego with their parents. Later, right? Tomorrow? Sunday? Not later. Now. In a couple of hours. They want to take two cars to California, see, not one. Becker's sister has this big Lincoln that's been modified for her to drive, but she can drive only an hour or two before she has to rest, so here's the deal: Becker wants to know if I'll drive his sister to San Diego in the Lincoln, following her parents down the Pacific Coast Highway.

"Love to. I just need to sleep for a couple of days."

"That's the thing, see. They have to go today. This morning. I figure you drink a pot of coffee, you'll be fine."

I try to focus on Becker's face. He's one of these steel-jawed, handsome blond surfer dude types. Surfer turned sergeant. Powers is the same type but with dark, curly hair. They're both looking at me, telling me I can do it, I can drive this girl to California. It seems to be very important that I do this thing. The reason is standing off to the side, a beautiful, fragile-looking Eurasian girl Becker has met at the party. As wrecked as I am, I get the connection. Becker doesn't want to go to California himself because this girl is waiting. He's trying to con me into taking his sister to California so he can stay with the girl. In his place, I'd probably do the same thing.

"You drive her down," Becker says, "my folks have this great beach house at Oceanside, outside San Diego. You crash with them, drink their liquor, get a suntan, come back all ready to finish basic."

Somehow, I manage not to tell him that returning to basic does not figure in my plans.

This is crazy. I am half drunk and two-thirds stoned. I have no idea what was in that acid punch, but I feel very strange and I keep seeing lights flickering out of the corners of my eyes.

I slept for two hours. I am in the advanced stages of exhaustion from basic training. I want to go north to Canada, he's asking me to drive all the way down the Pacific coast to San Diego. With a paraplegic girl. In a Lincoln. Less than a week before Christmas. He's a drill sergeant and I'm a deserter, only he doesn't know that. Eight, maybe ten hours since we were standing there looking at our shoes, figuring we would spend the holidays back in barracks watching the rain. And now we're talking about San Diego?

"You ever seen California, man?" Becker asks. No, I have not seen California. I am leaving my country forever, and I have not seen California.

"Don't feel like you have to to do this, man," Becker says. "No sweat if you can't. But if you can, I'd appreciate it. I'll owe you one."

Oh, no. I do have to. I have to see California.

"When do we leave?"

"I'll take you over to meet the folks, meet my sister, get a couple of pots of coffee down you, and you're on your way."

Becker's folks are nice, well-to-do suburban types, his father a blocky, successful-looking man with a mustache, his mother a kind woman with a tired smile. I hope they can't tell how messed up I feel, sitting there drinking cup after cup from a big pot of strong, black coffee as fast as I can choke it down. I have no clothes at all except my dress uniform, combat boots, and some army-issue underwear and socks stuffed in the duffel bag, so Becker lends me some of his clothes. He's four inches shorter and fifty pounds heavier, all of it muscle in the shoulders and legs, so the clothes are all too short and too wide in the shoulders and too big around the waist. I take a pair of green jeans, three or four T-shirts, an old sweater, a light jacket, cinch the pants up with my army dress belt. The cuffs ride four inches above my shoes, but they don't look too bad with the combat boots. Becker, pretty high himself although he hides it well, points at the shoes, giggling. "What'd you polish those things with, goat shit?"

"Nah, we had a little accident."

"I guess you had a fucking accident. You're lucky I came along, you'd be spending Christmas sitting on the base holding your dick. You woulda never passed inspection with those things."

"Yeah, I know. Thanks, by the way."

"You drive my little sister to San Diego, we're even. You get back from down there, call me and we'll find another party."

The sister arrives in her big black Lincoln and waits outside. I get behind the wheel. Her father leans in to give me instructions.

"We hold it at sixty-five all the way," he said. "I want you to stay right with me so we don't worry about you two. If for any reason we lose you, pull off at the next exit and wait. I'll find you."

I've driven tractors and hot rods and trucks with fifteen gears and twenty-ton loads. I'm pretty sure I can point this great big Lincoln down the middle of an interstate highway no matter what condition I'm in. "I won't lose you."

"Good. We're going to stop somewhere around Portland and have a big breakfast. Breakfast is important if you're going to drive all day."

I can't wait.

■　　■　　■

Pacific Coast Highway, the hour before dawn. Seattle to Portland following old man Becker's taillights down Interstate 5. Riding the purr of the big Lincoln, nothing to do but hold the road. Blinking, eyes burning, trying not to fall asleep. Sense rather than see tall pines, cedars, towering Douglas firs, fog coming undone as night fades, drifting into webs of mist back in the woods where moss trails down the north side of old bark. Clear creeks running December cold, the scrabble of tiny claws leaving precise tracks on wet ground, dying ferns under the tall trees already running to fossil. Dawn something smoky gray in the east, no light at all in the way it spreads across a Pacific sky choked with the urge to rain. It's dark, and then it's less dark, and then it's something you might call day although you couldn't point to the sun without a compass. Still the taillights twist round the next bend in the road, white lines blur, small-town exits loom and vanish.

Her name is Betsy. Pleasant, bright, cheerful young woman, paralyzed from the waist down. She doesn't say how or where or when and I figure it's not polite to ask. Strange couple, driving the coast highway a few days before Christmas, a deserter walking away from it all and a girl who can't walk. Make small talk, keep it light. What basic training is like, what Nebraska is like, how she feels about Seattle. Stop for breakfast at a House of Pancakes outside Portland. Hover around Betsy, help set up her wheelchair, unsure of the protocol. Offer to lift her into her seat? Stand back and pretend nothing is different? Wait anxiously, be there if she needs me? Once the chair is at the door she lifts herself smoothly into the seat; all I have to do is close the car door and open the door of the restaurant for her. She scoots herself into a seat across from her parents, I fold her chair and sit down with a menu.

The little ironies of franchise America, where everything is the same from one coast to another: At the *Detroit Free Press* I covered a press conference with the fast-talking wheeler-dealer who founded this chain. In Miami I had my first and last meals with Mariela at a House of Pancakes on Biscayne Boulevard, the last on that rainy Halloween morning lost under several thousand miles of moving on. Now the first breakfast out of the army at this pancake house near Portland—a cheese omelet, bacon, pancakes, toast, coffee, orange juice, no sergeants pushing me to choke it down. The Beckers ask polite questions about my background and get just-the-facts-ma'am answers. We don't talk about the real things, Vietnam or Mariela. Nothing about jets screaming low over a jungle tree line spitting napalm, or the knot of fear and pain you carry in your gut from the moment you decide to walk away, or the way Mariela comes walking out of the Atlantic on Key Biscayne, salt water streaming down her lean, tanned stomach and her long brown legs, or how when I think about it my lungs freeze and I forget how to breathe.

After Portland, Betsy takes the wheel for an hour while I try to doze. High on stray flashes from the acid punch at the party or the delirium of this run to freedom pumping through my veins, I can't even close my eyes. Awake and back at the wheel again, I want to drive all day and all night, through California into Mexico, push the Lincoln to the red line through mountain and jungle and swamp, to Guatemala, Panama, Venezuela. Drive until we run out of ground under the wheels, drive all the way to the tip of Patagonia. Park the big Lincoln down at the end of South America, make friends with the penguins, toss pebbles at Antarctica.

The Beckers are less ambitious. For them, northern California is a pretty good day's work. We cross the state line long before dark but they're already taking an exit west of Sacramento, putting in for the night at a comfortable motel just off the highway. I get a room of my own for the first time in weeks, sprawl on the double bed, get used to the luxury of clean white sheets. Too exhausted to do much, still too wired to sleep. Everything is happening too fast—no time to plan, no time to think things through. It's been five days since I decided to desert from the army, and I haven't had five quiet minutes to think about what I'm doing.

We're headed south. South to San Diego, which is next door to Mexico. I never felt the urge to go to Canada. I always wanted to go to Mexico. Books do that to you. You read, you want to be there: Malcolm Lowry's *Under the Volcano,* Graham Greene's *The Power and the Glory.* Mexico is exotic, but still close enough to the U.S. that you can get the baseball scores. Mexico is warm, Canada is cold. Mexico is cheap, Canada is—well, I don't know what Canada is, but I assume it isn't cheap. If I have to live underground, Mexico is as good as Canada—better, because it's warmer and cheaper. The only country in the world where U.S. deserters can definitely go is Sweden, and that's half a world away. And cold. And they speak a different language. So do the Mexicans, but I learned a little street Spanish growing up in a town that was one-third Mexican. Added a few words in Miami, along with a taste for warm climates and Spanish culture.

The fantasy begins to take hold: I'll go to Mexico, learn Spanish, write novels set in Mexico. Find a beach shack or rent a little room in a mountain village, live on tortillas and write all morning, standing up at a worktable, scribbling with a number two pencil like Papa Hemingway. Drink tequila at a neighborhood café where the owner's daughter, a beautiful señorita, will gaze at me with longing in the liquid pools of her dark eyes. At night she'll visit my room with a magnolia blossom in her hair. Her name will be Pilar and we will drink the good wine and eat the good bread and make love through the night and in the morning she will creep from my room before dawn so that her father will not know that she and the gringo have become lovers.

My college roommate Larry Grossman always talked about Oaxaca, in the mountains south of Mexico City. He made it sound as though Oaxaca were the most beautiful spot on earth. A good place for a new start, with a name like a creek running over rocks: Oaxaca. I drift off to a real sleep for the first time in two days, dreaming of Oaxaca. Lowry's twin volcanoes, Popocatepetl and Ixtacihuatl. Burros and white-washed buildings and lovely señoritas, sleepy in the sun. Yes. Mexico.

We start early the next morning. A solid wall of traffic crawling through the freeways around Los Angeles in the afternoon. Ribbons of cars all the way to the horizon, dry brown hills in the distance, no time to see Hollywood and Vine. Once out of L.A. we make good time and by late afternoon we're sitting at their condo in Oceanside, just north of San Diego, sipping chilled white California wine and watching the great Pacific waves roll in. It's 70 degrees, so I borrow a swimming suit from old man Becker and dive into an ocean so cold it's like a shock to the heart. Seems like centuries since we paddled in the warm Atlantic off South Beach, out where my toes barely brushed the sand, Mariela's legs locked around my waist, her arms around my neck. Alone here now in icy water off the California coast, a few surfers out where the big surf breaks, black dots in wetsuits riding tall waves. No one else here crazy enough to try swimming without a wetsuit, but I need this— ocean and cold at sundown, freedom in salt water that turns your skin blue. I need to stop spinning, get a fix on things, understand that I'm about to do an irrevocable thing. Make sure the line is plumb, follow where it leads.

Over dinner, Becker senior says I'm welcome to stay until my leave is up. Just enjoy the ocean and the condo and California. It's tempting, but my cousin Kenny lives in Chula Vista on the other side of San Diego, so I figure I'll be moving on, wanting to get closer to Mexico, wanting family at Christmas no matter what comes after. Kenny and his sister Carol spent most of World War II living with my folks on the farm in Nebraska while their parents worked in defense plants on the coast. They're almost like my older siblings, and a phone call to Kenny is enough to arrange it. I'm to hop a bus in Oceanside and Kenny will pick me up at the bus station in San Diego. Becker insists on giving me two hundred dollars to cover my air fare back to Seattle and another hundred for driving his daughter to San Diego. It's an unexpected windfall; I've got maybe fifty dollars in my pocket and no idea how I'm going to survive on that for even a week in Mexico. I thank him and say good-bye, thinking that whatever is ahead, I will miss good people like the Beckers.

Christmas with Kenny and his family is so normal it's eerie. Eating turkey, telling tall tales about farm life back in Nebraska during World War II, doing endless pushups with their kids on my back. Kenny worked for years for Boeing in Seattle before he ended up in Chula Vista. In between, he spent a couple of years working for a company in Montreal. We go through a big stack of photos of the city, the kids playing on snowbanks six feet high, bundled from head to toe. I figure no sensible human being would live in a place like Montreal, where it's cold and snowy half the year. Going hungry in Mexico has to be better than a full stomach in a place where the wind blows cold and they pile the snow higher than a tall man's head.

No snow this Christmas, just Christmas lights in the palm trees and a Christmas morning call from home, no way to explain why I lit out south instead of hopping a flight back to Scottsbluff for the holidays. A time will come when I have to tell them. Not yet, not until it's certain. Not until I'm over the border in old Mexico.

■　■　■

I make my way to Tijuana by bus the day after Christmas, lugging a duffel bag and a guitar in a cheap plastic case. At Mexican customs they pay me no mind. *Si, señor,* just an American soldier on leave, having a peek at the joys of Tijuana. Spend a day, drink a few tequilas, maybe check out the *putas*. Say a flamboyant good-bye to America, land of my birth. I'm an exile now, a refugee from Nixon and a collective if temporary insanity that can somehow justify a merciless war against peasants on the other side of the globe. A refugee seeking refuge, *por favor*. Seeking to tarry awhile in the land of Diego Rivera and Emiliano Zapata.

Tijuana is a hole. Filthy, garish, touts everywhere pushing the glories of strippers who loll in doorways, wearing makeup that is an invitation to anything but sex, flashing strips of raw anatomy that could put you off fornication forever. Trying to lure you into dark caverns masquerading as bars, where their cronies will be all too happy to relieve a wandering gringo of his wallet. I make the mistake of pointing a long and curious nose into one of these joints and retreat thirty seconds later, sensing that if I don't I may have to fight my way out, shadowy figures closing in from all sides. There are enough sailors and Marines in San Diego to keep these places in business for centuries. Let them get rolled in Tijuana; they have nowhere to go except back to base. I have other destinations, and an hour's stroll is enough to see that if Tijuana is not actually hell, it will do until Lucifer takes charge. Back to the bus station, making plans on the fly. I find a map and locate the next sizable town south of Tijuana, a place called Ensenada maybe an hour down the coast. Climb aboard a wheezing bus for the twisty, nausea-inducing ride to Ensenada, take a room in a clean little hotel near the bus station.

From my bed in a Sacramento motel room, Mexico was a beautiful fantasy, difficult to sustain now after the hard faces on the touts and whores in Tijuana, the bumpy bus ride to Ensenada, the difficulty communicating when the street Spanish you learned back in Scottsbluff refers mostly to intimate body parts and acts of sexual congress with donkeys. In Sacramento I thought of selling stories on Mexico to the *Miami Herald*. Once in Mexico I remember that the *Herald*'s people in Latin America all speak fluent Spanish, have an intimate knowledge of the region and its politics, and have been in place for years. A gringo with a North American income can live well down here, but a gringo with no money is just a nui-sance, especially a gringo wanted by the FBI. A six-foot-six American with a shaved head, so there is no way I can keep a low profile and blend in with the landscape. Ensenada is still a beautiful, unspoiled little town. There is a beautiful bay, the Bahia de Todos Santos, and a famous hotel resort that was once owned by Jack Dempsey. Unlike Tijuana, Ensenada is a good walking town. I set off aimlessly, carrying a cheap paperback. After a couple of hours of wandering, I find a small café and sit down to read, but the paperback is a thin and silly crime story. I want to be reading *Under the Volcano, The Power and the Glory, The Quiet American, To Have and Have Not, A Moveable Feast.* I want to read heady stuff and get drunk and twisted on mezcal, have visions that will lead to towering works of literature, stuffed with symbol-ism and pregnant with portent. But there is no English book-store here, nothing but a little candy store with a dusty week-old copy of the *Los Angeles Times.* I buy a couple of spiral notebooks to record the profound thoughts that inevitably oc-cur to wandering fugitives in exile—not yet understanding that when you are broke and on the run, the things most on your mind are hunger, fear, and loneliness.

After a cheap and fiery dinner back at the same café, I spend a sleepless night listening to a couple having raw and noisy sex on the other side of the wall. Miserable and lonely, I'm tempted to chuck it all and go back to Fort Lewis before my leave expires. I see them the next morning, the loving couple. A fat businessman in his fifties and a tiny, pretty, dark-haired girl who doesn't look a day over sixteen. Sit at a café over *huevos rancheros* and strong coffee, try to begin a short story featuring the mismatched lovers. Nothing comes. Perhaps I have to skip more meals. Like Hemingway in *A Moveable Feast,* prowling the streets of Paris hungry. Perceptions are heightened when the stomach is empty, and it should be easy to go hungry in Mexico. What observations I have don't seem worth entering in the little notebook. The color of the sea from high above the Bahia de Todos Santos, the fat woman on a log near the beach who rocks back and forth, singing softly to herself, the way the ancient bus wheezes along the main highway, the driver grinding gears as he fights his way uphill with a load of peasant women and their chickens. No inspiration here. I date the top of a page—December 27, 1969—and stop there with nothing to say.

I set out to find Jack Dempsey's Riviera del Pacifico, get lost, find her instead. Sitting on a beach, reading a book, the four or five hippies with her sprawled on their sleeping bags sound asleep. I can't even say why I walked up and started talking to her—loneliness, maybe. Hoping to get her away from the group, perhaps, talk her into spending the night in the little hotel by the bus station.

It's 1969, you flash the peace sign and smile, you can usually get into a conversation. She asks about the hair, thinking I'm a Marine from across the border in San Diego. I tell her about Fort Lewis, one thing leads to another, I find out she's a graduate student at Berkeley and that she works for a committee there that has been helping draft dodgers get into Canada. It shouldn't be possible, a big country like Mexico, but here she is, one person who can tell me the things I need to know.

It takes awhile. She kids me about why I let myself be drafted instead of heading for Toronto or Montreal, I mumble something about the cold. She asks why I'm so far from Fort Lewis, I mumble something about Mexico. Sometimes you just need to talk. I'm a little paranoid but she's a good listener, and I end up telling her almost everything.

Her alarm is genuine. She tells me I've been a fool. That I need to get my butt out of Mexico, *pronto*.

"You know you can work in Canada," she says.

"I'm a deserter, not a draft dodger."

"I know that. Pierre Trudeau changed the rules. Deserters

can work legally in Canada. As long as you have a college education and you can get a job, it shouldn't be a problem."

"Are you sure about that?"

"I'm sure."

So Powers was right. Canada is legal.

"You can't stay here, I know that much," she says, squinting up at me in the bright sunshine. "The Mexicans will extradite you for sure. But first they'll put you in a Mexican jail. Nobody told you that?"

Truth is, I didn't ask. She tells me there's help all the way up the West Coast if I need it. Takes out her phone book and copies out a list of numbers for me—committees for draft resisters all the way from San Diego to Seattle. She's attractive. I wouldn't mind spending the night with her, but now I have other priorities. Mexico was a pleasant fantasy, but I don't have to be told that I don't want to spend so much as a night in a Mexican jail. That quickly, my Mexican interlude comes to an abrupt end. I don't have to think about it. If Canada is a sure thing, then I'm going to Canada. Better a regular paycheck in a cold country than hunger and dysentery in a Mexican jail.

I mumble thanks, take the list of phone numbers (which I will manage to lose within a day), and stumble off in the direction of the hotel to stuff my things in the duffel bag and catch a bus to San Diego. Waiting for the bus I have a moment of the kind of irrational paranoia that catches up to you when you're on the run. The encounter with the woman from Berkeley is so improbable, I find myself wondering if she was planted on the beach to send me back the other way, into the arms of waiting Americans. It's no more than a passing thought, but the paranoia is real. It will get worse.

The important thing is that I have to move far and fast. It's already December 27, my leave expires at midnight on January 4, and I'm going to have to hitchhike to Seattle to save money. On the bus to the border, it all becomes terribly real in a way it hasn't been until now. Mexico was always a fantasy. Canada is a reality. I am going to make one last trip across the U.S. from the Mexican border to Canada, and then I may never see my country again.

But the world is a big place. Mountains and deserts and oceans and people who speak strange languages. It's a way to get past the heartbreak of exile: don't think about where you've been, think about where you're going.

And now I know exactly where I'm going. North to Canada.

The guards at the border harass the Mexicans, wave anyone who looks vaguely American right on through. I'm on my way.

■ ■ ■

We walk the straight and narrow with difficulty, we become outlaws without effort. You wake one morning, haggard and unshaven, and you feel the pursuit at your back even if it's not there yet. You see it in the mirrored sunglasses of every highway patrolman, every short-haired guy in a suit who might be an FBI agent. You become lean and nervous and watchful, you glance back along the street to see if anyone is following, you sleep with your pants and shoes beside the bed for a quick getaway. I'm not yet wanted for desertion, not even AWOL until midnight, January 4, when my leave expires. I have every right to be drifting around the U.S., a young soldier on leave, my destination no one's business but my own—but once you begin to think like an outlaw, you never go back. Never. Within a few days I will be wanted, within a month J. Edgar Hoover's crewcut FBI men will officially start looking for me. I have a head start, because I'm already looking back over my shoulder for them.

I should hitch straight to Seattle now, but there is unfinished business: if I am going to leave America forever, I have to see

San Francisco first. If America has a soul and a conscience, it is in San Francisco. The Berkeley free speech movement, Haight-Ashbury, Lawrence Ferlinghetti and the City Lights bookstore, Ginsberg and Kerouac and Gary Snyder, Henry Miller up in Big Sur, Jefferson Airplane, the Grateful Dead. By dawn the next morning I'm on a service road leading to an access ramp to Interstate 5, hitching north to San Francisco. Sitting on the ground, strumming Gordon Lightfoot's "In the Early Mornin' Rain," waiting for a lift. I bought a loose-fitting poncho in Mexico, and with that and the guitar I must look a little less like a soldier, because a group of hippies in a gaudily painted VW van stop to pick me up. There are four or five of them, with a live chicken in the back. One has a guitar too, so I keep my guitar out and he teaches me a couple of licks on the way to Los Angeles.

"If you're in the army, man," he says, "you should leave that scene behind. Nothin' but bad karma. You go to Vietnam, your karma is messed up forever. Like in your next life, you'll be in the Klan. You need to find a good place, stay stoned, blow a spliff the size of a banana, let 'em have their war." I want to tell him that's just what I plan to do, but these are the days of surveillance and paranoia, and you can't always count on J. Edgar Hoover's boys to wear crewcuts for easy identification.

They offer to let me crash at their pad in L.A. that night, but time is tight. They flash the peace sign and drive away after dropping me near a freeway on-ramp just outside Los Angeles. I'm thinking that hitching to Seattle will be a breeze when a California Highway Patrol car pulls up and two big, swaggering patrolmen get out, their eyes hidden behind their standard-issue badass cop sunglasses.

"Didn't anybody tell you hitchhiking is illegal in the state of California?" one of them says. "Let's see some ID."

For once, the army is on my side. I pull out my army ID card and leave papers, explain that I'm trying to get back to Fort

Lewis before my leave expires. Next thing I know I'm in the back of their cruiser, getting a lift to the far side of L.A.

"You shouldn't be hitching like that," one of them says. "Get your uniform on, you'll get to Seattle in no time. Way you are, 'cept for the hair, you could be a hippie."

He served in Vietnam, so he decides to clue me in about life in Southeast Asia. "It helps if you speak a little gook. You know what the gooks say for 'big'? They say 'boo-koo,' like 'GI have boo-koo big dick.' I must've heard that a hundred times in 'Nam, 'GI have boo-koo big dick.'"

His partner laughs. "You're so full of shit," he says. "I heard when you were down in the Delta they took you along on ambushes to rape the mosquitoes and keep 'em off everybody else. Isn't that what they used to call you? 'Needle-dick the bug-fucker?'"

Funny how I can slip right into feeling comfortable with guys like these two. They're like most of the jocks I grew up with—not bad people really, just a little crude. They let me off at a gas station north of Los Angeles. As they're about to pull away, the one who was in Vietnam leans out the window.

"Hey, man! When you get over there, kill a few gooks for us, huh?"

I nod and wave. Absolutely, boys. Second I set foot in 'Nam, I'm gonna start greasing gooks. Special for you. In the gas station restroom I put the uniform and the dress shoes back on. Mercifully, I haven't thrown any of it away. The highway patrolmen were right. On the highway, the uniform is a magic passport. Three quick lifts, the last from a retired couple from Phoenix on their way to see San Francisco for the first time, and I'm in the City by the Bay. I have friends in San Francisco, a couple of college girlfriends and a guy who was in our crowd. I call them all hoping to find a place to crash and a free meal, but no one answers. It's the holiday season, they're probably back in Nebraska. It's cold and getting dark and I'm tired of dragging the duffel bag and the guitar around the streets, so I find a cheap hotel and check in for the night.

Trying to get to the Golden Gate Bridge the next morning, I find myself wandering past buildings that look vaguely familiar, although I can't say why. I keep walking, pass two army officers in uniform, then another. I turn a corner and there it is: "Headquarters, U.S. Third Army, El Presidio." I've walked right onto the Presidio army base, home of the infamous Presidio stockade, one of the lockups for soldiers who decide to go AWOL from the armed forces of the United States. I'm stationed with the U.S. Third Army at Fort Lewis, so my chain of command leads right to this building. I pat the leave papers in my pocket and keep walking. A couple of noncoms look me over but no one says a word. Everything is cool, but if I'm going to be a fugitive, I have to be smart enough not to stroll onto an army base.

The Golden Gate Bridge gleams in the sunlight against the blue December sky. There are a few scattered fishermen along the shore under the bridge, all with their lines in the water. A tall, thin black man in his late sixties sitting in a comfortable folding chair nods in my direction.

"Good mornin'," he says.

"You catchin' anything?"

"Some, some." He points to a short string of fish dangling in the water. "Had better days, had worse days. But I got a few, I do. I got a few."

I sit down a few feet away and watch for a while without saying anything.

"What brings you down here?" he asks.

"The bridge. I just had to get a look at this bridge."

"Oh, it's a beautiful thing, all right. A beautiful thing. A lot of good men died building that bridge, but it's a beauty to look at. Especially on a day like today, shining up there in the sun.

I've seen that bridge almost every day of my life but I never get tired looking at it."

The Golden Gate Bridge must be like Scotts Bluff. A thing you can see every day, and every morning you find something new in it.

"You stationed up to Presidio?" he asks. Seems like everyone I meet smells the military on me.

"Nah. Further up. Fort Lewis."

"Fort Lewis! Fort Lewis, up in Washington? Boy, you're a long way from home. A mighty long way. We get a lot of soldiers down here fishin', Presidio bein' so close, but nobody from Fort Lewis. Seems like if you used to fish wherever you come from, it makes you feel better to go fishin' when you're a long ways from home. They catch a fish, some of 'em, they give it to me 'cause they got no way to cook it anyways. It's a hard thing, bein' in the army. A hard thing. You find it a hard thing, son?"

"Oh, yeah. It's hard, all right."

It's warm in the sun. I feel sleepy and lazy and right at home, like I could spend the rest of my days here with him, fishing under the Golden Gate, eating what I catch.

"You fish here a lot?"

"I come down here most every day, 'cause if I don't fish, we don't eat. The mizzus, when she don't eat, she gets cranky. Woman is big as a house, you'd think she'd have some to spare, but she got to eat her little fishes. She thinks if I don't bring home no fish, I been drinkin' or playin' cards when I oughta been fishin'. You married, son?"

"Nope. I had a girlfriend before I went into the army, but it didn't work out."

"You get one of them Dear John letters?"

"Something like that."

"Oh, yeah. You can't leave a woman alone. Can't leave her alone at all, 'specially not a young one. Next thing you know they up and found themselves a new fella and you back out tomcattin' around, trying to get a little bit. I know. I left more than a few myself, had a few leave me."

The day wears on. I'm supposed to be seeing San Francisco, but I feel like I'm seeing San Francisco just fine right where I am. The more I move on, the more I find places where I want to stay put. We talk some and stay silent some and I feel as easy with him as though we've been fishing side by side for years. He catches three or four more fish, begins to pack up. "What's your name, young fella?"

"Jack."

"Mine's Nate. Old Nate the Fisherman. You come anywhere round here again you ask for me. They all know where to find me."

"I'll do that."

Now I've seen the Golden Gate, it's time to move on. Walk around some that evening, saying good-bye to a city I don't even know. Back in the room I dig out one of the little spiral notebooks and jot down the conversation with old Nate. I'm saving the notebooks for deep thoughts, but deep thoughts have been kind of scarce lately, so this will have to do.

Before dawn the next morning, I put the uniform on for the last time, get a couple of short lifts to the interstate, and catch a ride on an eighteen-wheeler as far as Portland. The trucker is a Korean War vet, fifteen years a long-haul trucker. Chain-smokes cheap cigars, doesn't say much. I tell him about my cousin Bud, another long-haul trucker who tried to teach me to back the big rigs through a long line of trucks when I was about fifteen, how I could never get the hang of it. He isn't impressed.

"The trick is don't think about it," he says. "Just look where you want to go and haul ass." He shares one pithy observation: "Korea was a shitty war," he says. "Vietnam is a shitty war."

He drops me off near the same exit where we stopped at the House of Pancakes the first morning out of Fort Lewis, a week and a lifetime ago. It takes three short lifts to make it the rest of the way into Seattle, the uniform a ticket to ride. By the time I phone Powers from a truck stop restaurant near the highway, it's ten o'clock at night on December 30.

"I'll take you up to Vancouver Sunday morning," he says on the ride back to his apartment. "It looks like I'm gonna be joining you up there pretty soon. I'm supposed to hear from the Pentagon in a month, maybe sooner. If they turn me down, I'm heading north."

Powers stops at a friend's place on some mysterious errand and leaves me sitting in the car fiddling with the radio. I've never heard anything quite like the plaintive John Lennon–Yoko Ono chant on a Seattle station: "All we are saying / is give peace a chance." Over and over again. All we are saying is give peace a chance. It seems so simple. Why has this become such a complex, elusive thing? Bring the boys home. Give peace a chance. Staring out at the Seattle night with one day left in the '60s, listening to John and Yoko, wondering where we lost our way.

■   ■   ■

Barb is waiting at their apartment. She has made soup and sandwiches, Powers has a six-pack of beer in the fridge. She's small and bright and birdlike, so smart you can feel the electricity off her. We talk until 4 A.M. It's early morning on December 31. I tell them about the long, strange trip to Mexico and back, about the Beckers and all they did for me, Christmas with my cousins in Chula Vista, the woman from Berkeley I met at Ensenada, the California highway patrolmen and "kill a few gooks for us," the old black fisherman under the Golden Gate Bridge, the trucker and the "shitty war" in Vietnam. We talk about "Give Peace a Chance," the Hells Angels and the Rolling Stones at Altamont, the hard and bitter turn of the past six months, the big sappy family of Woodstock already breaking into fragments, life in America at the end of the '60s edgy and suspicious and dangerous as a knife blade, a place where peace has no chance.

I wouldn't mind sleeping on their couch, but Powers has other ideas. It's a small apartment and the couch is about a foot too short, so Powers has spoken with a woman downstairs who's away for the holidays and made arrangements for me to crash at her place. I suspect the real reason is they don't want anyone listening while they make love, but that's fine with me. Barb gives me the key with a warning: "I have to tell you," she says, "the place is a real mess."

I nod. I've been in lots of hippie pads over the past couple of years and I think nothing can surprise me, but this is unreal. The apartment is one big room with a small bathroom attached. The kitchen sink is buried in unwashed dishes, the bed and every inch of floor space covered in books and clothing and dirty plates and half-empty pizza cartons. I pick up a sweater to clear the bed and find a plate bearing the remains of some mystery meal underneath, all of it heavily overgrown with fungus. I step over a pile of dirty clothes and tip an overflowing ashtray, scattering ashes and cigarette butts all over the floor.

This isn't sloppy—it's closer to madness. Being here is like living in a deranged mind. Just to clear a space to sleep on the bed I have to move piles of books and dirty clothes and records, half-eaten sandwiches and encrusted coffee mugs and two overflowing ashtrays that have spilled butts and ashes onto the sheets, which are stained in every imaginable way. I feel sufficiently unhinged all by myself. I don't need someone else's lunacy to drag me down. I've hitched all the way from San Francisco and spent half the night talking with Powers and Barb, but I still can't sleep. I lie there wondering what kind of woman lives in this place and how she can endure it, whether her friends know about this private madness, about this woman's war with herself.

The next night Powers finds me a better place to stay with

two female teachers who share a house in the suburbs. They have no plans for New Year's Eve, so they cook a huge meal, we get reasonably drunk on decent wine, and at midnight I play "Auld Lang Syne" on their piano before crawling into a nice clean bed with crisp white sheets. I am in a deep sleep when I realize that I'm not alone. Someone is in bed with me. By the time I realize it's the smaller of the two women, she's on top of me and I'm inside her. We're making very noisy love when I hear the other woman banging doors and then tearing out of the driveway in her station wagon, laying rubber all the way down the street. The woman with me starts crying. It takes a while to sort it out, but it turns out they're lovers. The one with me occasionally wants a man, and they have this arrangement, only sometimes it doesn't go over too well, and it looks like this is one of those times.

At 4 A.M. she drives me back to the filthy apartment in the city. It's more horrifying than ever, but after that little drama in the suburbs, I'm too tired to care.

We see in the new decade without optimism. The '60s and all that craziness gone, the mad '70s looming like a rabid pit bull on a frayed leash. No reason to think things are going to get better, no reason to believe the war is going to end. Time left to see a little of Seattle, visit a couple of cousins who live in the suburbs (including Kenny's sister Carol), write a long letter to Mariela, put off the one thing that has to be done. The night of January 3, 1970, with Powers waiting to drive me to Vancouver early the next morning, I call home. My mother answers, and in the instant after I hear her voice I think I can't possibly tell her. Then I just blurt it all out.

"Mom, I'm not going back to the army, I've made up my mind, the war is wrong, I can't be part of it, I'm going to desert and I'm going to Canada tomorrow morning."

She catches her breath. She's tougher than I am, tougher than Pop, tougher than any of us. She knows I need her to be steady and she is. She speaks slowly. I can tell she's determined not to let her emotions get in the way.

"Well, you know we'll support you whatever you decide to do. I know you've thought about this a lot and you know I hate this war, but this is going to be hard for you, real hard."

"I know, Mom. I know it's going to be hard for you, too. But I have to do it. It's wrong to be a part of it, you know? I feel awful but I don't feel like I have a choice."

"You're sure you don't want to go back and wait to see what school you get in the army? What if you get into journalism?"

"That would just make it worse. If I did, I'd feel like I had to ask for infantry. Writing press releases for the army would be the most dishonest thing I could do. It would be like writing speeches for Nixon. It would make me sick."

"You know if you go you might never get to come home again."

"I know, Mom. I've thought about that a lot."

"And you know we might never see you again. We're getting old, your Pop and I. We can't afford to go traveling and we've never even been on a plane, anyway."

"I know. I'll find some way to get you up to Canada. You should see the world anyway. You can't just stay in Scottsbluff all your life."

"Oh yes, I can. You know what Faulkner said, how if a man was meant to travel he'd of been long-ways like a road or a wagon instead of up-and-down-ways like a tree or a fence post? Well, I'm like that. I was meant to stay put."

I laugh. At least she can kid about it a little. And she has to know that if not for her, I would not be going to Canada. She taught me about books, taught me to think for myself, taught me to be skeptical about people in power. If it wasn't for her I would never have become a reader, never have gone to university. If it was up to Pop I would do my hitch in the army and go back to Scottsbluff to haul hay and work horses with him.

"How are you going to live in Canada? Are the newspapers any good? Do you know anybody up there?"

I try to answer her questions, but we both know that I don't have the answers. Thousands of other young men have already done or will do the same thing. Each will have his own private drama, each will have to go through what I'm going through now. I ask her to call Sonny for me and tell him I'm about to do what he begged me to do in the first place—go to Canada. She has more questions.

"Are you going to be able to get enough to eat? I've got a roast here I could send, and a big pot of chili, and I could make that carrot salad you like and a corn casserole."

Her voice breaks a little then. She knows how silly that is, talking about sending pots of food all the way to Canada, but somehow it's a comfort to pretend that she can. We talk around it awhile longer, but the truth is out there, dangling along the thousands of miles of telephone wire between us. Given her age, their poverty, the distance, it's possible we will never see each other again.

She insists on passing me to Pop, and I have to explain it all to him, too. It's worse because he's hard of hearing, especially on the phone, and I have to keep shouting and repeating things.

"Pop, I've made up my mind, I'm going to Canada."

"How's that?"

"I said Canada! I'm going to Canada!"

"Canada! What the hell's up there?"

"I'm not going back to the army, Pop. I'm going to go live in Canada."

"How's that?"

"I said I'm not going back to the army! I'm going to live in Canada!"

"Well, I'll be damned."

"I'm sorry, Pop. It's what I have to do."

"How's that?"

"I said I'm sorry! I don't believe in this war, Pop. I think it's wrong. I'm going to Canada. I'm not going back to the army."

"Hell, they'll shoot you if they catch you, won't they?"

"They aren't going to catch me, Pop. And even if they do, they don't shoot deserters anymore, not in this war."

"Well, I think a man's got to fight for his country, but you know more about it than I do. I expect you have to do what you think is right. You know we'll always stick by you."

"I know."

"What's that you say?"

"I know."

By the time my mother comes back on the phone I feel so miserable I want to crawl through that phone line and hug them both and go back to high school, to a time before anyone thought about Vietnam or the army or Canada. I can't go back, and there's nothing else to say. I've been the golden boy in the family, the first to go to university, the one who made it all the way from poverty to the *Miami Herald,* the one my mother could brag about to all the genteel, snobbish aunts who are better off than we are. Now there will be no more clippings from the *Herald,* no more dreams of bylines in *Newsweek.*

Still, I'm doing what they taught me to do. To think for myself, to swim against the tide, to stand up for my beliefs no matter what the cost. It will hurt them both, but Pop means what he says, even though to him deserting from the army is about the worst thing you can do short of murder. They will stick by me.

Powers wants to roll at first light the next morning. I spend a sleepless night in the apartment downstairs. I feel the pain of old ties breaking, the sense of loss overwhelming: my parents, Mariela, all my old friends back in Scottsbluff, my lost career. All because of this war and the things it is doing to people. No matter what happens, I'm an American—as American as Richard Nixon or Spiro Agnew or Dean Rusk or Henry Kissinger or any of those generals in Washington—so why should I have to go into exile for my beliefs? Why should I have to give up my life in Miami and shatter my parents and turn my back on my country and go into exile when I was born in the USA, when I tried to become a Marine Corps officer, when my patriotism runs at least as deep as theirs and possibly deeper? I would fight any war except this one, so why does it have to be this one? Who turned my country over to these maniacs anyway, and when are we going to get it back? What kind of madmen decide to defoliate an agricultural country on the other side of the world in order to "save" it? I have been brought up to despise injustice, and this is injustice—massive, powerful, state-supported injustice.

There is nothing left to be done. I have written editorials and marched, protested and argued and carried placards, worked for Bobby Kennedy, hoped for Eugene McCarthy after Kennedy was shot. And still the war grinds on, madness carried along by its own momentum. The only thing left is to walk away.

I doze for a while and wake around 3 A.M. in an absolute panic, heart pounding, thinking I can't do this. I just can't do it. I can't leave my country. I can't become a criminal, I can't be a wanted man. I can't make it alone in a strange country, I can't give up my job at the *Herald*. It's too much: family, country, career, the woman I love. It's not too late to change my mind. I won't be AWOL until midnight. All I have to do is go back to Fort Lewis and it will be as though none of this ever happened. With that strange clarity you sometimes feel in the middle of the night, I convince myself that if I go back into the army I can make things work with Mariela. My parents will be relieved. Worried if I get orders for Vietnam, but relieved. I'll finish my hitch, go back to the *Herald*, do what I planned to do in the first place. I can't stop the war by going to Canada, and the personal sacrifice is too great. I'll go back to Fort Lewis, put myself into a two-year stupor, block everything out, get through it.

For half an hour I feel good about all this. Wonderful, like a terrible weight has lifted. It's so much easier not to go to Canada. Then I remember the chocolate bars. A gooey, awful chocolate mess in my footlocker. As soon as the sergeants see that, they'll know what I had in mind. Why would I make a mess like that if I didn't plan to go AWOL? I can't go back to Fort Lewis because I left unwrapped chocolate bars in my footlocker. I'll face a court-martial for chocolate. I feel paralyzed. The weight is back on my shoulders, the weight of a dozen chocolate bars. I curl up in a ball, feeling something like physical pain. I can't bear to go to Canada and I can't go back to the base to face the consequences of those chocolate bars. Finally I climb out of bed and pace back and forth, distraught and unable to think.

Slowly the panic ebbs. I have reached a decision that was years in the making. I can't let the dark-of-night jitters change all that now. I can't go back to the base, but I can't be swayed by a few chocolate bars. Even Mariela doesn't matter now. I love her, but she's out of my life. I won't go back to Fort Lewis because it's the wrong thing to do. I have made the right decision. Now I have to find the courage to carry it through.

Until I was fourteen or fifteen years old, I walked with my sisters to the Foursquare Gospel Church down the road on Sunday mornings. My father was an atheist, but he said we should go to church, so we went. There was another church much nearer our house, but Pop knocked out the preacher there, so we dressed in our Sunday best and made the weekly walk to the Foursquare Gospel. I went Sundays when we weren't out in the hay fields, and sometimes to Wednesday night prayer meeting, when the holiest members of the congregation rolled in the aisles and under the pews screaming,

"Hallelujah, Jesus!" and I even thumped the old piano for the hymns when the regular pianist was out—"What a Friend We Have in Jesus," "The Old Rugged Cross," "Rock of Ages."

I could use a little of that now. I have not grown up to be a religious man, but I say a little prayer to the darkness anyway. Help me through, Lord, help me through.

Part III

NOTHING LEFT TO LOSE

SOMEWHERE BETWEEN DARK and dawn, a soul migrates to the light. We are simple beings, simple as plants. Feed and water us, provide a little sunshine, and we're feelin' all right.

The sun rises over Seattle, daylight scatters the things that go bump in the night. I'm ready for a new world and a new life, up after an all-night vigil, sitting out on the front steps to admire a delectable Pacific dawn. Sunday, January 4, 1970. The air rain-washed and clear, the last-minute panic forgotten. No more anguish over chocolate bars in footlockers. If we're going to do this, sweet Lord, then let's do it. I gulp down a coffee or two at the kitchen table with Powers and Barb, grab the duffel bag and guitar, give Barb a good-bye peck on the cheek, and dive into the white Mustang with Powers at the wheel.

It's a good day for a drive. Due north, same direction I've been moving since Ensenada. Faster now, Powers pushing it up to 90, talking faster than he drives, looking at me while he talks and I keep a weather eye on the road. Roll the window down, sniff pine and Douglas fir, trees a hundred feet tall flashing by. Note the towns we pass, saying good-bye to America: Edmonds, Everett, Sedro Woolley, Bellingham. A quick run through the Cascades, less than two hours at the speed Powers is driving, not counting time for Canadian immigration.

Powers is in one of those moods when he wouldn't slow for a tank blockade. He isn't on anything heavier than coffee, but he acts like a man who sprinkled greenies on his corn flakes. Far as I can tell, he's pretty much like this day and night: hunched over the wheel of the Mustang, watching me as much as he watches the road, waving his arms, banging the dash, ranting about Trotsky and Hermann Hesse and Solzhenitsyn and Kerouac and Jimi Hendrix and Dien Bien Phu, where the French poured their blood down the same rat hole.

"Dien Bien Phu, man, Dien Bien Phu! It was all right there, all they had to do was look! Kissinger is an intellectual, right? That means he's read Bernard Fall on Dien Bien Phu, but he gets it all wrong, like the French are these faggots don't know how to fight. Man, they had Foreign Legion troops in there, toughest soldiers in the world except for the Viet Cong. It isn't about the soldiers, it's about the people, man, and if you're some poor peasant in Vietnam, all you want is to be left alone. They should have known after Dien Bien Phu. The Vietnamese, they pulled heavy fucking artillery over the mountains and just blew the French to shit. Kissinger read his history, he oughta know that. The guy is Dr. Strangelove."

I'm too wound up to listen. Speeding north, all of it happening fast now, running hard to the border.

And there it is, a mile ahead: Canada. We are in the flatlands of British Columbia south of Vancouver, but in the distance you can see the Coast Mountains where the Cascades soar on north into Canada, into this big, wild, cold country I have managed to ignore all my twenty-three years. I know more about England, France, Mexico, the Soviet Union, China. Canada is a complete mystery once you get past ice and wolves, igloos and hockey.

I have no time to think about it. Powers roars up to the border, still ranting about Vietnam. We hit the border and a cus-

toms officer leans out of one of the booths. Powers rolls down
the window of the Mustang. The Canadian looks the car over.
I feel my whole body stretch, taut as a 12,000-volt wire. If the
man can't see the tension he can surely smell it, waves of nervous energy crackling through the Mustang.

"Where were you born?"

We've agreed that Powers will do all the talking unless they
ask me a specific question. "The USA," he says.

"Both of you?"

"Yep."

"Where you going?"

"Vancouver."

"Staying long?"

"Couple of days, just seein' the sights."

"OK, go on."

And that's it. I keep expecting something else, a second
checkpoint, red lights in the rear-view mirror, but it's over.
We're through. Powers hits me with a straight right, a punch
that leaves a bruise on my shoulder that will last two weeks,
but I'm grinning now. I don't mind at all. Canada. We're over
the border into another world, the rest of the drive a dream
ride into the future. When I was a kid my brother Red used to
drive fast over a railroad crossing where the road dropped
sharply on the far side, and as the car floated through the air
you'd feel your stomach in your throat. It's like that now, the
car dropping into another world, fear and elation all mixed
up. This is Canada. I've crossed the fault line, the point of no
return, that other life on the south side of the border already
slipping away.

We speed on into Vancouver. I watch the side of the road for
strange and wonderful things, but the strange and wonderful
thing is that it isn't strange at all. I haven't fixed on it yet, but
this will be the warp of it—exile in a country that is so much
like home that every morning when you get up you have to re-

mind yourself that this is not home, that home is now a place where you can no longer go.

The hotel is just off Hastings Street on Vancouver's skid row. Because it's on Carrall Street rather than directly on Hastings and because it's relatively clean, the hotel is an upscale joint that charges upscale prices and delivers upscale service: fifteen bucks Canadian gets you a room for a week, the toilets usually work, and heroin addicts rarely break into your room to crank up. I hand the desk clerk a green American twenty and he gives me back a handful of this strange pink and blue money. I'm about to tell Powers the fucker is ripping me off when I realize this is Canadian currency, this Monopoly money in my hand. Powers sees me staring at it and laughs. I don't think it's funny at all.

This is the end of the line as far as Powers is concerned. He helps me haul my guitar and duffel bag up to the room. Worn linoleum floor, saggy double bed, the view out the window just another wall of the hotel three feet away, that sad, musty smell of worn-out rooms and worn-out lives. No television, no phone, a sink but no toilet or shower because the toilet is fifty feet down the hall. Back downstairs, Powers points the way up Hastings Street, says to walk as far as Granville and hang a left if I want to see the main drag in town. If he gets turned down on the conscientious objector thing, he'll be back in Vancouver in a month, two at the most. He says we'll get a place together. I figure I'd rather room with a wolverine.

Powers gets into the Mustang and drives off. I watch him go as far as the red light at the corner of Hastings, feeling desolate, fighting an impulse to run after him. The light turns green. Powers makes the turn and disappears. I fumble in my pockets for a cigarette and discover that I left my smokes, a fresh carton of Marlboros, on the dash of the Mustang. A whole damned carton of cigarettes gone, a big chunk out of my budget. I go back into the hotel and get change from the surly clerk to buy a pack from the machine in the hotel lobby. There are no Marlboros, no Winstons, nothing familiar—just these mystery smokes with names like Craven A and Du-Maurier. I wander off down Hastings Street in the throes of a nicotine fit. Big things are happening, but all I know is that I'm hungry and broke and I want a cigarette.

Walking along Hastings Street in January is like sticking your head in a sink full of cold, dirty water after the dishes are done. Winos, junkies, pimps, whores, derelict screaming crazies. Everywhere you look, the sidewalks have a coating of spittle and vomit, all of it frozen and slick now because the temperature is just below freezing. In the fading sunlight of a January afternoon, the air turns cold and the wind picks up, slicing through the poncho I bought in Mexico. Skid row in winter, a place you don't want to be. I walk carefully, eyes on the sidewalk, trying not to step in spit or vomit or puddles of frozen urine.

A few blocks up, the neighborhood improves a bit. A street leads off to the right, down to the waterfront. It's cold and windy near the water. Seagulls sweep low over the waves, blue-black water laps at the jetty in the foreground, black mountains drift white-capped in the distance, wind-driven clouds skim inland from the Pacific across a gray-blue sky. Down the street to the right is the Vancouver train station, above it a sign reading "Canadian Pacific." I used to hear a song about the Canadian Pacific on my pocket transistor radio, fixing fence and branding cattle on the rich man's ranch back in Nebraska, alone all day with Patsy Cline, Jim Reeves, Johnny Cash, and Eddie Arnold to keep me company. So this is it, the Canadian Pacific, a railroad through the valleys and the forests.

Down by the water, the cool wind whipping in my face, I tote up the ledger: I'm by my lonesome here. Adrift without a girlfriend, a job, a home, a bank account, friends, family, food, or enough money to last more than a month at the outside. Without a country. I figure it'll take at least a month to find a job and get legal status in Canada. I've got about two hundred dollars in my wallet. Minus fifteen a week for rent, that leaves a little more than forty dollars a week for food and smokes and everything else, and there's nowhere I can turn when the money runs out. But exile also means I have no ties, no obligations, no debts, nowhere I have to be, no one to please but myself.

I have to tear myself away from the waterfront. There is peace in that black water and the distant fault line where the land breaks to mountains, but I am hungry and I have to get my bearings in this new city, this new country.

Just off Granville Street in downtown Vancouver I find a little diner with a color television set in the corner showing a National Football League playoff game, the Minnesota Vikings beating the Cleveland Browns, 27–7. Some of the guys are probably watching this game at Fort Lewis right now. I find a seat where I can see the TV, order a Coke and a club sandwich with fries. The fries are OK, but the waitress puts a bottle of something clear that looks like water on the table instead of ketchup. I figure maybe it's some kind of clear mustard, shake a few drops on the fries and try it, recoil from the sour taste of vinegar. So Canadians put vinegar on French fries. What next? Tomato juice in beer? I eat slowly, trying to make it last to the end of the game. The waitress takes the plate away and brings a cup of coffee so weak it's like thin tea. I look around to see what people are smoking. A green and white pack seems to be the most popular, so I ask the cashier for a pack of Mac-Donald's.

"What?"

"A pack of MacDonalds," I say, pointing to the ones I want.

"Oh," she says, smiling. "You mean Export A."

Yes, of course. Export A. Everybody knows that. It's like asking for a pack of "R. J. Reynolds" when you want Marlboros. Another of those little jolts, like vinegar on French fries, weak coffee, the Canadian money at the hotel. The cigarette tastes strong and hot, so strong it feels like it's going to tear my tonsils off, but it's tightly packed and lasts twice as long as a Marlboro. I sit there drinking terrible coffee and smoking until the game ends, spending my first afternoon in Canada watching American football. By the time I walk back to the hotel it's dark and cold. In Vancouver in January the winter damp crawls into your bones. The winos and panhandlers, junkies and whores are still at their places on Hastings Street. This time on a Sunday afternoon in Miami, Mariela and I would be getting home from the beach, jumping into the shower together to wash off the salt and sand, soapy wet skin hot to the touch, tongues probing, Mariela's long hair wet down her back, her body slick against mine. I watch the sidewalk, stepping carefully.

Mariela, if you could see me now.

There's a pay phone in the corner of the tiny lobby in the hotel. I dial the operator, make a collect call home.

"Mom, it's me. I'm in Vancouver and I have a nice room and everything is fine."

"Well . . ." She pauses and I can feel the weight of it settling on her, like a death in the family. "I'm glad to hear you're OK. I thought when we didn't hear earlier that maybe you changed your mind and went back to the army."

"No, there was no way I was going back." No point telling her about late-night panic or the chocolate bar crisis. "I was hungry when I got in so I went out for something to eat, that's why I didn't call before. This is a beautiful city, Mom. You can see the mountains right from downtown, a lot closer than in Denver."

"What about your friend? Did he stay with you?"

"No, he went back. He's still trying to get his C.O. discharge. If it doesn't work out he's going to come back up to Canada."

"Well, I hope he does. I don't like the idea of you up there with no friends."

"I'm fine, really. I can take care of myself. It's just going to take awhile. You'll probably get a visit from the FBI or the army, but don't tell them where I am, OK? At least not until I get landed immigrant status up here. I don't think they can do anything, but I don't want them pounding on my door."

I'm involving her in a criminal act but I can't help it. We talk a long time, both of us staying away from the things we're thinking. We talk about my sisters, the weather in Scottsbluff and Vancouver, anything but worries and separation and heartbreak. Mercifully, Pop is out with the horses so I don't have to shout another explanation to him. I give her the address of the hotel and ask her to send two things: my clippings from the *Akron Beacon-Journal,* the *Detroit Free Press,* and especially the *Miami Herald,* and a box of clothes with my one suit and a couple of ties so I can start hunting for a job. She promises to get a box in the mail the next day. I promise to write. She will fulfill her promise, I won't. We say good-bye and I put the receiver down.

The night clerk steps out from behind the desk because he has to run me upstairs on the elevator, operating it himself with an old-fashioned hand crank. He's a burly character about my age, with close-cropped dark hair, a bushy black beard, a huge hoop earring in one ear, a lumberjack shirt, and blue jeans. All in all, he looks like a cross between a Hells Angel and a werewolf. I get as far away from him as I can, jammed against the far wall of the tiny elevator.

The room looks worse now in the light of the single bulb that dangles from the ceiling. Faded curtains, peeling wallpaper, faded linoleum, no carpet, cigarette burns on the bedspread. Loud, drunken voices from down the hall. I can't control the noisy radiator. When it's on, it heats the room almost to boiling. When it's off, you freeze. After midnight it's off. The thin blanket and thinner bedspread aren't nearly enough in this frigid room. I read myself to sleep, wake shivering in the night to the sound of a drunken argument between a couple of loggers out in the hall, slip on the jacket and poncho and my jeans, slide back under the covers fully dressed, and drift off to something like sleep again, thinking: So this is Canada.

■ ■ ■

Next morning I'm up on army time, well before dawn, reading until something that can pass for daylight filters through the window. I manage to drag the window open wide enough to get my head through. There's another wall of the hotel three feet away, but if I corkscrew my neck to look up I can see a patch of yellowish-gray sky.

I pack a full bladder down the hall to the locked bathroom and jog from foot to foot waiting until the sound of someone retching inside says this is a situation where you don't want to be next, pad down the stairs to find an open toilet, go back to the room to grab a thin towel and a bar of soap. Awful sounds are still coming from the toilet on my floor, but the room with the bathtub is empty. I manage to scrub it out a little and take something that resembles a bath in a trickle of lukewarm water and shiver dry. It takes a while to learn the tricks here. The toilets tend to be occupied a lot, so most of the men (and at least some of the women, no doubt) use the sinks in their rooms to urinate. When you take a bath, you pack your own little bag with cleanser and a sponge and clean the tub first, and if you want a bath it's best to take it either very late at night or before dawn when the water is still almost warm.

At a breakfast place on Granville the Canadian accents sound exotic to my ear. It seems like every other word is "eh."

"Eh, Bob, I seen ya the other day down on Hastings, eh, and I said hello but ya went right on by, eh? Like ya were lookin' for somebody else, eh?"

"Eh, Patsy, y'know what, eh? Maybe I had a few too many that day, eh?"

"So it was pretty much like every other day, is what you're tellin' me, eh, Bob?"

"About" becomes "abote." "House" rhymes with "dose." "Abote the hose" instead of "about the house." "Eh, Kenny, yer goin' to see Danny abote the hose, eh? Don't ya get lost ote there in Burnaby, eh?"

Patsy the waitress is kind enough to point the way to the building the *Vancouver Sun* shares with the *Province*. "Just keep goin' up Granville, eh? You'll come to a bridge, and that will be the Granville Bridge, eh? You walk over that, and you'll see a big building on your left, and that will be the *Sun*. But y'know, the *Province* is a better paper. Their horoscope is always right on, eh?"

Thanks, eh, and if I ever start saying "eh," it's time to go home, eh?

Trudging over the bridge, I pause in the center of the span to watch the tugs down below working the big strings of logs down False Creek to the mills along the river, the air smelling of fresh wood, sour pulp, and mountain water. In that mood when the whole world is new and luminous and full of promise. The gulls cry, the wind pulls at the floppy black hat with the paisley band bought to cover my shaved head, the tugs roar and snort down below, white-capped mountains loom. Even in January the city is a deep, smoky green. The winter sun when it trickles through the thin clouds doesn't do much to take off the chill, but I stand in the center of the span for twenty minutes anyway, huddled into the wind, hearing the rumble of a new city all around, a wild, thrilling Pacific place, a long continental diagonal away from Miami.

A couple of hours south, the remnants of my platoon—those who returned from Christmas leave, anyway—will be marching or standing at attention or doing pushups or squeezing off rounds on the rifle range. Maybe the MPs are finding the little chocolate surprise in my footlocker. Going through my things, looking for clues. Wish I had thought to leave a note: "Gone to Canada. Peace, brother. We shall overcome. Private Todd."

The Pacific Press building bears the logos of the two newspapers which share its space: *Vancouver Sun, Vancouver Province.* Not as appealing as the *Herald* building, set at the end of those twin rows of palm trees on Biscayne Bay, but it's a pleasant enough place, some of the windows looking out over False Creek to the city skyscrapers and the mountains beyond. I will come back in a week or two in jacket and tie, with an envelope full of clippings from the *Herald,* and they will give me a job or they won't. On the way back to the hotel, I stop at a downtown bank and exchange the rest of my American money. Somehow, the money seems like much less after it's converted to these strange multicolored bills, even though the Canadian dollar is worth slightly more than the American. I need a job badly, but for now there is nothing to do but drift and wait and try not to think about food.

Four or five days go by, exploring Vancouver on foot or by bus all the way from Chinatown to the University of British Columbia, trying to conserve my dwindling supply of cash by eating one meal a day, reading Dostoyevsky, waiting for my clothes and clippings to arrive from Nebraska. Rolling back into the hotel late one evening, I find the weird desk clerk on duty again. Big hoop earring, bushy beard, looks more like a Hell's Angel now than ever. Like a man who munches live rabbits for lunch. He slides the folding door closed and turns the crank on the creaky old elevator, bouncing me up to my floor. Just the two of us, no protection if he decides to lift my wallet.

"God, I hate shoes," he says. "I just wait till after eight o'clock. The boss never comes around after eight, so I work barefoot then."

Perfect. A Hell's Angel who munches live rabbits and works barefoot. I grunt something and slide a little farther away, which isn't easy in an elevator maybe four feet across.

"You're still here," he says.

"Mmm-mm."

"I thought maybe you'd go back to the States. A lot of guys stay in Canada a day or two, decide they can't take it."

Instant paranoia: a Hell's Angel who munches live rabbits, works barefoot, and rats for the FBI. He won't let it go. "Hey, I don't blame you. Can't be easy, leaving everything behind."

"Who says I left anything behind?"

"Sorry, I guess I'm wrong. I thought maybe you were a deserter from the States."

"The hair, right?"

"Well, yeah. The hair. You look like you just got out of the army, that's all. My mistake."

The clanking old elevator bumps to a halt. He steps out and stands in the hall with me. I want to go to my room but I don't want to be rude.

"You know people here?" he asks.

"Nope."

"That must make it tough."

"Nah, I'm fine. Thanks."

"Look, man, I don't bite. I can't leave the desk, but if you get bored in your room come on down and keep me company. Maybe I can help you with some things."

"Yeah, maybe I'll come down later."

"It's pretty quiet after ten. Come down and hang out with me for a while."

"Yeah, OK." Not meaning it, not wanting to be rude.

Back in my room, I sprawl on the swaybacked bed and try to read Dostoyevsky, a seventy-five-cent used copy of *The*

Idiot picked up out of a sale bin outside a bookstore on Granville, but this down-and-out hotel is too much like Dostoyevsky's world. Without a radio or TV, the hotel is creepy at night. Nothing to drown out the sounds, strange screams and cries, gurgles and moans, slammed doors and flushed toilets and arguments, always arguments. The hotel is full of drunks, and drunks argue. Best friends get furious and threaten one another for hours, remembering nothing of it when they wake in the morning. Finally I give up on the book. I haven't talked to anyone since Powers left, and even the rabbit-eating Hell's Angel can make conversation. Downstairs he's telling a couple of gawky teenagers how to get to a youth hostel, explaining that this hotel isn't really where they want to stay. I flop down in one of the seedy chairs in the lobby and wait until they leave, figuring he can't be all bad if he's trying to help these kids.

"So you got bored upstairs?"

"A little."

"It must be strange to be in a place like this when you don't know anybody. Where you from?"

"Nebraska."

He laughs. "Man, that is *really* strange. Nobody is from Nebraska."

"Johnny Carson."

"OK, Johnny Carson."

"Henry Fonda. Marlon Brando. William Jennings Bryan. James Coburn. Gale Sayers."

"Sounds stranger all the time. Your folks farm out there?"

"They used to. My dad lost the farm a piece at a time. We mostly hauled hay for a living when I was growing up. Now he just trains horses."

"And you are a deserter, right? I wasn't wrong about that?"

Sooner or later, you have to trust somebody. "Nope. You weren't wrong."

"Fort Lewis, right?"

"Yeah."

"Figures. That's the closest place. I've been to the committee a few times. They've been getting four or five guys from Fort Lewis every week."

"What committee?"

"Nobody told you? There's a Committee to Aid American War Objectors not far from here. Good place. They'll help you out. We've had a couple of deserters here before you. I know the look. They both stayed a few days and decided to go back. It's not easy for you guys."

I know he is asking a question. "I'm not going back. I'm here to stay."

He nods. I can see he doesn't believe me.

His name is Norm Wolfe. He's not a biker, he doesn't eat live rabbits. He is one of those charitable souls destined to do a lifetime of good works. He's a community activist, a genuine "freak" in the '60s sense of the word, a gentle soul who believes in peace and love and spends most of his waking hours trying to help people less fortunate than he is. We talk most of the night. Norm leaves at intervals to run the elevator. He's gentle but firm with the drunks, steering them into the elevator, helping some of them to their rooms. He knows most of the tenants in the hotel by name, and he sees the other side of Hastings Street, how lost souls retain a shred of dignity even when they've pissed their pants and passed out on the sidewalk. We're a couple of small-town boys in strange circumstances. By the time I head back upstairs to bed, I've made my first friend in Canada.

Two weeks vanish in wandering and waiting. Waiting for papers, waiting for clothes, waiting for a job interview at the *Sun*. Hair growing a little, money shrinking a lot. Aimless days wandering the streets in Vancouver. It's a beautiful city, but the light in January is flat and thin, the air damp and cold, my jacket much too thin even with the poncho I bought in Mexico worn on the outside. Vancouver is cold and lonely, and every day I feel the temptation to go back, do a little stockade time, finish my hitch in the army, and get back to Miami.

Norm discovers one day that I haven't eaten in twenty-four hours, so he drags me to a strip of back-alley restaurants in Chinatown a couple of blocks from the hotel. The Red Door, Yellow Door, Green Door, narrow, steamy joints accessible only through the alley, known only by the color of their doors and the fact that the food is plentiful and cheap—all you can eat for a dollar.

The menu is entirely in Chinese, with western numbers for the dishes. The clientele is almost entirely Chinese, old men hunched over the counters and tables, their conversation a tumult of Chinese between mouthfuls. Norm orders by number, a whole rack of dishes. I feel like I'm going to faint just watching them bring the platters. Norm digs in, I sit there waiting for someone to bring me a fork, but there are no forks, no knives, no spoons, and I have never seen a chopstick. Norm picks a little off this plate, a little off that plate. I try to copy him, but I manage only a grain or two of rice at a time while Norm giggles. It's maddening. I want to put my face down in the food and graze. At the counter, the Chinese men hold up the bowls right under their noses and use the chopsticks to shovel it in. The technique works pretty well, even for me.

Food becomes an obsession. Waiting to eat, thinking about eating, thinking about not eating, thinking about the last meal, thinking about the next meal. My goal is to confine myself to one meal a day, either in the back-alley Chinese restaurants or at the White Lunch Cafeteria, where the winos and junkies hang out, the two cheapest places I know. Within a week the prospect of a meal at the White Lunch isn't quite so appalling. If you can ignore the people around you, the food isn't bad. They usually have a good soup for about fifty cents and they give you enough bread and crackers with the soup so you can pretend it's a meal.

It takes awhile, but Norm finally persuades me to check in with the Vancouver Committee to Aid American War Objectors, known simply as "the committee." I don't want to go; I want to do this on my own, without help from anyone. I made the decision to desert, it shouldn't be anyone else's problem. Norm says that is a crazy attitude, these people know what they're doing and I need their help. Finally I run out of excuses.

The committee office is a fifteen-minute walk east of the hotel along Georgia Street. At this stage the committee is basically a two-man operation run by the two Peters—Peter Burton, a big, burly Canadian activist with long red hair and a bushy red beard, and Peter Maly, an American deserter with long black hair and a black beard. It's run from a place that looks like a bombed-out warehouse, with small groups of deserters and dodgers shivering around two ineffective stoves, Maly and Burton counseling them at small desks strewn with movement literature, grungy coffee cups and overflowing ashtrays, a busy place in January 1970. It's about to get busier, as resistance to the draft and the Vietnam War grows. After the bombing of Cambodia and the murder of four students by National Guard troops at Kent State in May, the committee will become an absolute madhouse, with nearly one hundred war resisters coming through every week and ten people working here almost full-time.

I expect a bunch of vague, crunchy granola types who will invite me over for a brown rice and broccoli dinner and an evening of whale-sound music, but Maly and Burton set this committee up for a reason and they have a harder, more businesslike edge. The committee exists to help draft dodgers and deserters come to Canada, and the people who run it do their jobs with remarkable efficiency, given the political tenor of the times and the tendency of so many initiatives to come undone in petty squabbles. Maly and Burton do most of the work, but the committee is also staffed by an endless series of volunteers, one of them an ethereal beauty who is sometimes dropped off in a chauffeur-driven BMW. Among the half-empty coffee cups and full ashtrays, the burnt-out druggies and desperate hippies who hang around the committee, she is like a rose in a garbage dump. I catch a glimpse of her only once or twice, but she's so intriguing that I ask Peter Burton about her.

"Forget it," he says. "She was just in Fiji with Pierre Trudeau. That's the prime minister's girlfriend."

"Yeah, right," I say. "And I'm Eric Clapton." The woman looks about twenty-two, much too young for Trudeau. Within fifteen months she will be on front pages across Canada: Margaret Sinclair, new wife to the prime minister of Canada. Apart from Maggie Trudeau, the committee draws the usual suspects from the radical fringe in the late '60s: crunchy granola hippies, Trotskyites, Maoists, wide-eyed do-gooders, zonked-out druggies, moochers, marchers, anarchists, macho types who babble endlessly about guns and bombs and revolution, deserters who have been to Vietnam and back (or claim they have) and who seem always on the verge of some kind of subterranean explosion. Among the draft dodgers a definite type predominates: a bespectacled son of the middle class who has just graduated from Stanford or Brown or Vanderbilt and has decided, after long and careful planning, to dodge the draft in Canada. They arrive, wives and girlfriends in tow, in Volkswagen Beetles piled high with their belongings. They usually pay a visit to the committee, but they require less assistance because they already have jobs lined up and places to stay in Vancouver, they have money and family connections and furniture. They are less angry, less explosive, more welcome in the homes of Canadian liberals opposed to the war.

Deserters are different. We tend to make people nervous. Antiwar Canadians who open their homes to draft dodgers often draw the line at deserters, who tend to be less educated, more troubled, and infinitely more likely to make off with the silverware—and quite possibly the youngest daughter's virginity. Deserters turn up alone in their fatigue jackets and combat boots, gaunt and desperate, with no belongings except what they can stuff in a duffel bag. Deserters usually come without college degrees, often without a high school diploma, and sometimes they're wanted for other crimes in the army, like dealing drugs or punching a drill sergeant. Even within the antiwar movement, deserters are outlaws.

Over cigarettes and coffee, Peter Burton takes me through the drill for American war resisters. He explains exactly what I need to do to get landed immigrant status in Canada: find a job, get my new boss to write a letter to an address in the U.S. offering employment, go back across the border, and present myself at Canadian immigration as though I'm entering for the first time in response to the job offer. Immigrants need fifty points to enter Canada, points that are awarded according to a strict system. The final ten points are determined by the immigration officer who conducts the interview. Burton is emphatic on one point: we are never to lie about our problems with the U.S. military. We will be asked about our draft status in the U.S. (or in my case, about my military status), and we are instructed to tell the truth. If the Canadian government discovers we lied, we can be deported.

It isn't easy to get landed immigrant status; as more and more draft dodgers and deserters head to Canada, the border tightens again. No more than 25 percent of all the American war resisters who head north actually get legal status in Canada. Some return to the U.S. because of family pressures, because they change their minds, or because they can't stand the homesickness; many more don't have the education or can't find jobs in a Canadian economy that is in a deep recession. Already, Burton and Maly are pointing those who may have difficulty getting landed to less popular destinations such as

Regina, Saskatchewan, or Thunder Bay, Ontario, where they get extra points for skills that are locally in demand. Even so, many war resisters will try again and again before they are forced to make a choice: live underground in Canada or the U.S. or turn themselves in. The Canadian government is willing to open its doors to us, but it is not granting political asylum. We are treated like any other immigrant; nothing more, nothing less. The dangerous part for me is that I can't apply to immigrate directly in Vancouver. I have to go back through the U.S. border and reappear at the Canadian crossing—with a prison sentence waiting if I'm caught by the Americans. If necessary, the committee has drivers who will take us across the border and then back to the Canadian side, but they prefer not to rely on their regular drivers because their faces are becoming too familiar. If possible, they want me to find my own lift.

I'm hungry, tired of waiting, anxious to get my clothes and clippings and apply for a job. I feel sorry for myself until Burton shows me a desperate letter from a deserter who has been in Sweden for two years. Sweden was the first country to offer asylum to American deserters from the Vietnam War, but it's a strange, cold place. The poor devil has copied into the letter a billboard he could see from his apartment window in Stockholm, a fifty-letter word in Swedish. He pleads for help from the committee. Now that deserters can live legally in Canada, he wants desperately to cross the Atlantic.

No matter how tough things are, someone always has it worse.

■   ■   ■

After nearly three weeks, two big cardboard boxes arrive from Nebraska. Inside are most of my clothes, along with two envelopes of clippings from the *Herald*, a copy of my birth certificate, my high school diploma, university transcripts—and a couple of boxes of homemade cookies. Now I don't have to wear the too-short green jeans and the jacket borrowed from Sergeant Becker with the sleeves that stop three inches short of my wrists. It's late on a Friday afternoon. From the pay phone in the lobby I call Pat Nagel, the city editor of the *Vancouver Sun,* and explain that I'm a former reporter for the *Miami Herald* looking for work in Vancouver. He seems pleased to hear from me. Better still, we have a mutual acquaintance in Will Jarrett, one of the editors at the *Herald.* Nagel gives me an appointment for a job interview at the *Sun* the following Monday afternoon. I get off the phone all but dancing on air. This is it: I will get that job, I'll get my landed immigrant card, and I'll move away from Hastings Street forever.

That Sunday I take the elevator up to the fourth floor with two native women, Nell and Doris, who have a room down the hall from me. I know them from the tavern, where I've seen them get into a couple of spectacular brawls. They share their room with a third woman named Annie, but she isn't with them this morning. They're real brawlers, always ready to fight when they are drunk, which is most of the time. The native women who end up on Hastings Street have been through a lifetime of abuse. Sober, they are shy women who won't look you in the eye and who speak so softly you can't hear what they're saying. Drunk, they yell and swear and pick a fight with anyone who gets in their way—male, female, or cop.

Nell and Doris have been to visit the bootlegger who plies his trade in the hotel on Sundays when the liquor stores are closed. It's not yet noon but they're already half drunk. I turn one way off the elevator and they go the other way. I open the door to my room and shut it behind me, not bothering to lock it. Two minutes later, Nell and Doris are banging on my door. They don't wait for an invitation, just push their way in.

"We gotta have a place to shoot up," Nell says. They shove past me, sit on the bed, take out short strips of rubber, and begin tying up their arms.

"You can't do that here. This is my room."

"Fuck you. Annie has a trick in our room. We can't shoot up there."

"Well, you can't shoot up here, either."

"Fuck you."

I feel helpless. They both outweigh me, they're big and strong, they're experienced brawlers who slug it out with men all the time. If I try to fight them I might win, but I'll be in for a battle even if I can stomach hitting a woman, which I can't. I have no phone to call the front desk, and the clerk would probably tell me to fuck off anyway. If I run down to call the police the women will go ahead and shoot up anyway, and they'll be gone long before the cops arrive.

"Look, you really can't do this here. If I have to, I'll throw you out."

They aren't impressed, but Nell figures she'll make nice anyway. She grins a toothless grin while she goes on tying up her arm: "Just take one minute," she says, "then we fuck you. Give good blowjob too. Free. Both of us, fuck and suck. You a nice boy, we do it free."

"I don't want a blowjob. I want you two out of here."

It's too late. They're already cooking the stuff in a spoon with a cigarette lighter, and then Nell fixes up the syringe, jabs it into Doris's arm three or four times until she finds a vein, pumps the syringe. Doris's eyes roll back in her head and her mouth lolls open. Her head falls forward and it looks like she has nodded off. Then she looks up at me again.

"Goo . . ." she says. "That's goo . . ."

Nell ignores her and begins cooking another spoon with her cigarette lighter. I try to get their attention again. "Jesus, this is sickening. You can't just come in my room and do this."

They pay no attention. Nell loads the syringe again, pulls the band tight around her arm until the vein stands out, jabs the needle in, sighs a long crooked sigh as the junk explodes through her arteries. For a second she looks startled. Then she stands, the needle still in her arm, staggers a couple of feet backwards, and falls across the boxes of clothing sitting on my floor, crushing them with her weight. She's out, her eyes rolled back in her head, the needle still dangling, blood trickling down her arm. Her body quivers a couple of times, then she's still. It looks like she's dead.

"Fuck!" I yell at Doris, who is still sitting stupidly on the bed. "Your friend just OD'd! She's dead!"

Doris looks at Nell, sprawled on my clothes, her fat legs open and her skirt up high enough so you can see she wears no panties.

"Nell? Nell's OK. She does that alla time."

"Christ, we have to get help for her." I don't know CPR and I have no idea where to start—whether to try to help her where she is or run downstairs to get the desk clerk to call an ambulance. I bend down to feel her neck, searching for a pulse, my hands shaking so badly I can't tell whether the pulse I feel is coming from my own body or from hers.

Doris is in no condition to do anything. I grab Nell's shoulders and shake her, press on her upper chest, trying to start her breathing, squeamishly avoiding her breasts. Still nothing. Try to remember how to do mouth-to-mouth resuscitation: press her nostrils shut, breathe into her mouth, but first you have to make sure she hasn't swallowed her tongue, you have to clear her mouth and throat of any obstructions. I have to decide— go for the police or try mouth-to-mouth. If I go for the cops, the woman will be dead by the time we get back. I have to try mouth-to-mouth. I pry her lips open and reach in with two fingers, trying to find her tongue. Probing for the tongue of a dead woman.

Then she bites down, just hard enough to break the skin. I jump back and yell like I've been bitten by a ghost. Her eyes roll open, her head lolls back and forth. She looks up and tries to focus. She blinks a few times, coughs, tries to sit up but can't move her weight off my clothes. Finally she focuses on me.

"Hey," she says. "You still here? Wanna fuck?"

"Jesus." My fingers are bleeding and I'm shaking like a leaf.
"You have to get out of here. You scared the hell out of me."
"Fuck you."
"No, really. You shot up. Fine. Now you have to go."
"Fuck you."
"I'm going to help you up, then you have to go. First get that
fucking needle out of your arm." She notices the needle still
dangling from her skin, swats the syringe onto the floor. I pick
it up and drop it in their little paper bag along with the spoon
and their remaining smack, wrapped in a ball of aluminum
foil, then grip Nell by both wrists and heave her onto her feet.
She doesn't come willingly, but she doesn't fight either. I leave
her standing there, swaying back and forth, and get Doris to
her feet and steer them both to the door, open it, and guide
them out into the hall. The heroin keeps them quiet and docile.
Nell drapes her arm over Doris's shoulders and the two of
them go staggering down the hall to their room. If Annie isn't
finished with her trick yet, she's going to have to finish now.

When they're gone I lock the door behind them and vomit
into the sink. Clean up, wash my face with cold water, sprinkle
some down the back of my neck, and brush my teeth. Then I
curl up in the fetal position in bed, beaten. Flat whipped. This
is the end of the line. No job, no money, no country, no girlfriend, no home—and a junkie woman almost died in my
room. I lie there most of the afternoon, hardly moving, not
reading, not doing anything at all.

The early winter darkness brings an end to a miserable day.
In the evening, hunger finally prods me off the bed. I pull a
sweater out of one of the boxes, slip it on to fend off the cold,
and walk down Hastings Street as far as the White Lunch
Cafeteria carrying my copy of *The Idiot*, figuring that Prince
Mishkin's troubles will take my mind off my own. I order a
hamburger and french fries and a Coke and a piece of chocolate cake I can't afford and sit there eating and reading. Annie,

Doris, and Nell are at a table in a back corner, Doris and Nell nodding out from the junk, heads down on the table. Annie is wearing her skirt up high, flashing her chubby thighs, keeping an eye out for customers who might be willing to ignore her missing teeth and her black eye. The chocolate cake tastes good so I go back for a second piece and wash it down with another Coke, living it up.

I have a job interview Monday. If it goes well, I'll be leaving Hastings Street. Annie, Doris, and Nell, they'll be down here till they die.

■ ■ ■

I must make a strange sight leaving the front door of the hotel on a chilly Monday afternoon in late January, wearing a somewhat wrinkled suit, a tie, and a pair of army-issue dress shoes, now carefully shined to hide the ravages of a cheap shoe spray carelessly applied on an army base, all my hopes tied up in an envelope of clippings tucked under my arm. Pat Nagel is an affable, sad-eyed man in his mid-thirties. I feel comfortable with him immediately. We chat for a while before he comes to the question: "What's your status with the U.S. military, Jack? I'm going to assume you didn't leave the *Miami Herald* and come all the way to Vancouver because you think the *Sun* is a fabulous newspaper."

"I deserted from Fort Lewis. I was at the *Herald*, I got drafted, I did six weeks of basic and when we got Christmas leave I cut out."

Nagel nods. "How old are you?"

"Twenty-three."

He scans my handwritten résumé. "That's quite a record for a kid. *Lincoln Journal, Akron Beacon-Journal, Detroit Free Press, Miami Herald.*"

"I didn't stay anywhere too long."

"So I see. You plan on staying here long?"

"Nowhere else I want to go."

Nagel winds up the interview. "I think we can use you," he says. "Let me take a good look at your clips, talk to some people around here. I'll call you tomorrow."

"Uh—I don't have a phone. Maybe it's better if I call you."

When I phone the next day, Nagel says that he put in a call to his friend Will Jarrett at the *Herald*. "He says you've got a lot to learn about reporting but you can write. That's good enough for me. I want to give you a job but our managing editor wants to meet you first. He wants to see you now. Can you make it this afternoon?"

The managing editor has one of the offices looking out over False Creek to the mountains. He has what looks like dyed black hair slicked straight back. He wears a striped shirt and keeps his back turned to me, staring out at the mountains as he asks questions. I see the envelope with my clippings open on his desk, the piece about the ball-peen hammer murder of the pilot's wife lying on top. He waves disdainfully at my stories. "This is all crime stuff," he says. "We don't do crime stuff at the *Sun*."

"I've covered budget hearings, city council meetings, county commission hearings," I say. "At the *Detroit Free Press* I spent time in the business department. I've written stories on the auto industry. I can write anything."

"All I see here is a bunch of crime stuff."

If he's trying to get my goat, he's succeeding. "Well-written crime stuff," I say.

"If you say so."

He stares at the clippings for a silent minute, two minutes, three minutes. Nagel shuffles in his chair. I shuffle in my chair.

"OK," he says, stuffing the clips back in the envelope and handing them to Nagel. "If you want him, you hire him." And he turns his back again, implying that if I screw up, it's Nagel's fault.

"I knew he'd say yes," Nagel says when we're back in his office. "He just wanted to see how you'd react."

"I wanted to punch him out."

Nagel laughs. "Everybody does. That's why he's the boss. Now, when can you start?"

"First I have to get my landed immigrant status. I need a letter from you on *Sun* letterhead, made up to my address in the U.S. I've got everything else. Then I just have to go back through the border, go through an interview, get my card, and I'm ready to work."

"What do we say then? Two weeks? I'll get my secretary to do the letter for you. You call us when you're ready to start. Glad to have you aboard."

Nagel doesn't have to, but he's sticking his neck out for me. I don't want to let him down.

Norm and I go to the Yellow Door in Chinatown for dinner to celebrate. I'm buying, splurging a couple of bucks from my dwindling cash on the cheapest dinner in town. All that's left is the tricky business of getting landed immigrant status in Canada. Norm would cheerfully drive me through the border himself, but he doesn't have a car. It takes a fair set of nerves to make the run through the U.S. border. In cases like mine where the passenger is a deserter wanted in the U.S., the American border crossing can be a high-tension experience. If you're caught, you are facing the full five-year sentence in a federal prison. Figure two years off for good behavior, that's still three years of hard time. And the drivers can be threatened with jail time themselves if they're caught.

Norm has a friend named Lenny, a reporter for the *Province*. A good guy, antiwar. He suggests we meet Lenny and see if he would be willing to make the trip. Lenny is tall, easygoing, soft-spoken, dressed in Carnaby Street hipster's gear with colorful bell-bottom pants, high boots, and a flared shirt. I can't believe he's willing to put himself at risk by taking me through the border.

"I'd be proud to drive you," Lenny says. "It's hard for Canadians to find something we can do to help stop the war. If I have a chance to do something tangible, I want to do it." Norm and I lay out the drill: I will carry two sets of ID to the U.S., hiding one in the car. For the Americans, I will show Norm's ID. Mercifully, his driver's license has no photo and it doesn't display the holder's height and weight, since I'm nine inches taller than Norm. We will cross into the U.S. at the same point where Powers and I came up nearly a month earlier, turn around in Washington, and appear at the Canadian border crossing, where I will apply for landed immigrant status. The interview and paperwork take an hour or two, and when it's complete Lenny will drive me back to Vancouver, a newly landed immigrant.

By the time I've got all my papers and Lenny is ready to go, my thirty days are up. I'm now officially a deserter, so we can't afford to screw up. We set out for the border on a warm, sunny morning—February 6, 1970. Tense, knowing what lies ahead, but optimistic. Everything is in order. There is no reason for the Canadians to turn me away. All we have to do is get through the U.S. border one last time. I have Norm's ID in my pocket, my own ID along with my birth certificate and all the other documents I need hidden under a pile of newspapers in the back seat.

I'm so tense I find it difficult to breathe, but the crossing into Washington goes off without a hitch. We're Canadians headed to Seattle for a couple of days. The American guard at the border asks Lenny all the questions, barely looks at me, and waves us through. We stop for coffee at a truck stop a mile into Washington, take a deep breath, and head back to the Canadian checkpoint. The Canadians are friendly enough, but there's a problem—I need an appointment. I can't just show up and expect an interview. Somehow, with all the briefing at the committee, no one mentioned this possible hitch. An officer at the desk shrugs.

"The best we can do," he says, "is give you an appointment at the truck stop border at 4 o'clock this afternoon. That's a mile east of here."

It means crossing the border into the U.S. a second time, but we have no choice. It's barely 10 A.M.; we have six hours to wait. We don't want to go through the border twice in fifteen minutes, so we get back into the car, head into White Rock—a little town about a mile inside Canada—and spend a couple of hours in the winter sunshine, throwing rocks into the water, killing time.

After a late lunch and more waiting at a café in White Rock, we cross into the U.S. a second time without incident. Again Lenny does all the talking. My heart is pounding in my ears, so loud I'm sure the guard can hear it, but a couple of perfunctory questions and we're through. We find the truck stop border point without difficulty, weave around the long line of waiting eighteen-wheelers, and pull up at a checkpoint for cars. Lenny gives my name and explains that I have a 4 o'clock appointment for an immigration interview.

"It's about time you two showed up," says the officer inside the booth. "We've been looking for you all day. You're wanted for running the border this morning. We've had the RCMP looking for you. They want to see you back at the main border point right now. You have some explaining to do."

"But we didn't know we couldn't cross the border. My friend is Canadian."

"Doesn't matter. You weren't cleared to enter Canada. You ran the border."

I'm white as a ghost and shaking. Lenny doesn't look much better. Not only are we in trouble with the Canadians, but now we have to turn around and reenter the U.S. for a third time—and this time, the Americans are no more than one hundred feet away. Two American border guards stand outside their booths, watching as we are refused entry into Canada.

Lenny does a slow U-turn, stalling for time. There's no question of making a run for it—they already have the RCMP looking for us. We're fifty feet from the Americans when I remember I have to switch ID because I still have my real papers in my pocket. Lenny pulls out Norm's ID, I get mine out of my wallet, and we're still frantically exchanging driver's licenses under the seat as we pull up to the U.S. checkpoint.

The American approaches the car. For some reason he comes around to the passenger side. I roll down the window, a handful of ID cards still wadded in my left fist. I have no idea what I'm holding—some of Norm's, some of mine. This has to be the end of the line. We've just been turned around at the Canadian border and anyone can see that something is wrong. The American leans his head almost all the way into the car and glares at me.

"Where are you going?"

My voice breaks. I try to say "Seattle" but it comes out "Se-AT-tle," going up an octave on the second syllable.

"Is that so. What for?"

"PLEA-sure?" I sound like a nervous boy soprano hitting puberty.

I can't help it. I'm squeaking like a cornered rat. I can feel the handcuffs already, see the MPs escorting me back to Fort Lewis, hear the judge's gavel when it comes down, see my prison cell.

"Is that so? Anything to declare? Alcohol? Tobacco?"

"Uh . . . no SIR?"

"All right, that's it. Go on."

Lenny hesitates a moment, not sure he heard right. I want to scream "GO!" but the officer does the work for me. "Go on, move it up."

Lenny floors it and we peel away from the border. I can't understand why the guard is letting us through. He saw us get turned away by the Canadians. The obvious explanation is that they're wise to us on both sides of the border, and we're being sent to the main Canadian checkpoint to be arrested there. I'm sweating and shaking, Lenny is tightlipped. We pull up to the White Rock crossing again. A hard-faced senior officer marches us into a little room, sits down on the edge of his desk, and launches into a tirade.

"You two ran the Canadian border this morning," he says to me. "This is an act that has serious consequences. I assume, from the way you're acting, that you are fleeing service in the U.S. military. You will be returned to the Americans, and they can deal with you as they see fit. As for you," he turns to Lenny, "you will be charged with running the border, bringing a fugitive into Canada. I don't know who you two think you are. Apparently you think you can just ignore the laws of Canada and get away with it. Well, that's not the way it works. You are going to face some very serious consequences for what you did this morning . . ."

He yammers on. I've gone from being shaky and frightened to simply deflated. After all the tension of the past month, it's over. I'll be deported and tried in the U.S. and sentenced to prison and the man is still lecturing us. I don't get the point. If we're in as much trouble as he says we are, why does he have to make it worse? Devastation turns to anger. I'm going to do five years in Leavenworth Penitentiary. I don't have to listen to this crap. I want to tell him to shut the fuck up and call the cops. A heartbeat before I open my mouth and blow the whole thing, he winds up his lecture.

"You've really screwed up—but we're going to interview you for landed immigrant status anyway."

I look at Lenny, slumped in his chair. He shrugs—he doesn't understand either.

"Follow me, please," the officer says. He marches briskly down the corridor with the two of us tripping along behind, uncomprehending. He opens the door to another office down the hall. "OK, here they are," he says to the man inside. "They're all yours."

This one is as friendly as the other one was sour.

"Good afternoon, good afternoon," he says, pumping my hand. He apologizes to Lenny: "I'm sorry, but I'm going to have to ask you to wait outside. I'll call you as soon as we're finished. There's coffee down at the end of the hall."

Lenny stumbles out of the room, completely confused. I sit down nervously, waiting for the other shoe to fall. He flips through my papers, studies the letter from the *Sun*. "This is quite a record you have," he says with a slight trace of a British accent. "So you want to work for the *Sun*, eh? Good paper, read it every morning."

He asks a few brief questions, beaming all the while. It's a trick, obviously: good cop, bad cop. They're just playing games with my head. Finally, he clears his throat and asks rather delicately, "I assume you have some kind of problem with your draft status in the U.S.?"

"Yes-sir-I'm-a-deserter-from-the-army." It comes out as one word.

"Yes, I thought so," he nods. "The haircut. I must say it's a terrible situation for you young Yanks. The U.S. has gotten itself into an awful mess over there in Asia. You have all my sympathy."

He whisks through the rest of the questions, giving me points for education, for speaking English, for having a profession, for having a job offer in hand.

"Now," he says, "as you probably know, we're allowed to give you points on the basis of our own discretion, from one to ten. I think you'll make a brilliant addition to the *Sun*, so I'm going to give you the full ten points. Congratulations, you are now a landed immigrant in Canada!" He jumps up and starts pumping my hand. I mumble my thanks and he takes me down the hall to still another office.

"Congratulations," he says to Lenny. "Mr. Todd has passed with flying colors. He's now a landed immigrant in Canada."

Lenny and I exchange glances. This is too weird for words.

We are still unsure of our status. If I'm a landed immigrant, what does this mean for Lenny? Is he still going to be charged with running the border? Will I be granted landed immigrant status—and then deported? It seems best to say nothing. The officer who did the interview shakes my hand again; his delight seems genuine. "This officer will type up your papers," he says, introducing me to the clerk at the desk, "and then you're free to go. Welcome to Canada."

The clerk, working on a big manual typewriter, begins laboriously typing my papers, page after page. The man can barely type. He has to hunt for every key, he keeps making mistakes and pulling the forms out of the carriage and starting over. It's maddening. I sit on my hands, feeling like I'm going to explode. I could jump back there and type these forms up in five minutes. Lenny and I are a bundle of nerves, looking back over our shoulders every thirty seconds, expecting the officer who told us we would be arrested to come bursting in any second with the RCMP and the FBI in tow. It takes the clerk a full two hours to do the paperwork. Peck-peck-peck, rip up a form, start over. Peck-peck-peck, peck-peck-peck, in that quiet room. Repeating over and over my mother's maiden name, place of birth, date of birth, address in Vancouver.

By the time he finishes it is pushing eight o'clock at night. He hands me my copies of the pile of forms, along with an appointment for a physical in Vancouver the following week, the last hurdle to legal status in Canada. As long as I don't have tuberculosis, beriberi, or malaria, I'm home free.

We leave the office like zombies, still keeping watch for the guy who wanted to put us both in prison. I've got the papers clutched tight in my fist: legal status in Canada. Lenny starts the car and we pull away in silence, afraid even to breathe, watching the rear-view mirror, wondering if it was all a mistake. It's not until we're well up the highway past White Rock that I start howling and yipping like a coyote, whacking

Lenny's shoulder so hard he almost runs off the road, the two of us exploding with elation, relief, joy, a dozen hours of constant tension evaporating in this last run to Vancouver. I still can't believe it. "What the hell was that about? I thought we were going to jail, and then he says, 'We're going to interview you anyway'?"

"I have no idea," Lenny says. "No idea at all. I guess he was just trying to give us a hard time."

"I felt worse for you. I got myself into this, but when he said you were going to jail . . ."

"You're telling me. I felt bad for me, too."

I stare out at the darkness, feeling the elation fade to black. I am now a deserter from the United States Army, a traitor in the eyes of most Americans, a traitor even in the eyes of a younger self I left behind a short distance down the road. An exile, cut off by a three thousand–mile border from all the places I love, barred from virtually all the people I care about. Parents, sisters, Sonny, Mariela, Rich, Larry, a dozen friends from high school, a dozen more from university. Some will now be ashamed to admit they ever knew me. Already the American border we have just crossed looms as the great divide. It might as well be the Berlin Wall, strung with razor wire and guarded by watchtowers manned with machine guns.

Heading north, letting go. Feeling the ties stretched and snapping, like rubber bands taken to the limit. Grateful to Canada, a good, wise country that has made us welcome. Grateful to Lester Pearson and Pierre Trudeau, the men who stood up to LBJ and Richard Nixon. Glad they helped make a country like this, a grown-up place compared to that big, noisy, meddling teenager next door. Happy to be here. Wishing it felt more like home.

We had called Norm in the afternoon to tell him the appointment had been rescheduled so he was expecting us to be running late, but not this late. He's frantic, waiting at Lenny's apartment where he has organized a little party with three or four women he knows and some hippie friends, including a couple of the guys from the committee. We burst in on a party that is already in progress. Norm has laid in a gallon jug of wine and some takeout burgers from the White Castle up the street. There are a dozen people waiting at Lenny's place, most of them friends of Norm's from up in the mountains.

Lenny and I tell the story over and over—the three separate crossings into the U.S., the bad cop, good cop Canadian immigration officers, the crazy ID exchange going on under the seat as we approached the American border the last time, my squeaky-voiced answers, the friendly officer at White Rock to whom I owe my freedom, the clerk who could barely type holding us up for two hours.

When the party winds down, Lenny's portable typewriter catches my eye. It's sitting next to a neat stack of pale green typing paper on a desk in his living room. I sit down in the middle of the party and start writing the Great American Novel, about a young man from Nebraska who goes to Canada during the Vietnam War. I keep at it for a week, read over the twenty-five pages I've produced—and dump it in the wastebasket, where it belongs.

During the party Lenny mentions that he is about to move into a bigger apartment and that he wouldn't mind having a roommate. It seems like a good idea. I'm about to get a job, we're both young reporters; if I room with Lenny, I won't have to spend months saving money for an apartment and furniture. A reporter's job at the *Sun,* landed immigrant status in Canada, a comfortable apartment. After the army, after the month on skid row Hastings Street, after losing nearly everything, the wheel has turned again. I can resume my career almost without interruption, rejoin society. Who knows? With hair and a job, I might even get a date. My hair is growing back, but something strange is happening. There is no baldness in my family, but my hair is falling out. Every time I brush it, I come away with handfuls of hair. Norm and Lenny are sure it's the stress of the past six months. Whatever the cause, at this rate I'll be bald by summer.

Next day I phone my mother to tell her I'm legal in Canada, I have a job, everything is going to be cool. She is pleased for me, but it's not a happy moment; from her perspective this makes it official. I won't be coming home.

I put the phone down, pick it up again on an impulse, call Mariela in Miami. Her father answers, says she isn't home and he isn't expecting her anytime soon. I can't resist. "Tell her I got a job at the *Vancouver Sun*. It's a beautiful city, I'd love it if she'd come to visit."

I finally get through to Sonny, too.

"Your mom told me when you left," he says. "She's pretty upset, but you did the right thing, man. You did the right thing."

"How are you making out?"

"Oh, you know. Pretty good, pretty good. Working a little, this and that."

I get the sense that Sonny is not doing "pretty good," but I don't want to push him. He poured his heart out my last night in Scottsbluff, said all he had to say. He's happy I'm in Canada, pleased to know his nightmares will not become my nightmares. That's as far as it goes.

"Hey, you gotta come up and see me sometime, eh? It's beautiful up here, eh?"

"Y'know I think you're Canadian already. You say 'eh' all the time."

It's true. The word drove me crazy when I first arrived, but it's already slipped into my speech.

"Sonny, y'know, I have to thank you for trying to talk to me before I left. I know it wasn't easy. I just wasn't ready to listen, but I think it had an effect on me. It took awhile, but I'm here now."

"You did a good thing, man. Don't ever think about it any other way. You did the only thing you could do."

The physical exam the following week involves little more than checking a bunch of boxes on a form and letting a doctor press his chilly stethoscope to my chest. All around me Third World immigrants are anxiously awaiting a far more thorough exam. I'm a big, healthy ex-jock North American. Even if I smoke too much, at twenty-three and with no physical disabilities the exam is a breeze.

We spend a long day of heavy lifting moving Lenny's furniture into the new apartment. My things I can haul up from Hastings Street in a duffel bag, two quick trips on the bus. After five weeks in that hotel room, the apartment feels like the Taj Mahal to me. No need to go down the hall for the bathroom or shower. A couch. A TV set. A stereo, and Lenny has the new Rolling Stones album, *Let It Bleed*. The first full day I listen to the whole thing, both sides, a half-dozen times.

■ ■ ■

On a gray, cold, rainy Monday, I put on a shirt and tie and jacket and go to work at the *Sun*. I can't wait: after three months off, I'm anxious to sink my teeth into some real stories. The huge trade in heroin at the port, the treatment of Chinese immigrants, life in Kitsilano, the booming hippie neighborhood near the *Sun* building. At the *Herald*, the *Detroit Free Press*, the *Akron Beacon Journal*, even the *Lincoln Journal* back in Nebraska, the drill was pretty much the same with varying degrees of pressure. From the first day you were loaded up with more work than you could possibly handle and left to sink or swim.

At the *Sun*, I fill out all the paperwork, get assigned to a desk, and sit. The morning passes without an assignment. After lunch there's still nothing. The assistant city editor is apologetic. "Sorry," he says. "Slow day. Nothing happening. Maybe tomorrow."

Next day it's the same thing. Check in, sit at my desk, talk to other reporters who are only slightly busier than I am, play with paper clips, try to look busy. No assignments. Around four in the afternoon the same editor notices me sitting there and wanders over. "Sorry things have been a little slow," he says, "but I have something for you tomorrow.

I sit up, all ears. Heroin gangs in Chinatown. Kickback scandals at City Hall. A ferry sinking on the Nanaimo route.

"A couple of years ago," he says, "I was up around Sixtieth Street and Granville and I found this real interesting old guy selling newspapers. Why don't you go up there and see if you can find him, chat a little, maybe do a feature? If it works out, call me and we'll send a photog."

It's not a riot in the streets, but it will have to do: an assignment at last. Next morning I take the bus up to Sixtieth and Granville, eager to probe the psyche of this fascinating character and show what I can do. No newspaper vendor anywhere. Walk up to Sixty-fifth, back down to Fifty-fifth. No one. Another walk, Fiftieth to Seventieth Street this time. There's one newspaper booth, but the guy selling magazines and newspapers in there isn't much older than me. I buy a copy of the *Province* and ask him if there used to be an older man working in the booth. "Maybe five, six years ago," he says. "I've been here five years myself."

I try striking up a conversation with him, just to see if he turns out to be a really interesting guy. He offers a few monosyllabic answers and I give up. I hate to strike out on my first assignment for the *Sun*, but this isn't working.

The next day I sit there all day with no assignments again, waiting for something to happen. Nothing does. Near the end of my shift, someone asks if I can take dictation from the *Sun*'s political columnist covering the provincial legislature in Victoria. I'm into my fourth day and I haven't written a word, done an interview, made a phone call. I roll some paper into the typewriter and get them to send the call to my desk: if there's one thing I can do, it's to take dictation quickly and well. At the *Herald*, it was an absolute necessity. You had to be able to compose stories from your notes in a phone booth and dictate them on the fly, and you had to be able to take dictation on the other end.

After three sentences, the columnist is already annoyed. I'm not typing fast enough to suit him. Three or four times I have to stop to ask him to spell a name because I'm unfamiliar with the cast of characters in Victoria. He grows more sarcastic with every name he has to spell, finally slowing down and spelling each name as though he's talking to a child. We're on about the sixth paragraph when he asks if I know how to type. That does it.

"If you don't like it," I say, "take your own dictation." I put the phone down, fuming. I don't know who this jerk is, but he has found someone with an ego and a temper to match his own.

Ten minutes later, Nagel comes out of his office. "Who just told our man in Victoria to get lost?" he says. I raise my hand sheepishly. Nagel laughs his way back into his office. Another reporter fills me in: the columnist is the paper's biggest star, bound for bigger and better things. Four days at the *Sun*, and all I've managed to accomplish is to piss off the big-wheel columnist.

Late the next afternoon the union steward comes around. This will be our last shift. The *Sun* and the *Province* are going on strike. Next week we will all receive our schedules for picket duty. I'll be paid for one week's work even though I did nothing, and on a union scale prorated for service time I'll get something like thirty-five dollars a week in strike pay. I have to talk to Lenny. The deal is that I'm supposed to pay my share of the rent out of my first two paychecks. He says not to worry about it, he has money in the bank, I can just help with the groceries until we get back to work and then pay him the rent. He figures we can't be out more than a week or two.

A couple of days later Lenny is on picket duty and I'm home on the couch listening to his Rolling Stones album when I hear someone pounding at the door. We've been warned: sometime in the first two months after you get your landed immigrant status, the RCMP will pay a visit. They might be intimidating, they might be polite—all they really want is to establish that you are living in Canada. Until then you are supposed to avoid illegal activities in your apartment, specifically the inhalation of cannabis. After one visit the RCMP will report to the FBI, and the FBI will stop looking for you in the U.S.

I don't want to answer the door, but it's a little hard to pretend I'm not home with the Stones going full blast on the stereo. I turn down the music and hesitate, hoping the pounding will go away.

"C'mon, Todd!" shouts a familiar voice. "Open the fuckin' door before I kick it in!" Powers. Wearing his army field jacket, combat boots, and jeans, carrying a duffel bag. Ruddy-faced, grinning like the cat that ate the canary, hair longer and curlier, full of hell as ever.

"Whatsamatter, you pussy? You afraid the MPs are gonna haul your ass back to Lewis? Why didn't you open the door?"

"Good to see you too, asshole." Locked in a Powers bear hug, trying to breathe while he whacks my back.

"Man, you're skinnier than ever, but you almost have hair now," Powers says. "One of these days, you might look normal."

Powers tosses his duffel on the couch, making himself right at home.

"How did you find me?"

"I was going to check in down at the hotel, but this guy Norm was working the desk," he says. "He gave me your address, said I could probably crash with you guys."

"I dunno, I've got a roommate. It's really his place, the furniture is all his."

"Hell with him. The more the merrier. Hey, is it true you worked one week at the *Sun* and now you're out on strike?"

"That's it. One week and I'm unemployed again."

"Man, that sucks. But don't worry—if it gets really bad we'll rob banks or something."

Powers helps himself to one of my Cokes from the fridge, sits down, and fills me in. The army has turned him down on his application for a conscientious objector discharge, even though it had been approved by everyone in the chain of command at Fort Lewis, including the company commander, the battalion commander, the post commander, priest, and psychiatrist. Someone in Washington had simply noted: "Applicant's views were fixed prior to entry into the military." Somehow, the fact that Powers had been a conscientious objector all along worked against him. Powers made up his mind to face a court-martial for refusing to serve, a court-martial which would sentence him to three to five years in a military prison. In the end, however, he decided that there was no point in martyrdom. "There are too many people in jail now and it's not doing any good. There are a lot of romantic notions about prison, but I think it's mostly just wasted time. A few more people going to prison isn't going to change the U.S."

"So what's happening down there, anyway?" I want to know. "Did anybody come back from Christmas leave?"

"I think your platoon lost three or four more guys besides you," he says. "I wasn't really paying attention. But I noticed one thing, brother—I saw the postings. You didn't get AIT. No Advanced Infantry Training for you, man. I didn't recognize the code for that category, but I know you weren't assigned to be a clerk and you sure as hell weren't going to the infantry. I'm pretty sure you got journalism. You'd be sitting on your ass somewhere now, writing press releases for Colonel Jerkoff. No rifles, no mud, no Viet Cong. But your ass is grass now.

You go near that border, you'll end up in leg irons, cutting weeds on a chain gang for the next five years."

"Hey, it was closer than you think." I tell him the story of our border misadventures, the three crossings into the U.S., the officer who told us we were going to be arrested. Powers thinks it's all spectacularly funny, but he's going to have to face his own immigration test if he wants to get legal status in Canada.

"So what are you going to do? What's happening with Barb?"

"I'm going to look for a job and get landed like you," Powers says. "When I get it worked out, she's going to join me up here."

When Lenny comes home from the picket line I introduce them, explain that Powers is going to be crashing with us for a while. Lenny looks a little uncomfortable with the whole idea, but he doesn't say no.

The next day Powers and I are standing at a busy intersection on Davie Street, waiting to cross. Suddenly he whirls and kicks me in the groin, full force with his combat boot. I'm down, writhing in pain and gasping for breath.

"You gotta be ready!" he says, bouncing back and forth on the balls of his feet over me, just in case I want to get up and fight. "You gotta be ready, man! That's the way it is in life. If you're not ready every second, it kicks you in the balls! That's the first thing I gotta teach you!"

I roll over onto my back, legs drawn up, fighting for air through waves of pain. People passing on the street stare, wondering what's going on with these two crazy people. Powers is in his karate stance, jabbering about how I need to be ready. I'm crawling on my knees to the gutter to vomit. The man is insane.

"Y'know, you are an absolute asshole sometimes. And you are the strangest conscientious objector I ever met."

"Yeah," he says, "but I'm your teacher, man. You are such a

naive pussy sometimes. You need a guru, somebody to teach you about life. You're lucky you've got me to take care of you."

Picket duty is monotonous and embarrassing. I feel like an idiot walking back and forth, holding a placard bearing a slogan I did not write. I want to alter mine, write "End the War in Vietnam!"—but self-expression here is not an option. I attend a couple of union meetings, but I don't even begin to understand the issues. All I want is to go back on the job and start getting a regular paycheck. The union members from the *Sun* and *Province* combine to publish their own newspaper during the strike, but it's a hopeless rag. I do a couple of editing stints but avoid working on the strike paper as much as possible.

Powers and I are both desperately short of money. I cash my one and only check from the *Sun* and hand it over to Lenny for the rent. We scavenge for pop bottles, exchanging them for food: in an afternoon we can usually scare up enough bottles for two Cokes and two packages of macaroni and cheese dinner, which I convert to something like a meal in Lenny's kitchen. It's becoming obvious we can't stay here much longer. It's the difference between Americans and Canadians—the Americans noisy and rude and boisterous and sloppy, the Canadian in this case soft-spoken and neat and polite. One of us Lenny could probably tolerate. Two is too many for anyone, especially when one of the two is as wired as Powers.

After a week with the two of us lounging around his apartment, Lenny has had enough. When Powers is out one afternoon, we have a talk. If I will ask Powers to leave, Lenny says, I'm welcome to stay—but we can't go on like this. I know how he feels, but I have to remain loyal to my fellow deserter. When Powers comes back, we pack our bags and leave. Powers wants to share a hotel room, but I can't imagine rooming with someone as hyper as he is, so I move into a deserter commune in Kitsilano for one night. Powers has spent time there himself and won't go back, but a friend of his says I can stay there for a month free until I get on my feet, and I figure by then the strike at the *Sun* will be over. For now, I'm so broke I can't afford even the hotel.

The "commune" is really just a crash pad in an old, ramshackle house in the Kitsilano neighborhood, the Vancouver equivalent of Haight-Ashbury. There are eight or nine deserters living there. They would be the dregs on either side of the border, in the army or out. Addicts and criminals, real badasses. Whatever their reasons for being in Canada, opposition to the war has little to do with it. Most of these guys couldn't tell you whether Vietnam is in Europe or Asia. Some are wanted in the U.S. for crimes other than desertion, most will soon be wanted in Canada if they aren't already. Two or three are more or less openly packing handguns. There are overflowing ashtrays everywhere, a week's worth of grimy dishes stacked in the kitchen, a couple of filthy toilets that barely flush and haven't been cleaned in months, dozens of roach burns in the bare carpet and the old, moth-eaten couches along the wall—one of which is supposed to be my bed.

There is a character here they call "Stillborn" because he sits day and night in a ripped easy chair in the living room, staring at the black-and-white TV and smoking dope. Even when the TV fades to the test pattern after midnight he's still in place, eyes open, staring at the screen. Except to go to the bathroom, he never moves. They say he's a veteran who got his head seriously turned around in Vietnam when the Viet Cong launched an assault while he was tripping his brains out on LSD. The other deserters think it's funny. I find it creepy trying to sleep in the same room with this character staring at a test pattern all night.

Young girls drift in and out, inevitably stoned, all of them looking about sixteen. There is supposedly a more or less perpetual gangbang going on upstairs with one or more of these girls at all hours of the day and night. You can hear them at it even in the middle of the night. I sleep with my jeans rolled up under my head so I can protect my wallet, sure that some of these guys would hack my kidneys out with a bayonet for the twenty bucks in my back pocket.

After one sleepless night it's back to the hotel. For two weeks Powers and I share a twenty-five-dollar room with two beds. It's like living with an infantry company. Powers is hyper day and night. Practicing karate, doing hundreds of pushups, going on his all-night talking jags about Solzhenitsyn and Gandhi, Malcolm X and Eldridge Cleaver and the revolution. Just listening to him wears me out.

Luckily, Powers is better at survival than I am. I tend to get depressed and withdraw into a shell and starve, Powers gets after it and hustles up a way to live. Once a week when the underground *Georgia Straight* newspaper comes out we stake out our own street and sell it, make enough money for two or three meals. Powers finds us a couple of day-labor jobs, hauling boxes or swabbing floors. But no matter how long or how hard we work, he's up half the night talking. Trying to keep up with him I feel like a sleepwalking zombie, as tired as I was back at Fort Lewis.

Mercifully, Barb finally arrives in Canada. She has quit her job, emptied her bank accounts, come to find work in Canada and get an apartment with Powers. They move into a place in Vancouver for a month or two, and then into a commune somewhere up in the BC interior.

After Powers leaves I move back to a fifteen-dollar room, this time on the sixth floor of the hotel. A room with a view of Carrall Street, a real prize. When the *Georgia Straight* comes out, I sell copies along the street we staked out as our territory when Powers was still rooming with me. If anyone else came along trying to sell papers, Powers scared them off, so now the territory is mine. I talk to the editors of the *Straight*, persuade them to let me write the occasional movie review for pocket money. For the first time in my life writing is a real struggle. For some reason I can't put sentences together. I feel like my mind is in fragments, pieces of it strewn all over the place from Miami to Nebraska to Fort Lewis to Mexico to San Francisco. Since I was sixteen years old I've been able to sit down at a typewriter and simply let it flow, but now I can't get it together. I have to work at the *Straight* offices because I don't have a typewriter; after one embarrassing afternoon spent trying and failing to do a short movie review I give up and leave, my face burning with shame because I can't find the words.

Norm comes through with a part-time job, persuading his boss to hire me as the weekend night clerk, replacing a middle-aged guy who has just been fired for being skunk-drunk on the job. Midnight to 8 A.M. Friday and Saturday in a hotel where weekend nights mean an endless stream of drunks and junkies puking in the lobby. One shift I work for my weekly rent, the second for cash. I make the mistake one night of trying to wrestle a drunken sixty-year-old logger onto the elevator. He throws me into a wall so hard it feels like my spine has been shattered. Another night, answering a complaint from an adjoining room, I pound on the door of a room where a half-dozen loggers fresh out of the bush up north are partying with a dozen women, most of them natives. A big logger opens the door onto a scene of mayhem: naked women and loggers passed out on the floor, empty whiskey bottles all over the place, a radio blaring Hank Snow, a hopelessly drunk fat man trying to screw a toothless native woman on one of the sagging beds.

"Waddya want?" says the man who answers the door.

"Uh, I'm going to have to ask you to hold it down in here. There's been a complaint about the noise."

He stares at me, wobbling back and forth, barely able to stand. "Fuck off. You bother us again, I'll fuckin' kill ya with my bare hands, eh? And I'll boil yer fuckin' kidneys and eat 'em for breakfast." And he slams the door so hard he almost breaks my nose.

Still, it's a job. Work two shifts every weekend, they let me stay in the hotel rent-free. With the strike money and the money from selling the *Georgia Straight*, I'm a wealthy man on Hastings Street.

We're into the second week of the strike, walking picket duty outside the *Sun* building, a lovely day in late February. Sunny, warm, the daffodils out. Walk a little, sit a lot more in the sunshine. Someone brings out mail for *Sun* employees on the picket line. Most of the reporters have a pile of press releases to throw away; I have one personal letter, a thick one from Miami, addressed in a feminine hand.

The handwriting isn't Mariela's. It's from another reporter at the *Herald*, a woman in her early forties who worked with me in the *Herald*'s Broward bureau. She's a kind, bright woman, married to an independent TV producer who was working on a documentary on the Bermuda Triangle. They screened it at a big party in the summer of 1969, in that other world when I had Mariela on my arm, beautiful in a flowing white dress, the two of us fresh from the beach, glowing with youth and health, sex and love.

It's a chatty, gossipy letter, eleven pages long. I sit down to read it on a bench outside the *Sun*, the picketers strolling back and forth behind me. She has bits about almost everyone I know in Miami, the reporters and editors I worked with in Miami and Fort Lauderdale. Who's sleeping with whom, who's drinking too much, who left for the *Washington Post*, who's angling for a job at the *New York Times*. I read it slowly, this lifeline to a world left behind. My old buddy Rich Wallace has never written, so this is the first news I've had from Miami since I lost contact with Mariela. I get to the last page, read the very last line, then notice that she has added a postscript on the back: "Remember that beautiful Cuban girl you were seeing last summer? The one you brought to our party? Such a lovely girl, I think her name is Mariela. Anyway, I ran into her in Coconut Grove last night. She just got back from her honeymoon in Haiti. She married that lawyer Tom Clagg right after Christmas, and they've moved into a house in Coconut Grove. But I guess you probably know that already. She is such a beautiful woman, and smart, too. You should have hung onto her."

The letter swims in a sunny haze. I put it down, pick it up, read the paragraph again. "She just got back from her honeymoon. . . . She married that lawyer Tom Clagg."

I leave the picket sign on the bench and stumble away down the street, clutching the letter. I need to get away. I walk over the Granville Bridge, pause in the center of the span, and read the letter one more time. Memorize the postscript about Mariela, rip it all into bits, and drop it off the bridge into False Creek. Let it float away in the water, along with the best part of me.

This is worse than the day at Fort Lewis when she told me it was over. Tom Clagg with Mariela. My Mariela. In Haiti, the bastard. And I'm in Canada, and there's not a damned thing I can do about it—although the one thing I want to do at this moment is to sneak back over the border, hitchhike to Miami, and throttle Clagg with my bare hands.

I keep walking, all the way to Hastings Street, all the way back to the tavern in the hotel. It's the middle of the afternoon, but there are a half-dozen drunks at the tables, working on their daily buzz. I've never been a drinker, but this seems like a good time to start. I sit down at a table and order two draft beers, drink them as soon as they hit the table, and order two more. Within fifteen minutes I'm reasonably whacked, but I keep it up until it's dark outside and I don't have a dime left in my pocket. I stagger to the elevator and down the hall to my room, bouncing off the walls just like the other tenants. Vomit in the sink, just like everyone else. Fall asleep drunk, just like they do. Get up and vomit again, wake the next day to a brass band headache, unable to stand the light. Stumble to the bank, take out twenty dollars from what little money I have left, and spend the afternoon getting drunk again. At fifteen cents a glass of beer you can do a lot of drinking on twenty dollars, especially if you don't eat. In the morning I tell the waiters to "make it red," meaning half tomato juice, half beer, because that's how the drunks here get their nutrition.

Norm comes into the tavern a couple of hours before his shift on the third day, finds me drunk again, insists we go out for coffee at the White Lunch. The sight of the place makes me gag. After about the third coffee Norm asks what on earth has gone so wrong.

"Mariela. She married that sonofabitch Tom Clagg."

"Married?"

"Married. They went to Haiti on their honeymoon. The son of a bitch. I'm gonna find him, break his fuckin' neck."

"Geez, I'm really sorry to hear that. But you know drinking isn't going to help."

"I don't give a shit. I don't care what happens to me now."

"Well, you better sober up. You've got no job. You start drinking, you're going to end up just like those people we help up to bed every night. The cops are going to be scraping you off the street with the rest of them. If that happens to you, you'll end up deported."

Norm helps me upstairs to bed, but the next day I'm back in the tavern. Somehow, I could take all the rest of it, but the news that Mariela married Clagg has put me over the edge. I'm living on skid row. It looks like there's a fair chance the strike could go on for a year or more. That one little candle of hope I kept going for Mariela is now officially out. A three-day drunk doesn't put you in the same category as the rummies, but I can feel the bottom falling out. I could have stayed in the army, taken a journalism assignment, maybe spent two years in Germany. But no, I had to do the big, noble thing and come to Canada to live with the winos. As long as I don't eat I can afford to keep drinking, and after the fourth or fifth beer (sometimes augmented with a mickey of cheap whiskey from the bootlegger on the second floor of the hotel) I feel a comfortable haze over everything, get into a zone where none of it matters and there's no reason to do anything else.

Late at night I write drunken poetry in my room. One poem about a junkie hooker, another about the Canadian flag and the way Canadian industry is tied into the Vietnam War, something about the tip of the Maple Leaf dunked in the blood of Old Glory. Evenings I jump into drunken, disconnected arguments about hockey and politics in the Hastings Street taverns, sure that I know as much about Bobby Orr and Pierre Trudeau as anyone else.

When the money runs out I have to ease up on the drinking. I'm living hand-to-mouth as it is, scavenging the streets for pop bottles. Eating all my meals at the White Lunch, uncomfortable anywhere else. A good part of what I have goes for Coca-Cola and cigarettes. If I have to choose between cigarettes and a meal, I'll take the smokes every time because they're like company. Sit there all afternoon in the White Lunch drinking coffee and smoking and staring out at the rain-soaked streets, so thin I have to cinch my belt in two more notches to keep my pants up.

Sober enough to take an interest in women again, I fall into a strange relationship with a thirty-year-old stripper who works at a slimy joint around the corner on Hastings Street under the name Candy May. She's blonde and pretty, but she had an operation which made her breasts hard as marble and she's self-conscious about anyone touching them. We meet in the White Lunch one night when I'm drunk and feeling talkative, and she's a good listener. When she finishes her shift some nights she comes to my room because she doesn't want to take a cab home. We talk until we get drowsy and sleep curled up like spoons, a couple of lost souls giving each other a little comfort. When I watch her act I want to slug the noisy drunks who make crude comments about her sitting on their faces, but she claims she never hears a word of it, tunes it right out, her mind somewhere else. Now and then she buys me dinner at one of the back-alley Chinese joints. A couple of times on sunny days we go out to Stanley Park together and just sit and hold hands. Then one morning she announces she's going back to Saskatchewan, and I'm alone again. She doesn't have a drug habit and I never find out why she became a stripper, why she had her breasts done, what she wants out of life. She's just there for a while and then she isn't. I don't realize how much I have begun to depend on her until she's gone.

After Candy leaves, it's hard to find a reason to get up in the morning. Lying in the dark at night, staring at the ceiling, thinking about Mariela with Tom Clagg. Whatever the principles involved, I'm beginning to think that I gave up too much by coming to Canada. Powers is right. I could be sitting behind a desk somewhere right now, writing press releases for some colonel, counting the days until my two-year hitch is up and I can go back to the *Herald*.

Drunk or sober, I sit in my room late at night writing poetry or playing the guitar, picking out Kris Kristofferson songs. Or I play out in the square, where I can learn how to pick bluegrass from some of the natives. I feel right at home with them now, Sunday morning comin' down, just another bum on Hastings Street, nothing left to lose.

■   ■   ■

There aren't many places on the continent worse than Hastings Street. Every town has its skid row, but Hastings is the skid row for an entire country. It's where you end up when you have nowhere else to go. You've bounced out of Winnipeg or worn out your welcome in Sudbury or taken the bus down from Prince George with the pay from a summer's logging fat in your pocket and forgotten the way back. It's warm enough

in Vancouver so you won't freeze to death in the winter, so
when the rest of it is gone—family and friends, jobs and
money and hope—you stop here in this beautiful place at the
tag end of the continent, two blocks short of the water, and
you try to get numb enough to die. I'm luckier than most. They've been taken down by cheap
rum, glue, smack, wine, beatings, rape, prison, frozen nights
sleeping on Toronto sidewalks or maybe just the demons
that live in the back of their minds. They end up here, dazed
and broke and bleeding, sitting in a doorway, sprawled on a
park bench, shuffling along sidewalks slick with frozen spittle
begging quarters from strangers, scraping together enough to
get a needle back into a ravaged arm or a flask of cheap brandy
or a few filthy balls of scavenged Kleenex soaked with glue,
jammed between the gum and upper lip so the fumes explode
behind their eyes. Days when they're almost sober, they sit for
hours in the White Lunch drinking coffee with extra cream
and sugar because the cream and sugar are food, sort of, trying
to eat a bit, hands shaking, the terrors of withdrawal nibbling
at the corners of their minds. Then they score enough for another bottle or another needle and crawl into a doorway and
pull the world shut behind them, nothing left except the warm,
dumb place at the end of consciousness when you go down under the water for the third time. Bobbing beneath the surface,
hoping not to come up ever again, not to go back to the shakes
and the terror and the cops whacking the soles of your feet
with their nightsticks when you've lost your shoes.

Hastings Street is a derelict's paradise, a symphony of mis-
ery. They come here all the way from Toronto and Halifax and
Newfoundland, chasing a warmer place to die. The only thing
that makes me different is the beast, because the beast has not
yet crawled behind my eyes and taken over, although if I stay
down here long enough it will get me, too. Beyond that there is
no pretense. No point remembering that not so long ago I had
another life, a job and a car and a beautiful woman and a fu-

ture. Tell people down here that you had all that and walked away from it and they'll just shake their heads thinking, hey, we all have our delusions. I'm one of them now, a scavenger like the rest, one more shadow in the kingdom of the lost. Running the rickety elevator at the hotel Saturday nights, swabbing up puke when the winos come in. I haven't started panhandling, not crazy enough or drunk enough yet, but that will come. That makes me different, maybe, but not different in a way you'd notice when we're all sitting side by side on a park bench at the end of an empty winter afternoon, waiting for time to pass.

There is a woman I see a dozen times a day on Hastings Street, a woman my age who might have been pretty once. She has stringy blond hair that hasn't been washed for months and her skinny butt is shrinking away under the tight jeans she wears to drum up business which is no longer there, and she stands in the doorway of a little café up the street in the evening, the needle tracks on her arms like infected mosquito bites and her skin the color of a fish belly upside down in the water. I see her so many times that I begin to nod and say hello. Her eyes spin, searching focus. Watery blue eyes, seeking mine. She finds me and a reflex kicks in from a place where she no longer lives: "Wan' go out, honey?" she mutters. "Honey wan' go out? Get a good blowjob? Suck your cock? Half and half? Ten dollar? Five dollar? Wan' go out?"

I don't believe she knows what the words mean anymore. She registers "male" and her tongue starts moving, because somehow that is connected to the fix down the line. She knows enough to stay out of the way when native women like Nell and Doris come staggering up the street. If she is in their territory, they will beat her as they are beaten by their men, their johns, each other.

Sundays when the taverns and bars and package liquor stores are closed they all come to the hotel bootlegger on the second floor and stand in line outside his room, waiting for a bottle. Drunks, whores, pimps, junkies, schizos, killers, lumberjacks, winos, glue-heads, panhandlers. It's a ritual, lining up at the bootlegger's door on a Sunday morning, a ritual like kneeling in the cathedral, except that here you will get the blood of Christ, not the body of Christ. The bootlegger will not spare you a cracker and you will not want one, because food just gets in the way. They line up every Sunday morning, shuffle out later with their bottles in brown paper bags to sit in the park, no matter how cold it is, on an icy bench pouring the alcohol straight down their throats until they can't feel the cold. If drink is not your poison, then you swap the bottle for glue or smack, speed or downers—anything to take you over the red line, anything to get you through a Sunday morning.

I get to know them by name. Know the ones to avoid, know the ones you can talk to, know at a glance how whacked my new friends are at any hour of the day or night. I sit with them for a coffee in the White Lunch at ten in the morning and share a smoke. See the tracks on their arms, the cuts on their foreheads from beatings they took in jail cells and back alleys, the missing teeth, like their conversations, full of gaps where the sequence just disappears, where you think they are onto something and then it vanishes like rain on hot pavement. See them at ten in the evening stretched out on the sidewalk, comatose.

On the bad days when all the copies of the *Georgia Straight* I can sell barely add up to one meal at the White Lunch, I come back to the hotel facing a long evening alone with nothing to do except read or look at the wall. Poverty is boring. You can't afford to eat, get drunk, go to a movie, go shopping, take a bus to see a friend if you had a friend to see, buy a six-pack of beer or a pack of cigarettes. On these nights I stop on my way through the lobby and scrounge cigarette butts out of the ashtrays by the elevator. Sometimes I get lucky, find one with a soggy puff or two left in it, try not to think about who might have smoked it before me.

*

Sundays are the worst. For the hundreds of lonely men and the few women on skid row, Sunday is a twist in the gut, a reminder of family, home, the lover you don't have. I dread Sundays most—but I find my redemption on a Sunday. Not in church but in the little square at the corner of Hastings and Carrall where the pavement is smeared with pigeon shit and the junkies and winos sleep in puddles of their own urine.

It's a sunny, chilly Sunday in March. I have exactly twelve dollars in my pocket so I'm feeling rich, the price of three or four meals riding on my hip. Sitting in the square with a book, waiting until it's time to eat at the White Lunch, carefully planning what I'll have to eat: a hamburger steak with mashed potatoes and gravy and peas and three Cokes to wash it down, followed by coffee and cigarettes. A gray-bearded, stocky man in a stocking cap and a navy pea jacket bums a smoke. We start talking. Turns out he is a sailor. Or was. Able-bodied seaman, Glasgow accent, been everywhere. Madagascar, Buenos Aires, Barcelona, Sydney, Cape Town, the Panama and Suez canals, before the mast for forty years under a dozen flags, merchant seaman in World War II when Nazi subs were sending half the fleet to the bottom of the Atlantic.

We sit out there all morning, him bumming my smokes and telling yarns. About a sailor at a port in Greece who killed two men with a broken beer bottle, nights in the North Atlantic watching other ships in the convoy go under, not knowing if he would ever see port again. Maybe the stories are true, maybe they're just yarns he tells. Maybe he doesn't know the difference anymore; it doesn't matter. He offers a pull from a mickey of rum to keep off the chill. I'm not about to decline. He's got an old woman and a couple of kids back in Glasgow, or at least he thinks he has, though he hasn't been back there in five years.

"But I'm goin' back, oh yes. Get me a ship, see how the old woman is doin'. She'll throw a few things at me when I come through the door, but give me two minutes I'll have her over the table bare-arsed. Woman could never get enough rogering. Drove me to sea, I tell ya!" He laughs until he coughs, bums another smoke.

"So what brings ya to Vancouver, lad? You have a peaked air about ya, like ya don't eat regular."

"I couldn't see eye to eye with the U.S. government over the Vietnam War. Decided to try my luck in a new country."

"I hear ya, I hear ya," he says. "I always say a man's got to follow his conscience. You steer by the stars, you'll never end up on the rocks."

"What about you, old-timer? What brings you here?"

"Me? I'm just between ships. I'll be sailin' out any day now. Any day now."

"How long you been here?"

"Vancouver? Oh, three years. Maybe more. Don't remember, exactly. But I'll be sailin' out any day. I'm between ships, y'see."

Yes. Between ships. That's it. I'm between ships. I haven't been sent to the bottom, I'm just between ships. He has an infectious cheerfulness that is like bellying up to the fire after a cold day bucking hay back in Nebraska. He's as down as any of these characters, but there's no out in him. He's profane and funny. Knows he's a drunk, but figures it's a temporary condition, and sooner or later he'll get back to the wife and kids in Glasgow. We talk a long time, until I feel the chill cutting into my bones despite the pulls from his mickey of rum, nearly empty now. I get up to leave.

"Say, you wouldn't be able to spare an old sailor a dollar for a bowl of soup, now would you?"

I reach into my wallet and pull out the ten-dollar bill.

"Here ya go, sailor. Don't drink it up now."

"Well thank ya, thank ya. This will provide a solid meal, yes it will. And I'll be stayin' away from the drink, ya know. I'm not a drinkin' man." He winks. Absolutely, mate. I'd know a drinkin' man if I saw one. He tags along with me as far as the hotel, gets off the elevator at the second floor. The bootlegger's floor. Time for a wee tot of rum, just for the warmth of it, y'know? I have enough left for a couple of bowls of soup at the White Lunch. I go up to my room first, grab my notebook, sit in the cafeteria sipping soup and scribbling the rest of the afternoon. For the first time in a month there's no urge to get drunk. The weather is getting warmer. Spring is here. I'm between ships. I'm going to make it.

■　■　■

The black cloud lifts. The old sailor points the way and I follow. There are good days and bad days, but on the bad days I repeat it like a mantra: Between ships, not at the bottom of the ocean. Between ships. Still lonely at night in that saggy bed at the hotel, homesickness a real sickness of the heart. But the memories of Mariela are bittersweet now, the anger beginning to fade. All around me people have it so much worse. There are things in this world worse than heartbreak.

The strike drags on with no end in sight. Some journalists have given up and taken jobs on other newspapers, but I have no contacts anywhere else in Canada and no way to get there if I did. I do picket duty when I have to, but give up all pretense of working for the strike paper. To fill the days, I start doing volunteer work at the Committee to Aid American War Objectors. I feel like a veteran now with my immigration nightmare in the past, my hair and beard growing out, ready to give advice to others who are just arriving.

I become less paranoid, less stonily determined to go it alone. Norm has a wide circle of friends, and there are a half-dozen places around town where all I have to do is drop in around suppertime to be sure of a meal. It might be brown rice and broccoli, but it will be food. We read Trotsky and Frantz Fanon, Hermann Hesse and Richard Brautigan, Ken Kesey and Tom Wolfe and Kurt Vonnegut, Che Guevara, Eldridge

Cleaver, and Mao Tse-tung's *Little Red Book*, Carlos Casta-
neda and Timothy Leary, Joseph Heller's *Catch-22*. We're
what they call the counterculture, but in Vancouver in 1970 it
almost seems like we *are* the culture. There are so many freaks,
acid-heads, hippies everywhere that it feels like we really have
taken over, that something spontaneous and joyful will eventually rule the world. Above all, there is a sense of community.
At concerts we dance together in big groups, exuding peace
and love and a genuine desire for a better world. Despite all
the horror, despite a war that goes endlessly on, there is this—
the defiant, communal joy of the young. Surely there is no way
they can kill it.

Everyone should live through a spring and summer in Vancouver. It is an aching riot of green, splashed everywhere with
strange and exotic flowers, steel-blue, white-capped mountains on the horizon, a sky that is blue kissed with something
deeper, streaked with pale cirrus clouds. There is nothing at all
cruel about this April. The dark winter on Hastings Street
lifts. My friends from Nebraska arrive. Mick Lowe, the writer
whose patient insistence finally turned me against the war, arrives alone. Mick wants to get landed, but he has a problem
that is common among draft dodgers and deserters: he is married, and his wife has refused to join him. If she isn't there to
apply for landed immigrant status with him, then she has to be
willing to send a notarized affidavit saying that she won't be
coming, or to grant him a divorce. Instead she has disappeared
and is traveling in Europe, leaving Mick in limbo.
    Mick is followed by a large group of friends, men and
women from the New Left circle at the university. Three or
four other men in his group are dodging the draft, and they
have arrived with more women than men, all of them headed
into the interior of British Columbia, hoping to find a piece of
land and start a communal farm, a venture that has no appeal
for me. The one thing I know about any kind of farming is that

it is a hard and perilous existence. Lots of sweat and worry, not much time for peace and love and Ravi Shankar. One of the women splits off from the group and stays with me for a time, a lover to mark the end of a long winter of the spirit.

They bring me up to date on the campus at Nebraska, which is now sweepingly antiwar. The conservative, buttoned-down university where football mattered more than anything else has become a hotbed of radical politics, the teachings of Students for a Democratic Society radicals Carl Davidson and Al Spangler finally taking effect long after both have moved on. It's that way at campuses across the country, but Nixon and Kissinger are still hunkered down in the White House, convinced they have the support of some unseen, unheard "silent majority" to continue waging the war in Vietnam—and into Cambodia—any way they see fit. After three years of working to change the U.S. from within, my Nebraska friends have all but given up. To them, "power to the people" has become an empty slogan, if it ever held any meaning at all. Pitted against the massed power of industry and government, the people who have been fighting for peace since 1965 have had little apparent impact. We may have prevented escalation of the war to a million troops or the dropping of nuclear weapons on Hanoi, but we can claim no more than that.

The gang from Nebraska has barely arrived in Vancouver when Nixon and Kissinger, having helped to install the corrupt puppet Lon Nol in place of Prince Norodom Sihanouk in Cambodia, decide to expand the war, more than five years after Lyndon Johnson first committed ground troops to Vietnam. The invasion of Cambodia—at a time when the conflict in Vietnam is supposed to be winding down—touches off the biggest demonstrations of the entire war, with campus after campus taken over by angry students. At Kent State University in Ohio on May 4, poorly trained National Guard troops fire on marching students. Four students are killed; the photo of a young woman screaming over one of the bodies becomes one of the most telling portraits of the war. Mick and I call Nebraska from a phone booth on a street in Kitsilano and get a blow-by-blow description of what is going on. Antiwar students have taken over the ROTC headquarters, the symbol of military power on campus. More than three thousand are camping out in tents, effectively occupying the campus of the state university in one of the most conservative states in the union.

It is the high-water mark of the antiwar movement. In the weeks after Kent State I spend more and more time working at the Committee to Aid American War Objectors, which is now all but overwhelmed with more than a hundred draft dodgers and deserters every week, similar numbers arriving in Toronto and Montreal. If this keeps up long enough, we fool ourselves into believing, the war will have to end because there will be no one left to fight it.

During the first week of May the unions finally reach an agreement with the *Sun* and the *Province* and we go back to work. By now Norm is looking for an apartment, so we find a place together in Kitsilano, a second-floor apartment in a pretty little house a couple of blocks from the *Sun* building. The place has only one bedroom, a long, narrow living room, a kitchen, and bathroom. Norm takes the living room because he's planning to move back to Castlegar in June anyway. After a week or two Mick joins us, and at intervals my friends from Nebraska crash with us. There are nights when we're sleeping eight or nine or a dozen people—and three dogs—in an apartment meant for one or two.

The next four months will be entirely without restraint. It's the summer of 1970 in Vancouver, like the Summer of Love in Berkeley three years earlier, and it seems like everyone is making love with everyone else—when they aren't marching, staging sit-ins, attending rock concerts, or dropping acid. The summer is one long drift of sun and sex, music and politics, cheap wine and pot smoke. The dreary winter on Hastings Street is forgotten. The army seems far away. Vancouver is like Haight-Ashbury two or three years earlier, still awash in peace and free love and the vague but powerful sense that our generation is creating a new world of hope and tolerance and peace. It is a fragile illusion, but for the better part of that summer we keep it alive, riding the wave, not wanting to come down. Every day there is a demonstration, or a meeting, or a coffeehouse folk protest, or a sit-in to protest clear-cutting by lumber companies in the interior of British Columbia, or a native solidarity march. With the Nebraska crew staying at my place, I spend part of that summer living with a woman named Suzanne and her friend Deborah in a big apartment on Davie Street. Suzanne is twenty-eight, an exotically sexy woman I meet in a Vancouver bookstore where she catches me staring at her legs when she's standing on a ladder in a short black dress putting books on a high shelf and basically dares me to take her home. Suzanne and I begin as a couple, Deborah (who is over thirty and qualifies as an older woman to me) moves in with her and within a week we're a trio. It's an exhausting ménage that leaves me drained night after night and swearing I will never go back, but then I finish my shift at the *Sun* at midnight and find myself walking over the bridge to Suzanne's apartment, where the two of them will already be entwined on the carpet in the living room, drinking wine and listening to Taj Mahal or Joni Mitchell, waiting for me to join them. My friends are envious, but there is little satisfaction in this three-sided arrangement. At times it feels almost like a second job, moonlighting in the sexual trenches.

■   ■   ■

I'm bored at the *Sun,* but in late July a story comes along that may have renewed my addiction to the adrenalin rush of newspaper work. For two straight nights, out-of-town hippies have been involved in minor disturbances at beautiful English Bay.

They've been crashing on the beach rolled up in their sleeping bags, offending the sensibilities of the people living in ugly high-rise buildings facing the beach. The police move the sleepers off the beach as roughly as possible, adding an occasional extra wallop because many of the long-hairs are French-Canadian.

"Clashes" follow, although the clashes on the hippie side involve little more than name-calling and tossing a few pebbles at the shields of riot police sent to disperse them. On the third night of the English Bay disturbances (the press will use the word "riots" throughout, although at no time did the activity on the beach approach anything resembling a riot), I draw the assignment. "Why don't you go down to English Bay tonight, keep an eye on what's up?" says the night city editor, a stolid middle-aged Brit of right-wing persuasion with whom I've already had several clashes.

I take the bus down to English Bay, arrive an hour or two before sundown. Hippies sit on the beach smoking dope, mill around talking, stare out at the water. It's like this on English Bay every evening from May to September: a gentle, good-time crowd, peace and love and pot. It doesn't look like it's going to be much of a story, so I stick my notebook in the back pocket of my jeans. My hair has stopped falling out; uncut since the last army clip job in December, it's nearly as long as theirs. I stroll along, talk to a few people who were there about what happened the night before, enjoy the scene and the beautiful hippie girls in tight jeans and T-shirts who seem to be everywhere. A perfect assignment for a reporter who is beginning to think that his place is with the footloose kids hitching back and forth across the country, not in some stuffy newspaper office.

I start talking with a group of young people from Quebec who are sitting on logs, playing guitars and singing songs in French. I want to find out what they have to say because many of the hippies who have been sleeping on the beach are French-

Canadian. One of the guitar players who speaks English says the people on the beach can't believe the way the cops have behaved. "We weren't doing anything, man. Just standing around talking, and they came charging in, waving their clubs around, beating the hell out of us." I write down what he says, but I'm skeptical. My experience says cops can sometimes be pretty bad, but usually not without provocation.

By now there are perhaps three hundred hippies clustered around the beach where Davie Street ends at English Bay. Some are chanting: "Pow-er to the people! OFF THE PIGS! Pow-er to the people! OFF THE PIGS!" It's more a party than a demonstration. A few of the leaders begin moving up Davie Street against the traffic, still chanting. Someone throws a rock that bounces off a bank window. Then the police arrive, a dozen vans carrying eight or ten riot cops in each van. I move toward the street, waiting to see how the police will handle this. I've covered civil disturbances in Omaha, Akron, and Fort Lauderdale and taken part in a dozen antiwar demonstrations. I've seen riot police disperse crowds before: they line up in V-shaped wedges with their shields forming a solid wall, and they march slowly toward the crowd, pushing it steadily in whatever direction they want it to go. Any police movement is preceded by several warnings given on bullhorns, a slow and steady escalation of force meant to defuse the incident without resorting to violence. Occasionally it gets out of hand, as during the police riot in Chicago during the Democratic National Convention in '68, but there is at least an attempt by the police to show that they are doing things by the book. And if things get out of hand, the demonstrators usually share some of the guilt.

This time, there is no warning at all. No chance to disperse, no effort at crowd control. The vans come screeching up, the helmeted riot police charge into the crowd as soon as they clamber out of the vans without waiting to form up, swinging their three-foot nightsticks at anything that moves. Within

seconds the entire English Bay area is a free-for-all, a wild me-
lee with a few hippies trying to fight back, hundreds more simply running for their lives, groups of two and three policemen
surrounding anyone they can catch and swinging their clubs in
long arcs. I try to hold my position on a traffic island at the
end of Davie Street and to take a few notes on the chaos all
around. The cops ignore me until I make the mistake of shouting at two officers who are beating a young girl twenty feet
away. They leave the girl lying there and turn on me with their
nightsticks. One of them lifts the stick with his hands held
wide apart and belts me under the jaw, a shot like a cross-
check in hockey. I see stars and my knees start to buckle just as
the other one swings his stick at the base of my skull. When I
come to they are dragging me by the hair to a paddy wagon at
least a hundred feet away. I grab their arms, try to twist free,
take another shot or two in the ribs. I understand the consequences. If I'm found guilty of any kind of crime here—resisting arrest, inciting a riot, whatever they come up with—I can
be deported. If I'm deported I'll be charged with desertion
and sentenced to Leavenworth. That quickly I feel the curtain
come down on the summer of love in Vancouver. For me this is
not just a ride in a paddy wagon; it's a potential prison sentence and the end of my life in Canada.

The cops are throwing people into the wagons like so many
fire logs. I land on top of a few of the others, male and female,
find a place to sit down. I can feel bruises on my ribs and back.
My jaw aches, the back of my head is pounding. There are a
dozen of us packed inside, some bleeding, some crying, some
screaming. Everyone stunned and angry. It has been swift and
violent and unpredictable. No one saw it coming. One moment it was a peaceful demonstration, the next moment the
police were just charging around, randomly clubbing people.

At the city jail a fat blond cop with an enormous beer gut
hanging over his belt—the spitting image of the pigs we're al-

ways talking about—takes us up in the elevator. "So these are
the beautiful people," he sneers, surveying our battered, bleeding, frightened crew on the way to a holding cell, confusing us
with wealthy jet-setters who spend their time in Paris or on the
Onassis yacht. "Well, I never saw an uglier bunch in my life."

Somehow I have managed to hold onto the notebook, so I
start taking down names and doing interviews. If I'm going to
prison, I'm going to write one helluva story on the way. I've
been an eyewitness to a police riot—and a victim too. There
are perhaps one hundred of us jammed into a big holding cell
at the police station. Once the word gets around that there's a
reporter in the cell, I'm surrounded by people wanting to tell
their stories. It's all I can do to slow them down so I can get
names attached to individual stories. A *Sun* photographer who
saw me being dragged away alerted the city desk to send out
another reporter and find someone to get me out of jail. It's after 1 A.M. when Pat Nagel himself arrives to bail me out. A cop
comes to get me and I find Nagel, even more sad-eyed than
usual, waiting in the corridor. I tell him what happened at English Bay, and he's completely sympathetic. "If you're sure you
don't have a concussion," he says, "I'll drive you back to the
newsroom."

"I don't feel dizzy at all. I just want to write this."

Nagel nods. Nagel has been an outstanding reporter and
will be a reporter again. He understands. Unfortunately, after
he drops me at the door of the *Sun* building, the story is out of
his hands. The night city editor isn't nearly as sympathetic.

"Oh, Todd," he says, "you're back. We didn't know you
were going to get yourself caught up in all this, so we sent Paul
Musgrove down to cover for you. If you like you can write a
couple of paras to insert in Musgrove's story."

"You're kidding. I talked to all those people in jail, I saw the
cops clubbing people, I got hit. It was a police riot, for God's
sake."

"You heard me. A couple of paras to insert in Musgrove's story, that's all. We don't need you to write editorials for us, thank you very much."

Seething with anger, I write three paragraphs and fling them on his desk. I want to call Nagel at home, but I figure he's already been dragged out of bed once tonight to get me out of jail; twice might be pushing it. Anyway, this is my third or fourth run-in with the same editor. The last time I went to Nagel with a complaint about the way this editor slashed a story I wrote on the American lawyer Melvin Belli, Nagel listened politely to my rant, then offered a response that was pure Zen: "Do you realize there is more timberland in British Columbia than in all of Scandinavia?"

There's no reason to think things would be different if I called Nagel now. I leave the office fuming. The *Sun* has some terrific people, like Nagel and city columnist Bob Hunter, but the *Sun* is not the *Miami Herald*. I feel certain the *Herald* would have ordered me to write my story on the spot, a dramatic first-person account of what I see as a police riot. I spend a sleepless night. The vague discontent with the job I've felt all summer now has a focus: the *Sun*, hidebound and sleepy, is part of the problem. I want to be covering the enormous events south of the border, not meetings of suburban council meetings in Vancouver. If this is how they are going to handle one story that is worth writing, then I want out.

■   ■   ■

There is something about Vancouver that makes you feel restless and claustrophobic. That ring of snow-capped mountains, gleaming in the August sunshine. The ocean, freighters shipping out across the Pacific every day. In Vancouver, the ineffable perfection of being can seem attainable as it does nowhere else, but the transcendental experience you seek—pure love, pure harmony with the universe, pure something—is always just out of reach. In a grimy eastern city, any grimy eastern city, you learn to be content with the occasional glimpse of spring sunshine. In Vancouver you want to soar, break out, walk through a mountain pass, hop on a rusty tramp steamer bound for Fiji, hitch a ride on a pickup truck headed for Newfoundland. A body in motion stays in motion, a body at rest stays at rest. In a sense, I've been in motion since the night we flew out of Fort Lewis in Sergeant Becker's Led Zeppelin wagon. Something in me yearns to keep moving.

Pat Nagel clears the way for me to write a long follow-up piece on the English Bay incident, but he's already a day late. He deserves better, but he gets a letter of resignation with a lengthy rant on the shortcomings of his night city editor instead, with a treatise on the way they treat young reporters at the *Sun*. Nagel tries hard to persuade me to stay, even asks Will Jarrett to call me from the *Herald* to explain that I'm making a mistake I will regret deeply in the future. Nagel and Jarrett are right—I am making a mistake and I will regret it deeply. The truth is, they've treated me well at the *Sun*, but I've made up my mind to leave for reasons that have nothing to do with the newspaper. Norm is living up in the mountains, the Nebraska crew is about to pick up and move to the interior of British Columbia, Powers is living in a commune somewhere, I'm weary of the nights in the sexual trenches with Suzanne and Deborah. I want to be on the road with a guitar and a backpack, not stuck in a newspaper office quarreling with an editor who has the sensibility of a minor functionary in the British Raj.

In a wild summer, the three or four days after the English Bay incident are pure, distilled lunacy. I testify at a hearing for some of the people who were arrested at English Bay, and the charges are dismissed. Mick and I attend a series of meetings of a radical group called the Northern Lunatic Fringe of the Vancouver Liberation Front. The lunatic part is accurate. People are seriously talking about getting rifles to battle the cops. About killing police, starting a revolution in Vancouver that will somehow spill across North America. People are spouting revolutionary rhetoric, cooking up absurd fantasies about apocalyptic battles with the cops and the army. Most of them are no better with a rifle than poor Fillmore—it's just talk, but it's stupid, dangerous talk. I didn't walk away from one war to get into another one. It's time to go.

With my last check from the *Sun* I buy a good sleeping bag and a backpack. I've met some young French-Canadian students about my age who are returning to their small town in Quebec. I invite myself to come and visit, maybe learn a little French. I abandon the beautiful little place we have on the top floor of a pretty house in Kitsilano and say my good-byes. The plan is to hitchhike to Quebec, see what follows. It's crazy, but it's been a crazy year. I get a ride with the Nebraska gang as far as Castlegar, where Norm is running his crisis center. Here we spend one last night together, a group of long-haired radicals who were short-haired, earnest freshmen at the University of Nebraska in the fall of '65. All that antiwar ferment on campus has led to this, a small town in the British Columbia mountains in the summer of 1970. We sit around Norm's kitchen table, drinking wine from a gallon jug, playing guitars, talking politics and old times. Someone lights a joint, someone plays the opening chords of a Bob Dylan song, and we all join in. We pitch our tents and sleeping bags in Norm's yard. The ground is hard, and it's cold and damp and hard to sleep, but this is the life I think I want.

Shortly after dawn, my old friends from Nebraska pile their dogs and gear into the vans and head north. They are my last link to that other world, the world of Cornhusker football games, pep rallies, debates in the student senate. I'm sorry to see them go. I stay one last night with Norm, who has agreed to stow the stuff I can't fit into my backpack. He would like me to stay and help with the crisis center, but I'm anxious to hit the road and start hitching to Quebec because I don't know how long it will take. On that last run up the West Coast after

Christmas, I made good time, but I was riding the army uniform all the way. With long hair and a beard it's going to be a different trip. Norm gives me a lift to the highway at dawn the first day. After a full twelve hours of hitching, I'm still in British Columbia. In a small town a hundred miles east of Castlegar, I duck into a tavern in mid-afternoon to get something to eat. Three tough guys at a nearby table take a look at my long hair and patched jeans and start muttering about fucking hippies. The waiter orders me out of the tavern. I'm outnumbered here about fifty to one. There's nowhere else to eat in town, no choice but to wait two hours in the hot sun for another lift.

I finally get a ride in the back of a pickup truck, make it another fifty miles down the road before dark, crawl back under the tall trees a half mile off the highway to spend a jittery night in my sleeping bag, jumping at every sound. There are bears in these mountains, but I'm more afraid of my own kind. I've seen *Easy Rider.* I keep expecting those rednecks from the tavern to come and club me to death in my sleeping bag. It doesn't make for a good night's sleep.

It takes most of a week to get to Toronto. After a couple of days on the road, the romance of it all has vanished. Lone drivers in empty station wagons pass without a glance, even though I'm clearly stranded in the middle of nowhere. I break down and take the train for one stretch, go back to riding my thumb, spend a night in a cheap hotel in Toronto and a terrible night in a small Ontario town halfway between Toronto and Montreal, sleeping in a youth hostel populated by hostile, dangerous-looking druggies. I curl up in my sleeping bag with my wallet stuffed down around my toes where no one can get at it. It's impossible to sleep. People are screwing, shooting up, arguing all night, doing drug deals. This is the ugly side of the counterculture. I want no part of it.

Montreal is better. I arrive on a beautiful day in late Au-

gust and stay at a tourist room in the city's East End near
Lafontaine Park, sit in the sunshine for an afternoon playing
guitars with a group of French hippies. Montreal is green and
lush this time of year, and I love hearing the sound of French
on the streets, the differences in style and fashion, the old gray
stone walls, the three-story houses with their staircases out
front, the view of the blue-gray tile roofs from the lower slopes
of Mount Royal.

I've had enough hitchhiking, so I take the bus from the
Berri-de-Montigny station the last hundred miles, drop my
pack and guitar in this small town, and figure I'll stay awhile.
A couple of students I know rent the place, and friends and ac-
quaintances drift through. Hanging my head out the window
of the house, I hear neighbors chatting in French. It seems im-
possibly exotic, like being in a little town in Provence. It's still
hot and sticky. My Quebecois friends make me feel welcome.
Winter is coming, and when the wind is wrong the air reeks of
the pulp mills, but for now this is a beautiful place to linger in
the valley of the mighty St. Lawrence River, at the end of the
road.

We settle into a kind of life on the top floor of the old stone
house. I become the designated cook, making chili and meatloaf and potato soup from my mother's recipes. Someone has
set up an old, upright manual typewriter in the kitchen. I lay in
a supply of paper and write every morning, coming up with little more than fragments of short stories, poems, another futile
attempt at a novel about a young farm boy from Nebraska
who goes to Canada during the Vietnam War. Afternoons I
read in the library, which, among its thousands of books, has
only a few in English. Dashiell Hammett, Plato, Kipling and
John O'Hara, Walter Scott and Raymond Chandler, an English translation of Marcel Proust and Graham Greene's *The
End of the Affair*, which I will read three times while the tem-

perature drops and the first snow clouds drift up the wide river.

Before the end of August the leaves have started to fall. Winter here is going to be long and bitter. After the library I take long walks, usually along the St. Lawrence, so wide here it looks like one of the Great Lakes. Freighters flying all kinds of foreign flags dock in the port, their flags feeding my perpetual restlessness.

I take a few French lessons from my friends, learn more sitting around the kitchen table at night listening to them talk. At first I can pick out only an occasional word—*puis, tu, la. Puis toi, la-la. Puis* sounds more like "pee," and the aspirated *t* turns *tu* into something more like "tsu," so I hear "pee-tsu, pee-pee-tsu, tsu-la, pee-tsu-la-la," a beautiful language reduced to baby talk and gibberish by my clumsy ear. On my third or fourth day in town I wander through a park not far from home and stumble into an encounter with a local cop, who confronts me, saying something over and over in French. My hair is down to my shoulders, my beard is filling in, my old jeans are patched in the knees and seat with gaudy red paisley patches. I can imagine how I look to him. I put my hands up, waiting for the arrest, saying the one phrase I've learned: *"Je ne parle pas français."*

He grins. "How tall?" he says. "How tall?"

I put my hands down.

"Six foot six." Grinning.

"Ah, very tall, very tall. Six feet and six inches. Very tall."

He walks off smiling, repeating it to himself, as if he just met Wilt Chamberlain. My friends teach me the French for "How tall are you?" along with the response. I practice it over and over:

Six-pieds-six.

The French-Canadians I meet are mostly sympathetic. They don't know much about Vietnam, but they accept my decision to flee as a moral and political necessity. What is known as the Quiet Revolution in Quebec—the transformation of values that has made the younger generation rebel against both the Catholic Church in Quebec and the government in Ottawa—was born in part in the conscription crisis of World War II, when numerous French-Canadians refused to be drafted into what they saw as an English war. Many French-Canadians did choose to fight and fought heroically; many others refused conscription with equal heroism.

My friends here are apolitical, but there is a strong separatist movement in Quebec, people who want the province to break off from the rest of Canada and establish a free, French-speaking state. Their battle cry is *"Vive le Québec libre!"* ("Long live a free Quebec!"), famously uttered from a city hall balcony in Montreal by Charles de Gaulle during a visit with Montreal mayor Jean Drapeau. As separatists, their spiritual ancestors are those who opposed conscription during World War II. They admire Pierre Vallières, whose book *White Niggers of North America* chronicled the way their fathers and grandfathers and great-grandfathers toiled for the English. They resent the fact that the one English word every French-Canadian knows is "boss." At first, instinctively, I back the underdog separatists, but it is not my fight. After a short while, I'm bored with the whole thing. I find the attitudes here small-town and provincial and xenophobic. After listening to the separatists in the taverns for a while, the truth is obvious: they don't care at all about building a better world. Quebec separatism is just one more narrow and fiercely intolerant nationalist movement, dedicated to hating English Canadians above all else. They are willing to grant me temporary exemption as an American and a deserter, but for me this is a new experience, being hated for the language that I speak.

I don't belong here and I want out, but I'm too broke to leave. Homesick for old friends and people who speak English, I spend too much on a round-trip bus ticket to Ontario, where George and Deanna Kaufman, more friends from the *Daily Nebraskan,* are working for the *Kitchener-Waterloo Record.* When I get back to Quebec it's October, there is a chill in the air, and my money is dwindling. I write to the *Miami Herald* and propose a lengthy feature on draft dodgers and deserters in Canada, similar to one I wrote for the *Vancouver Sun.* The *Herald* agrees to pay three hundred dollars for the story. With my notes from Vancouver and some personal observations, I finish the story, send it to the *Herald,* and wait for the check. I've seen enough of Quebec, and it's time to move on; when I get the check I'm going to go to Toronto and try to get a job at one of the newspapers. I know very little about Canadian papers, but I do know that Hemingway wrote dispatches from Paris for the *Star, so* I've decided I want to write for the *Star.* The problem is putting together enough money to get to Toronto.

In Vancouver, everyone talked about revolution. In Quebec, the battle for what the separatists see as their political liberation has long since turned nasty. A terrorist group, the Front de Libération du Québec (FLQ), has bombed and threatened and blown up mailboxes and killed a cop. The FLQ is a loosely connected string of tight little political cells, each dedicated to mayhem. In October, they pull off two kidnappings that electrify the entire country, grabbing first the British consul, James Cross, then Quebec minister of justice Pierre Laporte. Everyone is frightened. We watch the news on a fuzzy little black-and-white TV with rabbit ears, flickering images of soldiers on the streets of Montreal, provincial police raiding suspected terrorist hideouts, which always turn out to be empty buildings.

Then Laporte is found dead, his body stuffed in the trunk of a car. This is no high-spirited student prank—it is cold-blooded murder. The terrorists have shown the world what they are. This is real and horrifying, a reminder that you don't play at revolution. The October Crisis takes a nightmarish turn. Pierre Trudeau invokes the War Measures Act, reviving a wartime emergency measures clause to give the federal government almost absolute powers for the duration of the crisis. The army is sent into Quebec in force. Hundreds of people with the vaguest connections to the separatist movement are arrested and held without bail. You can be jailed because you have a tourist book on Cuba on your shelves, or because you once attended a party at the home of a known separatist. Opposition politicians find themselves behind bars along with famous actors and musicians.

It seems that everyone I meet is cursing Trudeau. I stay on the sidelines, outside the argument. Pierre Trudeau is the reason I have my freedom. I will never denounce a man with the courage to stand up to the U.S., nor should we be surprised that he has the courage to stand up to the FLQ. I imagine the FLQ terrorists are not much different from the juvenile fools in Vancouver who wanted to get rifles and shoot cops. Violence is always the first solution of small minds, in government and out.

The weather turns cold, and then colder, and then colder still. My twenty-fourth birthday comes and goes in October, twelve days after Mariela's twenty-fourth. I send a happy birthday letter care of her parents' address, but I have no way of knowing if she ever receives it. We have a party on Halloween night, exactly one year to the day since I left Miami. Everyone is speaking French too rapidly for me to understand. I sit watching them laugh, feeling as alone as I have ever felt. All I can think about is Mariela and Miami and all the things I left behind. I haven't heard from Mariela for nearly a year, since that Sunday morning when I called from Fort Lewis—but the ache has hardly diminished, even now. Mariela is rarely out of my mind. Everywhere I go I see her, disappearing around a corner, drinking coffee behind the steamy glass of a restaurant window. I hurry to catch up to a woman on the street so that I can get a better look at her face, suddenly convinced that Mariela has come all the way to Quebec to find me. Up close, the resemblance vanishes and the woman gives me a strange look, wondering why I am peering at her so intently. Some of the bitterness and anger toward Tom Clagg has faded, but the feelings I have for Mariela burn as intensely as they did the day I said good-bye to her in a pouring rain in Miami. I have a dozen or more images of Mariela that I carry in my mind like a deck of cards, shuffling through them constantly, an exercise that is nothing more than scratching at an open wound. At least once a week I take out the one letter she sent while I was in the army, the letter I still carry in my wallet. I smooth it out carefully and read it over and over, wishing there was some way we could go back to "I love you, Jacko" and start over.

At home, my parents are still getting regular calls from an army sergeant. My eldest sister, Linda, takes the calls and keeps insisting that the family doesn't know where I am. My mother writes at least three letters a week, sometimes stuffing a note in Pop's scrawl into the envelope. She has elegant penmanship and a clear, beautifully cadenced style. At another time, in a place where she could have finished her education, she might have become a writer. I write Sonny every month or so, get a couple of postcards in return. He always says he's fine, usually responds with a joke of some kind. I'm pretty sure he isn't fine, but I can't afford to call.

At American Thanksgiving, Larry Grossman, my old college roommate, comes to visit over the long weekend, taking a break from the U.S. State Department, where he's undergoing intensive Vietnamese language training in preparation for a two-year posting in Vietnam. We meet at the airport in Montreal and spend a couple of days exploring the chilly streets of this great winter city. The October Crisis is still very much in progress, the terrorists still haven't been caught, and on Ste.-Catherine Street, Montreal's main drag, we're stopped by rifle-toting soldiers outside the A&W near the big Hudson's department store. They want to see some identification, and all I have is my landed immigrant card. Larry flashes his diplomatic passport from the U.S.; the soldiers all but bow and scrape as they let us pass.

After Larry goes back to Washington I feel lonelier than ever. Every morning I wait anxiously for the mail, feeling that my whole future is tied to that check from the *Herald,* my stake to get back into the newspaper business in Toronto. Finally, with twenty dollars left in the bank, no prospects, and no check from Miami, I have to do something. On the way back from the library one afternoon in early December, I see a Help Wanted sign in the window of a neighborhood snackbar. The proprietor says he needs a dishwasher, I can take off my coat and start right away.

It's a job. I roll up my sleeves and plunge into a kitchen in the back that looks like an accident in a grease factory and start on the towering piles of dishes. There is no automatic dishwasher, just me and a huge, greasy sink and an inexhaustible supply of dishes. It takes four hours to finish that first batch, and still the dishes are coming from the hot dogs and french fries being served out front. When I'm finished—my fingers wrinkled like prunes, back aching—he punches open the cash register, hands me six dollars, and tells me to be back for the morning rush the next day. The job breaks into three separate shifts, three or four hours each, morning, noon, and evening, but I get a meal with each shift—fried eggs and bacon in the morning, hot dogs and french fries for lunch, a hamburger and fries for dinner. I keep the news of the job to myself because life has grown very uncomfortable with the people I'm staying with, and I don't want to have to start paying rent. I figure I can make sixty dollars a week cash, maybe put enough money aside to get out of town in a couple of months or less.

Long before Christmas, the first big snowfalls bury the

town. The snow is already as high as my head in all the neat little front yards, and still the trucks keep hauling it away to the river. Only the dishes in the greasy spoon are piled higher than the snow. The café is across the street from the biggest cathedral in town, and the most regular customers are the pallbearers and hearse drivers in their somber, charcoal-colored suits. While a funeral is in progress they drink coffee, smoke cigarettes, argue about the Montreal Canadiens hockey team.

I wash dishes, watch the storms howl outside the little café, watch the mail every day hoping for the check from the *Herald*. To keep warm, all I have is my unlined letter jacket from Nebraska, which I wear with the Mexican poncho on the outside and a pair of gloves Larry bought me when I was freezing in Old Montreal. I shorten the walks along the river, the days disappear to a sliver of sunlight between dawn and sunset. At two in the afternoon it's already getting dark. No wonder it's taking so long for the check to arrive. Miami is a million miles away.

■   ■   ■

In that narrow bed in the little town by the St. Lawrence, I have the nightmare for the first time. It begins like a dream I had in grade school, when I thought I could fly like Superman. In the dream I'm playing basketball, always in Scottsbluff. Sometimes with Sonny out in the driveway, sometimes with my high school teammates: Rod Ehler, Kenny Beeman, Hal Teague, Jim Hohnstein. Without effort, I can soar above the rim. The dunks are easy. Every shot falls. I leap so high I can touch the top of the backboard. Rod, Kenny, Hal, they just toss the ball up there. I go get it no matter where it is and dunk on the way down. I've never felt so light and agile.

Then a cloud passes over the dream. A warning bell rings: You're not supposed to be here. You're not supposed to be here. You have to get out. You have to run.

Sonny runs with me. We leave the gym and pile into his car and start driving north, headed for South Dakota, North Dakota, the Saskatchewan border. We never make it. The car breaks down and I take off alone across the frozen winter wheat fields, certain that I can outrun the pursuit. I can see where I have to go, across miles of frozen prairie, all the way to the Canadian border in the distance. The scenery changes, becomes more hilly. Now there are barbed-wire fences everywhere, looming out of the snow. At first I soar over the fences with ease. I'm a high jumper; these little fences are no test at all. But as I run, mile after mile, the fences get higher. I've lost my track shoes, I'm wearing heavy combat boots, and the barbed wire has been replaced by razor wire that slashes my hands. In the distance I hear sirens and then I see them closing in, sheriff's deputies in their cars and on foot and on horseback, and dog handlers turning loose a pack of German shepherds and Dobermans.

Overhead, helicopters circle, their spotlights trained on us. Armored personnel carriers move along the highways. The deputies release the dogs and they close in, pursuing me through deep drifts of snow to the last razor-wire obstacle, a fence twenty feet high with a wide, ice-clogged river on the far side, the Canadian border beyond that. I try to climb the fence but the razor wire cuts my hands to ribbons. The dogs get me by the ankles and drag me down into the snow and then they're on me, tearing at my legs with fangs like chain saws. I look up and Sonny is there with the cops, already in handcuffs. Shaking his head, saying, "I told you to run, man. I told you to run."

I wake drenched in sweat, my heart pounding so hard the bed is shaking. I get out of bed, pad to the bathroom, towel off the sweat, change to a dry shirt, pull a beer out of the fridge and sit alone and shivering in the kitchen, waiting for my heartbeat to slow down so I can get back to sleep. The nightmare will return, with variations, night after night, three or four nights a week, for years.

■ ■ ■

A few days into January, I get the bad news: the *Herald* has rejected the piece on war resisters. There will be no check. A couple of weeks later, I'm on my break after washing the morning's dishes in the greasy spoon. I sit down in my filthy apron for a coffee and a cigarette, and I see that someone has left a copy of the *Montreal Star* on the counter. I haven't seen an English newspaper for months, so I read it front to back. For some reason I check the classifieds to see if anyone happens to be looking for a writer, knowing very well that no one ever advertises for a writer in a newspaper. But there it is: Writers wanted. There's an address in Montreal, a phone number to call for an interview.

As soon as my shift is over, I rush home, call the number, and set up an interview for the next morning. I know it has to be something sleazy, but at this point anything is better than washing dishes. I'm so certain I'll get the job that I tell the owner of the greasy spoon I'm quitting and blow the money on a round-trip bus ticket instead of trying to hitch to Montreal in the middle of winter. I have nothing to wear to the interview except my heavily patched jeans. Somehow I have the feeling it isn't going to matter.

The address is on the eighth floor of a nondescript office building. The lobby looks so dressy that I wonder if I haven't made a mistake by wearing the patched jeans, but when I go around the corner into the office, the first guy I see has hair down to his waist and a beard to his chest. He might as well be wearing a sign that says "Hippies welcome." My guess was right—it is a sleazy job, writing fake news stories and soft-core sex for a chain of tabloids. But the pay is good, so nothing else matters. I have to take a writing test, pounding out a couple of dubious stories based on dubious translations from dubious German magazines. Marlon Brando, Jackie Onassis, and Frank Sinatra for one tabloid. For another one they want softcore sex and a crime piece with lots of gore. I knock off something about a couple doing it in the bottom of a boat. After a couple of hours I've written so much that I'm beginning to suspect it's all a scam—they run this ad in the paper all the time, print the stuff they get from applicants, and avoid paying money to writers. I'm about to bolt, assuming I've been had, when a scruffy-looking editor with a snowstorm of dandruff blowing over his shoulders comes out to say I've got a job in their writers' room if I want it. Pay is $120 a week, which seems like a small fortune. It's late Friday afternoon. I'm to start Monday morning.

I take the bus ride back up the St. Lawrence, then blow half the money I've saved from the dishwashing job on one last party. I've made some good friends in this town, despite the language barrier, but I'll always feel like a stranger here, permanently detached from the things that matter to people who call this cold country their home. It's a closed book, another stop along the road.

In eighteen months, I've gone from Lincoln to Miami to Scottsbluff to Denver, Fort Lewis to San Diego to Ensenada, Los Angeles to San Francisco to Seattle to Vancouver, Vancouver to Quebec, now on to Montreal. From a Florida apartment to an almost complete breakdown on Hastings Street, from the *Herald* to the army to the *Sun* to unemployment to dishwashing in a Quebec greasy spoon to a sleazy job in the tabloid trade. The only constant seems to be this endless flight, running on and on and getting to no place at all. Always wanting to be somewhere else, the one place I am not allowed to be. On South Beach with Mariela on a Sunday afternoon, lazily oiling her back while we listen to the waves roll in.

Part IV

FAULT LINE

"HE CAN RUN but he can't hide." Joe Louis on Billy Conn. Conn ran for twelve rounds but he got tagged in the end, and Louis remained the heavyweight champion of the world. Your demons run with you—patient, hungry, cutting off the ring, ready to throw a left hook to the jaw the second you think you are secure in whatever little illusion you've been able to cultivate for yourself.

"Don't look back, something might be gaining on you." Satchel Paige. It all catches up in Montreal. Great, chilly Montreal, the most European and ancient of North American cities, buried under mountains of snow in the record winter of 1970–71. Once you decide to run, it's hard to stop. Something feels wrong, you throw everything in the backpack, roll up the sleeping bag, grab the guitar case, and move on down the line.

"We have kept our erasers in order." Ezra Pound, the "Homage to Sextus Propertius." I try to write about Mariela, find I can say nothing except that she remains with me, in revisions and dreams and revisions of dreams. Memories that vanish in smoke like the vapor that rises from the great sheets of ice on the St. Lawrence on the coldest winter days, wisps of ghost ice floating in the pale cold air on this early morning bus ride down the line to Montreal, leaving small-town life behind.

I listen now to the clean, gleaming Métro in Montreal, silvery on its tracks, hiss out of the Berri-de-Montigny station with an ascending three-note scale: "Whoo-whoo-whee!" Bleary morning commuters see a tall hippie in a big black hat with a paisley band, an athlete's letter jacket from some university that begins with the letter N, old jeans liberally patched with flamboyant paisley patches, a heavy pack with a sleeping roll, a battered guitar case, a curly black beard, hair now down past the shoulders. Exclamation-point thin from too many missed meals and too many cigarettes, perhaps the beginnings of a haunted look around the eyes.

I get off at the McGill Métro stop with hundreds of students on their way to classes and wander into the mammoth Eaton's department store. I can find everything but the exit; I'm lost and panicky among the perfume counters, dragging pack and guitar, afraid of sweeping a rack of perfume bottles to the floor, creating a sticky chaos of shattered glass. It's too easy to imagine. Jerry Lewis meets Franz Kafka in the cosmetics department. Wandering a labyrinth of powerful, almost nauseating odors, late for a first day's work, desperate to find a way out. (This too will become the stuff of nightmare: the huge blue man stalking me among the perfume bottles, the certain-age women with their too-much makeup, the clerks with their frozen smiles. The blue man stalking, stalking, finally rounding a perfume counter to point an accusing blue finger, saying over and over, "It's you! It's you!") Find the escape hatch at last. Take the long, cold walk, shoulders aching from the pack, slipping and sliding on the icy streets on my way to work in the tabloid factory.

Later, we will christen the company Mother Earth because of its role in our lives. She's the giant, pillowy breast that succors a couple of dozen writers, artists, musicians, scholars, professional beatniks. We float in for a few months, long enough to put together a stake or to qualify for unemployment, then go off to paint or sing or write rock operas based on the early work of Little Richard. Existence in the tabloid factory is pretty much like life in factories anywhere, only different. We're expected to work nine to five with an hour for lunch and a couple of coffee breaks, pounding out on manual typewriters stories based on the shakiest hints from European magazines or, more often, nothing more than an editor's imagination. We're given a headline—"World's Oldest Poet Writes Epic Love Poem for Virgin Bride!"—and we write.

There are a dozen writers pecking away at Earth Corp. Two will go on to become university professors, one the managing editor of a metropolitan newspaper, one a famous movie producer, one a newspaper columnist. There is Egon, a German-born Jew who protests when he can't persuade building management to turn down the heat by working in his black bikini underwear and nothing else; a former soccer goalie from England who fancies himself a rock star, mostly on the basis of his hair; a gentle folksinger, and a painter working in the art department who lives for summer weekends, when he and his artist girlfriend like to take LSD and make love in cemeteries late at night.

Within weeks I become close friends with two of the writers: Ray Brassard is a deserter from Massachusetts who was in training to become an air force MP before he left. He arrived in Montreal in May 1969, on the lam from an air base in Texas. We both grew up blue-collar, both went to university, both discovered radical politics and worked on the student newspaper, both were drafted, both deserted. His crossing back into the U.S. before he applied for landed immigrant status was more traumatic than mine: Ray and his driver, a Canadian activist named Morton Bain, were forced to pull over while customs agents began removing the side panels of their car. Finally, to distract the agents from a closer look at Ray's identity cards, he and Bain dropped a few subtle hints that they were gay men on their way to a dirty weekend in Boston. The embarrassed officers waved them on their way, and Ray became a landed immigrant six months before I crossed the border. Ray reads history and politics and knows more about the good pop music of the '50s and '60s than anyone else I know. He has flaming red hair and a red beard, and within a month he sends the management at Earth Corp. into a panic when he and Egon decide to organize a union.

John Cooper is an ex–football player for Queen's and Mc-Gill who was working on his master's degree in literature at the University of British Columbia when he dropped out and came back to Mother Earth to put together a stake for Europe. We talk about Gaston Bachelard and Ezra Pound when we're supposed to be tapping out stories about Jackie O's mysterious attraction to Marlon Brando or The Sex Fantasies of the Single Librarian. John was born Jani Xiros in Athens during a Nazi bombardment in 1944. After the war, his mother left his father and moved to Italy, where she eventually met and married a soft-spoken former British naval officer. They moved to London and eventually to Montreal. John is an intellectual in the best sense of the word—widely read, curious about everything, with a deep and detailed knowledge of literature, art, music, history, politics, and the Montreal Canadiens. Above all he is a good listener; I am full of myself and inclined to blab, and it will be months before I discover that he knows infinitely more than I do about almost everything.

The atmosphere at Mother Earth is meant to be oppressive. Writers and editors are fired almost every payday, on the whim of the managing editor. The work varies from scandalous to monotonous to disgusting. Upper management reminds John of the Renaissance popes without the aristocratic tastes—narrow little men whose souls have long since departed, preserved in the formaldehyde of money. The product aspires to be trash, but it's not really that good.

And yet we're a merry crew of like-minded artistes, probably because we don't give a flying fandango about the junk we're turning out. There is a dart board in one corner which is in more or less constant use despite the protests of the managing editor, who thinks we might produce more if we didn't spend half the day playing darts and the other half talking. Pay is good compared to what we would make elsewhere, even on the daily newspapers, which we disdain because you have to be a corporate sellout to work on a daily paper. Discussions are wide-ranging and more or less constantly in progress, to the detriment of the daily quota of trash. Story meetings, always desperate for cover headlines, yield legendary exchanges, as when the Jewish editor of one of the tabloids asks, "What's Hitler done for us lately?"

The assembled editors scratch their heads for a moment, and then John responds, "I've got it! 'Charlie Manson Is the Illegitimate Son of Hitler'!"

I find a place in a rooming house on Aylmer Street in the McGill student ghetto for twenty-five dollars a week. A nicer building, but the room is less than half the size of my room at the hotel on Hastings Street. Even allowing for deductions, I have seventy or eighty dollars a week to spend on books and movies, meals in Indian restaurants. All this for a couple of dozen pages a day of unrevised copy, most of it from an imagination that is rarely more than half-engaged. Type with one hand, play darts with the other. I have a regular weekly assignment, a diary called "I, A Lesbian," about a beautiful, footloose young woman with a yearning for her own sex on the prowl in Europe.

"I was on the cross-channel ferry from Dover to Calais," I write with the help of a fourth cup of coffee, "when I met Ilsa. Ilsa was from Norway, tall and blonde and athletic, a former cross-country skier with muscular thighs, hefty breasts, and a pouty underlip that simply begged to be kissed. At Calais we could wait no more. We checked into a beautiful little bed and breakfast, and there Ilsa unzipped my skirt and tugged it down my thighs, then playfully licked that little spot in the back of my knee, knowing instinctively how to drive me crazy. I watched as she stood up and peeled off her T-shirt and those luscious globes sprang free . . ."

Upstairs to the cafeteria with John and Ray for another coffee and twenty minutes' talk about Leonardo da Vinci and the motif that recurs in so many of his paintings, where a character in one corner points to the sky or the deity with a subtle forefinger as if to say, "It's all His fault."

Then back to the diary: ". . . her full, pink nipples already erect, her flat belly inviting my tongue to explore her navel, her luscious perfume invading my senses as my tongue-tip trails down, down . . ."

It's lunchtime. Time to go eat samosas with John and talk about Pound, Leonardo, and the Montreal Canadiens, who have made a trade for the great Frank Mahovlich. Then back to Ilsa, who stands fully revealed at last, her statuesque form silhouetted against the white lace curtains in the little bedroom in Calais, the salt sea breeze stirring the fabric around her breasts, her thighs, her silky, satiny, sultry, salacious womanhood.

The snow swirls in foot-high storms, the cold between storms crackles its warning: this is the way the world ends, frozen into storm-banked silence. Ilsa stretches on the bed in Calais, turning her breasts to the sunshine.

■   ■   ■

The storms leach all the color out of the city. A swirl of white in the foreground, streaks of gray in the distance where old stone walls laid down centuries ago mark the boundary line for hospitals and nunneries, the spine of this city the coiled vortex of an old order spun in Catholic mystery, gray stone and stained glass, half seen in glimpses when the wind dies down and the snow curls in on itself and a heavy cast-iron gate announces the way to something ancient, severe, not of this world. The gate not opened. The snow falls, boundaries and certainties vanish. The snow falls, the wind howls, the world shrinks and you lose yourself in white, crossing a street through enormous drifts of snow until a squeal of protesting sheet metal underneath says that you are walking over the hood of a car, submerged in the middle of a thoroughfare by a storm that can make a city of three million souls vanish like a magician's prop. The great steel and glass towers downtown, glimpsed through a break in the storm, are no more than a midwinter night's dream.

Walking by a house one snow-driven night, John and I see an elderly woman inside rocking by lamplight, reading a letter. We take the story and invent it from there, spin the rest in little gasps through half-frozen lips, the grainy snow whipping into our faces: the letter is nearly sixty years old, the last she received from her husband in the trenches before the Battle of the Somme. She was barely more than a girl then, pregnant with his child, almost lost herself when she received the news that he went down in the first wave to go over the top, German machine guns taking down the flower of the Commonwealth. Young soldiers in their innocence kicked soccer balls into battle while young women waited half a world away, thighs stiffening on pews in the great Anglican cathedral on Sherbrooke, where they sent their silent pleas to heaven: "Please let him come back safe, Lord. I hardly remember him now . . ."

The cold chokes off the story. The vision of the old woman reading by lamplight trails off into the night. Another walker in the silence looms like a wraith, heavily bundled, white puffs of breath, from the shadows where a face ought to be, freezing to crystals in the cold.

Above ground in Montreal in the winter, the best way to get around is on foot. Below ground you streak past whole sections of the city on the Métro and emerge to the same scene, the disorienting snow sending you a dozen blocks in the wrong direction, all landmarks obscured by the storm.

We date things in blizzards. Every two or three days we get a half foot of snow, or a foot, or a foot and a half: fourteen inches on Valentine's Day and seventeen inches on St. Patrick's, or perhaps it was twenty-one inches on St. Patrick's Day when the city shut down and snowmobiles ran up Ste.-Catherine Street because the cars couldn't pass. The night before Valentine's Day, John and I meet two women from British Columbia at a club called the Mustache and offer to take them to the top of Mount Royal the next day. We keep our promise through the storm, John slipping and sliding to the top of the mountain in loafers because he owns no boots, too stubborn to turn back, me in army combat boots but shivering in my thin, unlined letter jacket from Nebraska because I own no coat, both of us too proud to admit to these mountain-born women that we are near expiring from the cold.

On another February day, a day of fierce glare when the sun breaks through and the temperature plummets and the light off the banks of white snow tears at the retina, we make an epic march from the city's extreme west end to the north-central Plateau, walking a hundred blocks or more in bitter cold on our way to a movie because John is preoccupied with the subject of the grotesque in art and literature, so we wander out of our way to see a stray gargoyle here or a unique decorative scroll at the entrance to an old tunnel there—the gargoyles conveniently popping up when John reaches a point in the discourse where he needs an appropriate illustration of the theme. I'm far too cold to care, shivering and protesting all the way, John reassuring me again and again that the theater is only a couple of blocks away while he takes a frigid detour past the façade of yet another cathedral.

My room on Aylmer Street is on the top floor of a rooming house run by a fierce old ruddy-faced Polish giant with eyebrows like paint brushes. There is a miniature desk and a single bed that sags badly in the middle and a bathroom down the hall. I try just once to make love to a woman there and give up—no one can have sex on a bed that sags like a swaybacked horse. After that, when a girlfriend comes to visit we roll out our sleeping bags on the floor. I have the entire upper floor of the house to myself, so I tend to pad naked to the bathroom in the middle of the night, a habit that has evil consequences when I accidentally lock myself out of my room after a late night at a jazz club. Given a choice between rousing the ferocious Pole from his bed at 4 A.M. and making a circuit of the house through the snow, I decide to brave the cold and head out the front door, climb naked through four-foot snowbanks, scale the emergency exit steps in the back to the balcony outside my room, and crawl in through the window (which is mercifully unlocked), diving between the sheets in the overheated room one step ahead of massive, total-body frostbite.

The snow falls without end. Even Montreal has never seen a winter like this; all the records for snowfall in a single winter are shattered, and still the mountains of snow in the tiny front yards of the houses along Aylmer Street pile higher and higher until they're much higher than my head and still climbing.

Weekends when John is shut away in his apartment reading, I like to get up early and take a long, wintry walk, end up somewhere like the Bistro on rue de la Montagne, drink espresso and eat croissants and read Rilke and the *New York Times* until the winter afternoon darkens. Then I meet John at a cheap curry house and spend an intense hour or two talking about our weekend's reading, catch a Bergman film at a repertory house and walk home through the snow, head teeming with half-baked ideas for novels, plays, poems, stories, revolutionary tracts that will change the world. I switch from smoking DuMauriers to Gauloises, black French tobacco redolent (or so I think) of Paris cafés after the First World War, when writers of the Lost Generation were busy making novels and legends.

My taste in art, literature, and music runs to the severe. I respond to clean lines and an economy of emotion—etchings rather than paintings, Dürer before Rembrandt, Bach before Beethoven, Manet rather than Monet, Paul Cézanne before either, Ezra Pound before anyone else. In the great poet's voice, heard on a scratchy recording at John's apartment, I hear my father's voice—cantankerous, skeptical, quarrelsome, very much the product of big-shouldered, turn-of-the-century America, even if the differences in learning and perception between the two men are as wide as the Atlantic. But it is Pound's precision that appeals, the gift for honing a line to a knife blade of sense.

I long to match that precision, but my work comes out stilted and choked. I worry at the theme of exile, the meaning of existence on what is, for me in this endless winter, the wrong side of a three thousand–mile border. Seated at a tiny desk in an overheated room in Montreal where the snowbanks almost obscure the window, this puny exile in a frigid city seems to lack the stuff of literature. Exiles go to Paris, not to Montreal; they leave stuffy bourgeois conformity, not the U.S. Army. This paltry tale seems as unexceptional as a trip to the supermarket. Afraid to tap the deep vein of pain and frustration inside, I reject every line long before a publisher can do it for me. Fragments of poems, short stories, plays, and novels are ripped up and thrown away. John understands what I have to do—simply to write and let it build, layer after layer—but I get lost trying to construct a single paragraph that will not seem hopelessly inept the next day. Random words typed on sheets of yellow paper rolled into the typewriter sit there for days, taunting me with their refusal to become clauses, paragraphs, chapters.

■　■　■

Even in Montreal, winter can't last forever. The ice on the river breaks with a rumble like artillery fire in the distance, the days lengthen, the mounds of snow begin to melt, and on the first really warm afternoons the entire city turns to the sun, palefaced, shedding clothes, seeking light. I pick a sunny Saturday to give up my two-pack-a-day cigarette habit. Long walks, showers, and orange juice are the cure, and for three days I stay high on the absence of nicotine. At the end of the first week of May, the leaves come out, the grass turns green, and you feel the sap flowing everywhere, the long winter banished from sight and memory.

On one of the first warm afternoons in May, John and I hike up to Mount Royal and sprawl in the sun with the city down below, the reach of the St. Lawrence where it bends to the north in the distance, the blue green tile roofs of the Hôtel Dieu hospital below. We're loafing there in the sun, watching women and thinking about nothing much at all, when I remember that I have an unopened letter from my mother stuffed in the pocket of my jeans. I rip it open and a clipping from the *Scottsbluff Star-Herald* falls out. The headline is set over a single slender column of type: "Sergeant Ronald Bales Killed in Vietnam." Ron Bales, the big kid from down the block who played Friar Tuck when Sonny and I dreamed up our Robin Hood games. Gentle Ron Bales, who would get angry and stalk back to his house when Sonny and I launched one of our kerosene and firecrackers assaults on a red ant pile, saying we were dumb and cruel.

I can't even speak to tell John what has gone so suddenly wrong, so I hand him the clipping. Ron Bales has been killed in a war that seems destined to go on forever. I've been in Canada nearly eighteen months. American ground troops have been fighting in Vietnam for more than six years, and more than three years have passed since the Tet offensive proved that America could not win in Vietnam. Any fool can see that there is no good or wise or honorable way out, that the troops should have been brought home long ago, that they never should have been sent to Vietnam in the first place. I feel a terrible, shattering guilt, although there is nothing I could have done to save Ron, who has died for no reason at all. I weep on the mountain.

The war goes on.

Ron's death in Vietnam colors everything that follows. We were occasional childhood playmates, nothing more, but I can't get it out of my mind, can't shake the guilt. Somehow, I feel I have abandoned my generation, walked away from the great conflict of our time, the war to stop the war. Like many of the war resisters in Canada I have left active politics and tried to forget about Vietnam, but now the war is back with a vengeance, the particular horror of a single death weighing far more than all the body counts of enemy dead, the rows of body bags awaiting shipment home.

I write Sonny to see if he knows any more details about what happened to Ron, but Sonny has dropped off the map. I send a letter or a postcard every couple of months, but he never answers. Sonny is the only person on the planet I could talk to about the death of Ron Bales, and he has either vanished or pulled so far back into himself that he can't answer. Sonny has vanished, Ron haunts my dreams. I can't imagine Ron in the army, can't imagine him a sergeant, can't imagine him getting killed. It is just wrong, a picture out of kilter.

In June, one of the writers at Mother Earth leaves for Europe and I inherit his apartment on rue de l'Esplanade and buy most of his furniture, including the barber chair he has in his study with a plywood desk, a circular hole cut in the plywood so the desk fits around the chair, the perfect desk for a writer in a tidy little room looking out onto the street. It's a good place to write, my first real apartment in Canada. I work away at a half-dozen projects simultaneously, especially a kind of prose-poem called "Paragraphs," a rough sketch of the run to Canada in its most cryptic form.

In July I meet Danielle, a pretty French blonde who works for Radio Canada. She has a cozy apartment in Outremont, a dozen blocks from where I live. We are very different, but Danielle is what I need. She is firmly grounded, not in the least intellectual, calm, so old-fashioned she refuses to allow me in the kitchen at all. We have our first fight when I go to the refrigerator to get myself a bowl of ice cream instead of asking her to get it for me. She is beautiful and sexy, patient and kind and supportive. Still obsessed with Mariela, I treat her miserably.

Another scene is beginning to break up. At the end of August, John leaves for England. A month later he's back, briefly, this time on his way to Vancouver to return to graduate school. Ray slips back through the border—something I would never have the courage to do—to help a close friend edit an underground newspaper. In October I call Pop on my twenty-fifth birthday because it's his birthday too. He's turning seventy-three. I'm ready for bed; Pop can't talk much because he's getting ready to go out to a dance.

November is so depressing I feel I'm going to suffocate. The leaves fall, the air turns progressively colder, the first snow falls. I am fond of Danielle and she does her best to take care of me, but we have little common ground. She knows I'm a deserter, but we never discuss any of the things that are eating me up—especially the job at the tabloid factory. November 13 is the second anniversary of my induction into the U.S. Army. Had I remained at Fort Lewis, I would have been discharged on this date, a free man, on my way back to Miami and the

Herald. Perhaps I could have found Mariela again, persuaded her to leave Clagg. None of that will happen now. I feel close to a nervous breakdown, ashamed of what I'm doing, barely able to work enough to keep the paychecks coming.

At the end of November I decide to quit the job at Mother Earth, leave Danielle, and return to Vancouver to hook up with John and get his help to finish a brief collection of poems and short stories. The lax Canadian rules make it possible to live on unemployment for a full year (I've learned they won't deport me if I apply), and I figure that's a year I can devote to serious writing. I take the three-day train ride to Vancouver, sitting up in coach all the way to save money. Danielle is angry and hurt, but there's nothing she can do to stop me.

As usual, I haven't thought things through. When I get to Vancouver I can't find John. He's crashing with a friend somewhere, so he has no fixed address and I have no phone number for him. I still have other friends in Vancouver, but they're people like us, without addresses or phone numbers. I can't find anywhere else to stay, so I check into the hotel off Hastings Street again. It snows the first day and then the snow turns to rain, a frigid three-day downpour. I walk the streets cold and drenched, the water pouring through my old black hat, trying to find John. When I finally locate him he's sleeping on a friend's couch, and there is no room there for me. I stay at the hotel for a week, with the dismal feeling that after nearly two years in Canada I've made no progress at all. Another day or two and I'm down with what is either bronchitis or pneumonia, too sick even to stagger out to the White Lunch for a bowl of soup.

I know when I'm licked. I can't bear another winter on Hastings Street. At the end of the week I feel well enough to get back on the train and make the three-day ride east to Montreal sitting up in coach, sleeping in brief snatches, nearly getting into a fight with a bunch of drunken loggers who stumble on the train in the middle of the night somewhere in northern

Ontario. They're going fifty miles or so and I've been on the train for more than two days, coughing my lungs out. The way I feel, a beating would almost be a mercy.

For some reason, Danielle takes me back. By Christmas I'm well enough to spend the holiday with her parents in Longueuil, a suburb of Montreal. That's the limit of my social life. Danielle is all I have and she's at work all day. I write lively letters to John and Ray, to Larry in Vietnam, less often now to Sonny, who never answers. I write short, happy letters home, careful never to hint at the emptiness, the gnawing unhappiness of exile in a strange, cold country. Now and then I write Mariela, too, keeping the same tone: life is good, Montreal is a fascinating city, I am going to write that elusive Great American Novel. The reality of life in Danielle's apartment on Bloomfield Street is utterly different. I have withdrawn completely. I read a lot, write very little, see no one but Danielle, and go to movies only because we live right next door to the Outremont Theatre, where for ninety-nine cents we can see an entire retrospective of cinema running seven days a week— Luis Buñuel, Orson Welles, Akira Kurosawa, Federico Fellini, Bernardo Bertolucci, Jean-Luc Godard, Ingmar Bergman. I see Bertolucci's *The Conformist* six or seven times, but the movie I find most disturbing is Bergman's *The Seventh Seal,* his medieval knight playing chess with Death. I watch it again and again and think about almost nothing else. I am twenty-five years old, lost in a cul-de-sac, unable to find a way out.

Through most of that long winter, Danielle is the only person in my life, and we never talk about the things that are on my mind—the books I read, the stories I'm trying to write, my preoccupation with Bergman and death, the fact that I am now cut off from everyone but her. We talk about Danielle's job at Radio Canada, her family, what we're going to eat. In the mornings I write on a little portable typewriter propped on Danielle's coffee table next to a pile of yellow paper appropriated from Mother Earth. In the afternoons I take long, solitary walks and stop every day at a little bookshop called Bonder's on Bernard Street, owned by a kindly Jewish couple who survived the concentration camps during World War II. One day Mrs. Bonder tries to start a conversation. When Danielle comes home that evening I'm sitting in the dark on the couch.

"What's wrong?"

"I can't go back to the bookstore anymore. The woman there tried to talk to me today."

"What's the matter with that?"

"I can't talk to people now. I can't do it. I don't want people talking to me."

"Those are nice people in the bookstore."

"I know. They're wonderful. But I can't talk to them. I just don't like it when people talk to me."

Danielle holds me for a while. When she turns on the light, I can see that she's crying.

■   ■   ■

By late March I've decided to leave for Vancouver again. I try to explain it in a letter to Ray: "Well, in a week or so I'm going to try running away, to Van of course, hoping mostly for a breath of fresh air. I must get away from Danielle because I can't work while I'm with her, I'm not meant to be salt to anyone's pepper, but I'm very, very sorry I must hurt her, something about knowing it's all a tragedy and wanting not to dump any more of the badness on people around me, especially the more defenseless ones like D. But a cul-de-sac is a cul-de-sac, for all that."

On April 15 I leave Montreal for Vancouver again by train, sitting up in coach for three days because I don't want to hitchhike. In my journal, as we pull out of the station I note that it's the first day in 1972 that the temperature has gone over fifty degrees in Montreal.

Spring in British Columbia and I feel like I'm rising from the dead, waking to the light. John and his girlfriend Cheryl have moved into a beautiful house near the University of British Columbia campus. The house is owned by a friend of Cheryl's, a wealthy professor at the university who is mortally afraid of dogs. There are a dozen big dogs on the street, so she has rented the place to John and Cheryl for a song and moved into a high-rise apartment. I spend a couple of weeks recuperating in this lovely house, coming back to life in the warmth of their intellectual energy and joie de vivre. The house is full of books, the back yard a tumbling garden full of flowers and trees. We sit in the sun with their cat Vico and talk about Pound and the things we want to write. John is a serious poet now, hard at work on a long series of difficult and complex poems. I can feel him pulling me out of my shell and back into life. The nightmarish winter in Montreal is over; I can bear to be around people again.

The day I arrive, John fails to pick me up at the train station because Cheryl has just been busted. She and a group of female artists, writers, and intellectuals have been making a tidy living performing dances vaguely reminiscent of Isadora Duncan at a little beatnik spot in town where herbal tea is served instead of alcohol. No difficulty there, but the dances are performed nude, the clientele mostly men in raincoats, and the constabulary has finally got around to arresting the dancers. The trial is a hoot, stolid Vancouver cops testifying in minute detail about visible pubic hair and undulating hips. John and I spend the week in the company of a dozen very attractive young women who are facing charges. One is the sexiest woman I have ever met—she can't even open a door without caressing the knob. But to my frustration, she is deeply in love with a rodeo cowboy.

Rattling around the city, I manage to locate most of the radicals from the summer of 1970, the people involved in the Committee to Aid American War Objectors and all the rest of it. All our conversations go the same way. They say hello, and then they want to know exactly where I'm at. Vancouver is not the answer they seek.

"So, are you a Marxist-Leninist now?"

"Uh—not really."

"Trotskyite?"

"No . . ."

"Maoist?"

"Definitely not."

"You're not still talking to those assholes from the Northern Liberation Front, are you? You know that they no longer accept the need for revolution and that they believe the class struggle is an outmoded social model."

"Well, it probably is."

"You're kidding."

"Marx was writing—when? After the Paris Communes in 1848? There's a good chance that doesn't apply to North America in 1972, don't you think?"

"I can't believe you said that. You're worse than the socialists."

"I am a socialist."

"Which kind of socialist?"

"This is pointless. Do you still see Dara Culhane?"

"Please. She's with *them*."

"Angela?"

"The last time I saw her she told me that she's a feminist now, and she's not taking part in any more of our patriarchal peacenik bullshit, and the world will never be a better place until all men are castrated at birth. She's a fanatic."

The lively, inventive scene of 1970 has fragmented into all these competing, bitchy, ferocious little cells, each group more preoccupied with getting its dogma correct than with effective political action in a world where the logging companies are still clear-cutting timber, women still get knocked around by their husbands, and the Vietnam War drags on without end.

*

I can't face Hastings Street, so I find a room in a shoddy boarding house downtown, not far from the Vancouver library. I can collect unemployment for a year, so I still have six months to go at ninety-two dollars a week. My grand ambition as a writer remains largely unfulfilled. A letter to Ray sums it up:

> Still having trouble getting much work of any quality off the ground. Something jumps up and happens, and then there's this long nothing until something else happens. Trying to get a quartet rolling now, four long stories on themes of love, terror, revenge and hope. Got a good start on the terror story and then bogged. Long poem Canticle/Compendium for Hank Williams completely stuck in the mud. Guess I told you I sent a short poem to New Yorker which will of course be recircuited. Frustrating, anyway, and sometimes the loneliness of it, writing and reading and reading and writing, gets to me & I want to be back in the middle of something, even if it's old Mother Earth. Have pretty well sealed myself from people for a year, beginning to wonder what it's like to have them around. And on days (today one of those) when I can't write a reasonable sentence to save my left testicle, well . . .

The problem may be that I keep attempting vast, ambitious projects instead of mastering the craft a step at a time. I keep going back to that long, disjointed Hank Williams poem, inspired by a poem cycle based on the life of Billy the Kid written by a young Canadian poet I admire, Michael Ondaatje. I spend more than half of every day reading, usually in the library because I can't afford to buy books.

Late one afternoon I come back to my room from the library, groggy with Pound and the vortex and John's ideas about counterpoint in the "Pisan Cantos," unlock the door and find Pop sprawled on my narrow bed in his cowboy boots. A Las Vegas casino wanted someone who could train horses to pull a chariot on a conveyor belt, and after several trainers failed, one of the investors remembered a crazy old man back in Nebraska who once coaxed his horse into a trailer when no one else could get it to budge, and so Pop left Scottsbluff for the bright lights of the big city. The hot summers he spends at home in Scottsbluff with Mom, winters he trains horses for the rich and famous in Las Vegas—including the ultimate lounge singer, Wayne Newton. He's nearly seventy-four and he's working fourteen-hour days, seven days a week, finding success in his seventies at a profession he loves after a lifetime of backbreaking work to make ends meet. One of the Las Vegas papers has done a long profile on him, and a Japanese production company looking for the archetypal American cowboy has featured the old man, a lifetime nonsmoker, astride a horse in a cigarette commercial. He is more grizzled, his hair a little whiter, his gray eyes a little watery, still whip-lean and tough as whalebone.

"Damn, it's good to see you, Jack boy!" he says. "I got to thinking. Hell, I've never seen Vancouver, so I decided to come on up."

"How'd you get here?"

"Hitchhiked! All the way from Las Vegas. Helluva trip, but I wouldn't care to do that again. I imagine I'll take the bus back."

"Jesus, Pop, you shouldn't be hitchhiking. How'd you get into my place?"

"I talked to your landlady," he says with a wink. "Helluva woman, that old girl. I told her you were my boy, she let me in."

The landlady weighs close to three hundred pounds, his kind of woman. No doubt he has flirted with her shamelessly to get her to break into my apartment.

"So how long are you gonna stay?"

"I imagine three, four days. I thought you'd have a bigger

place than this with a spare bedroom and all, boy with a college education."

"I'm not working, Pop."

"Well, what you do with yourself?"

"I'm trying to write." I point to the typewriter in the corner, a doubled sheet of yellow paper rolled into the carriage, a fragile half sentence under a page number, the same half sentence that has been staring at me for a week.

"How do you make a living?"

"Well, right now I'm getting unemployment."

"Is that like welfare?"

"Not exactly."

"Well, I'll be damned. A boy of mine on welfare. Hell, you can work construction, drive a truck, buck hay, there must be all kinds of work in a place big as this."

"I don't want to work construction. I'm trying to write."

"Well, have ya written anything?"

"A bit. Not much. It takes time."

"It don't sound like much for a man to do with his life."

I feel my temper rising, the impending explosion. We haven't seen each other for three years, and already it feels like we're about to go at it in this little room. I decide to change the subject.

"Pop, you wanna see Vancouver?"

"Hell, yes," he says, reaching for his straw cowboy hat. "That's why I came."

We walk for three hours. Through downtown, Stanley Park, English Bay, over the Granville Bridge to see the *Sun* building. He's tireless and curious about everything. He wants to know how the bridge was built, what they use for the foundation for those tall buildings, where the logs come from, where the ships are going. When I don't have the answers he starts wondering again, wanting to know why I went to college.

In the evening I take him for a dinner I can't afford at a

cheap steak house on Davie Street. He has the biggest steak on the menu and two baked potatoes and two pieces of apple pie with ice cream, and while I'm at the cash register paying the check he goes next door and buys a dozen peaches and eats them as we walk down the street, dribbling peach juice onto his best cowboy shirt, bringing out the father in me.

"You shouldn't eat all those. You're going to make yourself sick after all that steak and pie."

"Hell, a man's got to eat."

We pass two enormous young women, their ample behinds crammed into hot pants. They're his type. He sweeps off his cowboy hat and bows as they pass, then belts me one on the shoulder. "Hot damn, Jack boy! That's enough to make a tadpole slap a whale!"

I shake my head, uptight and embarrassed. I'm afraid he's going to dispense some more of his rough-hewn advice about the birds and bees, like "Find yourself a woman with enough behind to keep your balls from draggin' on the sheets."

I haven't forgotten the time I was twelve, when we loaded a mare onto the truck and took her to be bred. We sat on the top rail of the corral fence with a couple of cowboys and watched the stallion sniff the mare's hindquarters before mounting her two or three times, and then loaded the mare again and headed home. On the way he cleared his throat a half-dozen times, and then we had our one and only talk about sex. It lasted about ten seconds.

"Did ya see that, boy?" he asked.

"Uh, yeah, Pop."

"Well, don't ya reckon folks do it pretty much the same way?"

Every morning in Las Vegas he gets up before dawn, saddles a horse that some wealthy doctor will ride twice a year, and heads straight out, four or five miles into the desert, to take the salt out of it before they settle down to two or three hours of serious work. I imagine that at sunrise, alone on horseback out in the desert, he's as happy as a man can be. It's a life to envy.

I sleep on the floor in my sleeping bag that night and give him the bed. He starts snoring within thirty seconds, and I lie awake wondering how we can be so different, father and son, what I'm going to do with him for three or four days, how I can afford to feed him, what to do to entertain him now that we've walked all over the city. There's no need to worry. He's up at 4 A.M. the next morning.

"I expect I'd best be getting back," he says. "I've got horses to work."

For the return trip, he's going to take the bus. I drag myself out of the sleeping bag and we walk to the bus station, arriving five hours before his bus.

"You're not young for long and you're old for a helluva long time," he says while we're eating breakfast. "You gotta by God take care of it while you got it."

I understand that he's trying to tell me something about life, but I'm in no mood to listen to this bizarre old man in a bus station. I just want to see him back on that bus before he does something outrageous. He is quite capable of pinching the rear of a passing female or starting an argument about religion at any instant.

"Y'know, you never answered my letter."

"What letter was that?"

"I wanted to see if you could explain to me just what the 'soul' is. I figured a smart young fella like you, been to college and all that, would be able to straighten it out for me."

"Jesus, Pop. Don't start. You know I don't know any more about that than the next guy."

"Y'see, that's what I mean. If smart fellas can't explain it, then there is no soul. And if there is no soul, how the hell are ya gonna go to heaven?"

"Aw, Pop. I don't know."

He's quiet for a while, then he picks up a new tack.

"You got a girlfriend?"

"Sorta. She's back in Montreal."

"Whatever happened to that Cuban woman down in Miami? You said she was a real beauty."

"She was. She broke up with me."

"That's right. You got a Dear John in the army. I saw that happen to fellas in France in World War I. They'd get a letter, just go plumb crazy, wanna fight the whole damned German army by themselves."

"Yep."

Finally it's time for his bus. Back in the library that afternoon with the "Pisan Cantos" open in front of me, I can't concentrate. As always, Pop makes me feel half alive, like a drained and pale shadow of the real thing, like there's something about life I just don't get.

By June I've decided, typically, that the little room in Vancouver is too depressing, too much like the West Hotel all over again, and that I need more congenial surroundings if I'm to write great works of literature. I pack up and hitch the three hundred miles to Castlegar. I haven't seen Norm since I passed through here in the summer of '70. He's as busy as ever running his crisis center. I find what may be the only apartment in this tiny town, a little room over a shoe store, and begin writing again and stay at it through the summer. Late every afternoon I knock off for a couple of draft beers at the tavern, where half the songs on the jukebox are Hank Williams tunes. I pump quarters into the jukebox and sit there scrawling notes for the Canticle/Compendium poem and watching the junkies nod off. My lover for most of the summer is a hippie girl with hair almost to her knees who likes to make love late at night on the railroad tracks, because she thinks it's a kick to do it where a train might come barreling through any minute. Night after night we have a few beers in the tavern and make love on the tracks. She says we're closer to the heart of life like that, having wild sex, waiting for the vibration of the train, knowing that if we don't hear it we'll be crushed or dragged to death. Then late one night after a drunken party, a tough kid named Danny, a friend of Norm's who did two years in the provincial penitentiary for assaulting a couple of RCMP officers, drives his car off a bridge into a gorge on the Columbia River. After that, death seems much too close. We leave the railroad tracks and go back to making love in my cubbyhole apartment.

Through Norm I meet a couple of young printers who have a government grant to produce several volumes of work by young BC writers. Their committee approves my work, and they set out to print it, a slender volume of poems and short stories called *Stiff Blue Ground*. I want to include the Canticle/Compendium for Hank Williams, but it isn't ready. Because I never see the proofs of the book, it has at least one mistake per paragraph, and when it is published I find it unbearable to read a single line—although I do wrap a copy and mail it to Mariela, care of her parents' address in Florida, and one to my parents and another to Sonny care of his mother in Scottsbluff.

By the end of the summer I'm back in Vancouver. There's a political campaign in progress, and the bizarre right-wing Social Credit Party which has governed British Columbia for decades is about to lose to the socialist New Democratic Party. When John finds "Vote Social Credit" signs on his street, he scribbles underneath, ". . . and watch your genitals fall off."

I find a small apartment and persuade Danielle to join me in Vancouver, confident that I can get the *Sun* to take me back. We're going to try living together yet again. When she arrives, it's a bad time. I still haven't found work and my unemployment is running out. I visit Pat Nagel three times at the *Sun*, all but begging for a job, but he won't hire me. He doubts I'm sincere about wanting to return to newspaper work, and he's right. It rains every day, a heavy, oppressive downpour. Danielle and I are both job-hunting all over the city, getting one rejection after another, coming back to the apartment late in the afternoon soggy and depressed, making love to comfort each other and then lying there listening to the rain, wondering what we're going to do.

On September 20 I write a letter to Ray describing life in the Vancouver apartment:

Slight cool Van drizzle tumbling earthward, large picture window on street and people hustling by with umbrellas, work crews tearing down a couple of lovely old houses across the way as this is high-rise paradise—if ya can't see the sky well ya know the reason why. In 1st week we lived here the old drunk next door set his mattress afire twice, left us scrambling out at midnight to stand and sweat and pray it didn't get the manuscripts or the typewriter, nothing but smoke here except one night the smoke was strong enough to drive us to John's. That night the old drunk went out with a sheet over his face. So it goes. Then yesterday a fire across the street, two days before that a false alarm here, we've only lived in this hole ten days.

I give up first, take the train back to Montreal, move in with Ray. Danielle, who quit her job in Montreal to make a life with me in Vancouver, stays on another month, then surrenders and heads back to Montreal to move in with her parents. Fed up with being broke, I go back to working at Mother Earth, make enough money to get an apartment in Outremont not far from where Danielle and I had once lived. She finds a job too, moves in with me yet again. Every couple of months I break up with her again. Finally she has had enough. During one of our breakup phases she meets and marries a French-speaking schoolteacher. Alone again, I figure this is as good a time as any to start that Great American Novel about a young

Nebraskan who comes to Canada during the Vietnam War. I work on it for a month, read it over, shred the canary-yellow manuscript pages into confetti-sized bits, and toss them into the wind from my third-floor balcony on Bernard Street. No one needs to spell it out for me. I understand perfectly well. I've lost my way.

Finally, I decide the reason I can't write is that I am not in Europe. I want to live in Paris, scribble in cafés like writers of the Lost Generation. I have a little money saved after another stint at Mother Earth, but I have no travel papers. I can't get a U.S. passport, and I can't get a Canadian passport until I've been here five years.

One Sunday afternoon in October 1973, three of us are sitting around watching American football on Ray's TV—Ray, a navy deserter named John, and me. We start talking about how I want to go to Europe and John says he has a solution. He researched it, he claims, because he wanted to go to Europe too. If I renounce my American citizenship I will be stateless, and the Canadian government will issue travel papers to a stateless person if I want to go abroad.

It's tempting. There is no possibility we can ever go home, and we all plan to become Canadian citizens after five years in Canada anyway. To us, the U.S. has become unrecognizable. Every day there are new Watergate revelations in the papers. As the Senate hearings drag on, it is obvious that Nixon and his henchmen have attempted nothing less than the wholesale hijacking of the American government—but it appears that Nixon will ride out the scandal, no matter how ugly it gets.

October turns to November. One night after watching the CBS news at Ray's I take a long, chilly walk by myself. All the work we have done, all these years of marching and writing and demonstrations—what happened to all of it? Where *is* everybody? In 1968 it seemed that we could take the world with our notions of peace and love and racial harmony. Four years later all that has vanished like a mirage. What has happened to my country? How did we let this gang take charge? I feel like a German exile in 1936 watching Hitler consolidate his power over Germany. It has been nearly three years since I crossed the border, but I have never felt so bitter, so disenchanted, so out of touch with what America has become.

I begin thinking seriously about giving up my citizenship, getting travel papers, moving to France. As always, I feel that I can write if I just move to a place more congenial to writing. As far as America goes, it's a chance to make one final grand gesture short of self-immolation on the steps of the Capitol building in Washington. The gesture will matter to no one but me, but at least I'll know that I was true to my beliefs. If America won't do something about Nixon and the war, then I no longer want to be an American.

Within a week, my mind is made up—I'm going to renounce my American citizenship. I have so much frustration pent up inside that it needs some kind of outlet or I'm going to explode. I don't even double-check with the Canadian government to find out whether it really is possible to get travel papers if I am stateless. I want so much to make the grand gesture that I'm not going to be sidetracked by details. Ray tries hard to talk me out of it, but I'm in no mood to listen. Sometimes you look back at things and know you've made a terrible mistake. This time my impulsive nature is carrying me into a self-destructive, unnecessary blunder. What's worse, I can see it coming. I just can't stop myself.

I visit the American consulate in Montreal twice. It's a beautiful old building on the side of Mount Royal. The consul is a Yale graduate, a tall, blond-haired scion of the prep school classes—vague and plumpish, already patrician at twenty-eight. He is sympathetic. He understands my frustration. The Vietnam War was a mistake. Nixon has rather overdone things. True, the political winds are blowing a certain way at the moment, but political winds always change. He advises me not to do anything rash, not to throw away my citizenship in the greatest country in the world. The United States has taken some bad turns of late, but it will recover. It always has. He begs me to reconsider.

I will not be talked out of it. Sitting in his office, I explain my position. Amnesty for people like me at this point is unthinkable, a time when we can return to our country as citizens in good standing unimaginable, citizenship in a country that has become foreign to me pointless. Because of our opposition to the war, we have been cast as criminals, while men who are genuinely guilty of real crimes are still running the government. I have not deserted America; America has deserted me. America has deserted itself, deserted its young people, forgotten its own highest principles. I still love America—the America of Thomas Jefferson and the Declaration of Independence, the ideals set forth in John F. Kennedy's inaugural speech. I don't love what America has become. The destruction of Vietnam has not been limited to that embattled nation in Southeast Asia; the war has also torn apart the social fabric of the United States. Those of us who are on the losing side (and it's impossible to see yourself otherwise if you oppose the war) are already something less than full citizens of the U.S. We may own the moral high ground, but we are utterly powerless, scorned by the cynical men in the White House who see power as an end in itself.

I argue that great countries require great sacrifices, certainly, but this time what is required to support the war in Vietnam is nothing less than the sacrifice of intelligence, the liquidation of thought itself. When your country is doing something monstrous, it is monstrous to acquiesce; having deserted from the army, I have to take a further step now and signal my absolute opposition to an America I no longer recognize as my own. If this is the great sacrifice that is required to stand up for what I see as the most basic of freedoms—the freedom to refuse to fight an unjust war—then it is a sacrifice I am required to make by the very patriotism I feel for the United States of

America. Thomas Jefferson's America, not Richard Nixon's America.

The consul disagrees. He thinks it is possible to foresee a day when we will be able to return to the U.S. I don't. I believe we are all doomed to live as exiles until our dotage. Perhaps then we can toddle back to visit the graves of our parents, not before. There is no point in dreaming that we will be allowed to return to the U.S. If I am doomed to life as an expatriate, I want to see the world, and as a stateless person I will be a citizen of the world.

The consul hears me out, carries the argument as far as he can, finally shrugs and shakes his head. It is not his decision to make. He agrees to have the papers prepared. Ray comes along when I return to sign them a few days later. The consul makes one last pitch, offers to tear up the papers and forget about it. I refuse. Ray shakes his head sadly and watches as I sign multiple copies, renouncing my citizenship in the United States of America. We shake hands with the consul and leave, strolling down the hill toward Sherbrooke.

It is November 21, 1973, three years and eight days after my induction into the U.S. Army. One day less than a decade since the assassination of JFK in Dallas. A cold wind has whipped the last leaves off the trees, the first snowstorms will roll in any day. We have nothing to look forward to but five months of winter. I expect to feel some kind of elation, perhaps a sense of freedom similar to what I felt when I first crossed the border into Vancouver. Instead, all I feel is an overwhelming despair, the sure and bitter knowledge that I have just made a terrible mistake, that my thoughtless pride has led me into a blind alley from which there is no escape. I don't feel that I was wrong politically, only that there was no reason at all for me to throw away my citizenship. I wanted to hurt those who have wounded me. Instead, I have managed only to do more harm to myself and my own future. I am stateless now. A man without a country.

Back at his place, Ray jots in his diary: "Today Jack threw it all away." He is more accurate and more prescient than we know. Three months later I receive a reply from the Canadian government to my request for travel papers issued to stateless persons: the travel papers are available only for Hungarian refugees who fled after the uprising against the Soviets in 1956. American deserters need not apply. I failed to do the research, and I have signed my citizenship away for nothing at all except the empty satisfaction of making a grand gesture.

Six months later I receive an undesirable discharge from the United States Army. Not "dishonorable," which carries all sorts of penalties. Simply "undesirable," which is a category above "dishonorable." It seems the U.S. military is quietly discharging all deserters who are not U.S. citizens. For a brief time my friends envy me; I can't return to the U.S., but at least I've been discharged from the army.

■   ■   ■

Nixon, of course, will fall. Brought down by journalists not much older than me, working for a paper where I once aspired to work. Carl Bernstein and Bob Woodward and the *Washington Post* perform what is without question the greatest work of sustained investigative journalism in history. Nixon is through. Agnew falls before him, tainted by an unrelated scandal. H. R. Haldeman, John Erlichman, John Mitchell, John Dean, Jeb Magruder, Gordon Liddy, the whole sorry lot—all the president's men, the men who attempted to subvert the government of the United States to their own ends and failed. From the perspective of November 1973 it was impossible to foresee how they would fall like dominoes, but the ink is barely dry on the papers I signed renouncing my citizenship when all that journalism begins to take its toll. The republic is stronger than I thought, strong enough to right itself. From Canada we watch with disbelief as the scandal spreads, until Nixon himself waves his final histrionic good-bye in front of that helicopter on the White House lawn in August 1974.

It is too late for me. Too late for Sonny, too late for Ron Bales, too late for tens of thousands of others, American and Vietnamese. Once Nixon is gone, successive waves of amnesty from Gerald Ford and Jimmy Carter mean that most of my friends can return to the U.S. if they choose. Draft dodgers are pardoned, deserters discharged. Ray returns to the U.S. and his discharge is quickly processed; he is free now to work on either side of the border, but he chooses Canada. It is not the choice I would have made. I still feel the deep emotional pull of America, especially now that the entire Watergate process has restored my faith in the power of democracy. Had I not signed away my citizenship in a fit of pique with Nixon, I would have applied at every newspaper in the U.S., beginning with the *Miami Herald*.

The war, left to the South Vietnamese, goes on until the spring of 1975. Inevitably, their forces collapse. With Saigon falling, my old friend Larry Grossman, still with the State Department, is called to the Philippines to translate for Vietnamese refugees pouring out of the country the United States destroyed in order to save. I was a late convert to the antiwar movement in the fall of '67, but by the time the war finally ends I have spent nearly eight years fighting it one way or another. I have given up my country, my citizenship, my profession, my family, my belief in myself, my true love, everything but my life. For this I will be called a coward, and perhaps the people who say that are right. I feel it's the hardest, bravest thing I ever did, but it's not for me to judge.

It is April 1974. Another woman has moved into the apartment I once shared with Danielle. Very late one night the phone rings next to my bed.

"Hello, Jacko." It has been nearly five years, but I know that voice—like bells ringing in the distance.

"Hello, Mariela."

It is the first time we have spoken, the first time I have heard from her since the Sunday morning in 1969 when she told me it was over. Since then I have not had so much as a postcard. Now she is distraught. She and Tom Clagg are close to breaking up. Clagg has moved out.

"Can you come to Miami, Jacko? I need you."

I want to leap out of bed and walk naked two thousand miles to Miami to be with her, but I can't. I'm a man without a country. I can't even cross the border.

"Mariela, if I try to cross the border, they'll arrest me. It's five years in prison if I get caught. And I'm with someone now."

"I need you here. I wish you could be here now."

"So do I, but I can't."

"I've missed you."

"It didn't have to be this way."

"I know. I'm sorry. I really am. I think all this hurt us both. A lot."

"You know how many times I wished you would call?"

"I couldn't, Jack. I really couldn't. If I let myself think about things . . ."

"It's all right. Really. Maybe it was just meant to be."

"Would they really throw you in prison? What about the amnesty?"

"It didn't apply to me. I gave up my American citizenship."

"Oh, Jack! You didn't! Why?"

"It was just one of those dumb, impulsive things, Mariela. I was mad at Nixon, I thought I could never go home. I wanted to punish someone. I just ended up punishing myself, I guess."

"I wish I could have stopped you."

"So do I, but we were never much good at stopping each

other, were we? You hung up on me and married Tom Clagg, I ran off to Canada. Maybe we're both a little impulsive."

"Uh-huh. It's strange sometimes, the things that happen to people."

Hearing her voice makes me dizzy. "Mariela? Whatever you do, please stay in touch. Write, call, don't disappear again. I don't want to lose you."

"OK. I'm sorry. I just needed someone to talk to. I read all your letters, you know. And your book."

"I'm sorry I can't do anything now."

"It's all right. It's all right, really. I understand. It's good to hear your voice."

"I still love you. That won't change."

"I know, Jacko. I'll keep in touch. Thanks for listening."

The woman beside me stirs, asks who is on the phone at this ungodly hour.

"Sssshhh," I say. "Go back to sleep. It's no one."

■   ■   ■

In the hot, flat summer of 1981 a fat buzzard flaps away from the tire-flattened carcass of some poor road-killed critter on a state highway somewhere west of Bridgeport, way out in the Nebraska panhandle. I brake hard, not wanting buzzard blood all over the grill of my sister's old station wagon, a carload of cousins screeching with the thrill of a near miss, the car groaning and skipping a gear as it lopes up to third, grinding, hoping for a fourth gear that won't come.

This is my third, maybe fourth trip home. Old hat now since the first time in the late summer of '75, four days driving two thousand miles from Montreal with newly minted Canadian citizenship papers in the glove box, neglecting to warn anyone I was coming, just strolling onto the back porch of that tiny white house and finding my mother, gray and stooped and frail, bending to lift clothes from the dryer. The son she hadn't seen in six years hugging her old bones then, in a wash of tears and lost time. An hour later I'm out bucking hay bales with the old man as though the world since 1963 had remained fixed and unchanging, as though Vietnam and Nixon, Canada and the *Miami Herald* and Mariela and all the rest of it had never happened.

Now I'm on this back-road errand, driving my nephew to summer camp, his sisters and my two young sons shrill and cranky in the sticky cavern of this big old car, the bands on the automatic transmission fumbling and slipping. Hell of a place to be stranded on a hot August day with the buzzards and the silent corn fields baking in the heat, but the old car grinds all the way back to Scottsbluff. I drop the kids and my sister at the swimming pool and drive the wagon, stuck in second gear now, out to the Scottsbluff-Gering highway to a garage where yellowing *Playboy* pinups with their rose-nippled bodacious blondes say that 1961 was a very good year. The boss, gruff and skeptical, listens to my ignorant description of the car's aches and pains, nods, and reckons they'll get to it this afternoon or tomorrow, depending.

A smallish mechanic rolls his trolley out from under an old Dodge Ram pickup truck and gets to his feet, wiping grease from his face with the back of a greasier hand. He comes at me grinning.

"Hey, Jack," he says, "are you still in Canada?"

This is not a place where I care to advertise dissent and desertion and all that goes with it.

"Uh—yeah." Trying to place him. He has a mustache, the hair gray running to white, smeared grease like a Halloween mask on his face, but there's something in that grin that oils rusty gears of memory.

"You like it up there?"

"It's all right."

"Not too cold for you?"

"Winters, yeah . . ."

"You don't know who I am, do you?"

"Well, not exactly . . ."

Still grinning: "I'm just your oldest friend, and you don't know me."

A beat, two, three, and then a crash like a dam breaking.

"Sonny! My God! Sonny!"

I throw my arms around him, grease and all. Lift him off the concrete floor, the other mechanics looking at us like we're either crazy or queer, the two of us slamming each other on the back, both talking at once.

"Sonny! Jesus, I thought you were in Phoenix!"

"Came home last year. Things didn't quite work out in Phoenix, so I'm back now, living with my mom, working here, y'know, trying to keep it together."

"Man, we gotta go out, get drunk, catch up. God, it's good to see you. I figured you had pretty well run off the map."

"Hey, I ain't that easy to get rid of."

There's no point talking here, gawking grease monkeys staring at us, the roar of a mistimed engine hitting on no more than three valves from the back of the shop, the two of us lost boys trying to home in on a reality that is about three shards short of a full pane of glass. All we can do is make plans: Sonny will come by my sister's place after sundown, showered and shaved and shined up, and we will go out on the town—which means the Oregon Trail Lounge, a sizable den of iniquity and country music on a back highway outside Gering, where Sonny has been making regular mischief stops since he came home from Arizona.

I nod to the other mechanics, squeeze his shoulder again, walk back to my sister's place with more on my mind than a man can carry. The sun twists in the pale blue sky so I have to squint to see. Then I'm squinting through something else, wet and salty, a dozen years of hurt. Sonny and Ron Bales and Mariela and me and bridges that went down behind us so that now there is no way back. Ronnie's dead, Sonny's hair is gray, I lost Mariela a long time ago, my marriage is going south. The lot of us, '60s kids who wanted nothing but a Chevy with a rake job and a girl on our arm and time to hang out at the A&W, and what we got instead was Tet and My Lai and LBJ and body bags coming home from Southeast Asia.

Taking big gulps of air now, trying to hold it back, until on my sister's front steps with her and the kids still at the pool I sit down and let it go, thinking: My God, Sonny, what happened to us? One minute we were out there with our guns waiting for Charlie Starkweather and then you were showing me pictures of GIs wearing Viet Cong ears for necklaces and oh, my, look at us now. No way out, no way to rework it so that it didn't happen, to get back to Scottsbluff in 1964 when the world had ways it could go that would not lead to this—sitting here blind with sunshine and old hurt, planning a night at the Oregon Trail Lounge to wash some of it away. Knowing that there isn't enough beer in St. Louis to make us forget.

If somebody asked, some wandering soul curious as to why a tall man is sitting on the concrete steps in front of a yellow frame house on Twentieth Street in Scottsbluff blubbering like a kid who has just lost his new bicycle, I would have to say that I am crying for my generation, although that sounds as wrong as a one-winged crow trying to fly a straight line. There is something in all this, some sour point of cross-grained misdirection that I can't cut through. It has to be found and released, just to be able to get on with the simple things like buying milk and picking up the kids from the swimming pool and checking the box scores. And it will come out, willed or not, a good hour of gut-wrenching release until stomach muscles creak, breath comes in longer circuits, and I feel like a swimmer breaking the surface after an underwater crossing. Sonny. Goddam. Sonny. After all these years.

Sonny turns up that night looking slick, a man I would recognize now. At the Oregon Trail Lounge the women come by, run their fingers through his gray hair, want to know why he hasn't been by, not even bothering to drop a little coy into their invitations. "Sonny," one of them says, "you know I was waiting for you in my trailer three hours the other night and you didn't come by. Dammit, you know how I get with thunder. I saw that lightnin', I said Sonny's comin' by, I was just achin' for you baby. How 'bout tonight? You don't have a thunderstorm, but you can sure have me."

Sonny grinning, head down as though he didn't know the faintest thing about how she got with thunder—pleased, though, that I see him like this. Trying to explain what happened.

Sonny had some good years in Arizona. Six, seven years, the war fading in the background. He had a wife he met in Phoenix, a little business cleaning swimming pools for the rich, a home. Then one day he just couldn't go outside. Couldn't leave the house. Couldn't, for a time, even leave his bedroom. His wife would go to work and he would say good-bye and close the shades and lock the bedroom door and kill the lights and lie there all day in the dark, day after day, not able to stroll out onto the patio to light the barbecue.

Things happened in sequence: He lost the business, lost the house, declared bankruptcy. His wife left him. He got a little better with time, but there was nothing in Phoenix for him, so he came back to Scottsbluff and moved in with his mother, got so he could work and found a job doing what his father had done, fixing cars. It took him awhile to figure out what it was that made him pull down the shutters on his life in Phoenix, but other Vietnam veterans had been through the same or something like it, and now it had a name: post-traumatic stress disorder.

"I can't explain it. I was goin' along fine, y'know, feelin' like I put the war behind me and I could get on with things. It took a long time for it to hit me. Seven, eight years. Then I just shut down. Couldn't talk to people, didn't want to see nobody, didn't want to go out."

Sonny figured being home would make it better. Start over,

get a fix on something he could do and stay with. He gets about that far with his story and a brawl starts on the dance floor and comes at us like surf breaking, tables and chairs and bottles and bodies flying everywhere. Sonny dives under the table, I follow not too far behind. Another Vietnam vet who lost a leg over there sits up on the bar behind us, takes off his artificial leg, and starts whaling on anyone who comes near. When it calms a little we slip out the door, laughing. It's the first time I've seen a free-for-all in a bar, and it's not one bit like Hollywood.

The brawl puts an end to Sonny's story. We touch on it again, later, but we never really get back to it. That's as much as I know, as much as anybody knows. I go back to Scottsbluff a half-dozen times in the next two or three years, and every time Sonny and I end up at the Oregon Trail Lounge, but we never get back onto Vietnam, not even the night after Pop's funeral. Pop is hit by a drunk driver while walking home from the corrals where he keeps his horses a few days before his eighty-fifth birthday. He's still busting broncs twelve hours a day even though the horses have nearly killed him a half-dozen times— but the truck finishes him off before the horses can. The truck runs a stop sign, knocks the old man twenty feet in the air, breaks almost every bone in his body. When I visit him in the hospital in Scottsbluff, he doesn't know who I am. Walking out of the room, I hear him tell my sister, "That big fella that was just in here would make one helluva athlete." He lives another three months, gets well enough to walk a horse a few feet one day, fights the drugs they supply to keep him quiet in an old folks' home, staggers out of his wheelchair, and dies of heart failure in January 1984.

Sonny is there the night after the funeral, the wake just me and Sonny at a hole-in-the-wall bar on East Overland patronized mostly by Mexicans, because no one else in my family drinks. Sonny still hasn't sorted out what he wants to do with his life but he seems all right, cheerful and funny if you're close enough to hear what he's saying, because he isn't the type to shout. There's still that sadness down there somewhere you can't touch, sadness that comes down like a curtain after every belly laugh.

I go back again in the summer of '85 for our twentieth high school reunion. Stay with my mother, who sits up until the wee hours every night waiting for me to come home. When I stop to pick up Sonny for the reunion, his mother takes us out in her back yard to snap a Polaroid, me wearing a black T-shirt and a white tuxedo jacket I bought for five bucks on Canal Street in New York, Sonny in a neat sport jacket and tie. The sight of us together makes her laugh. "You two," she says, "you two were always Mutt and Jeff. You were always together, and every time I saw you I thought the same thing: Mutt and Jeff."

On the way to the reunion, I tell Sonny about my plan. He's all for it. We're going to sit down with a tape recorder, and he's going to tell me the whole story, and then I'm going to write a book about it, all the things that have happened since the night we wanted to ambush Charlie Starkweather and Caril Ann Fugate. Sonny is going to come stay with me for a while, maybe get a job back east, give us at least a few months to work through it all, and then I'll put it down for the record: a book about two boys growing up in Nebraska and what the war did to us.

It's a good reunion. A good party, good friends twenty years later. There's an ex–Green Beret in the room and a couple of ex-Marines, including my cousin Terry Todd and my old friend Salome Blanco. For some unearthly reason they vote me the one in the class who has changed the least, which has to be impossible. I come close to falling in love again with an old flame, dance until the wee hours. If anyone has a problem with what I did, they're too polite to say so.

Sonny and I have breakfast at a truck stop on the highway the day I leave Scottsbluff. Sonny wants to take two or three months to get some money together, then he's going to jump on a plane and we're going to finish this thing once and for all. Get it down on paper, do us both good. We finish breakfast, Sonny walks me to my car. We shake hands and say good-bye, he slaps me on the shoulder. I get behind the wheel and hit the road to Denver to catch a plane back east. I never see him again.

Epilogue

August 1999

TO GET THERE from Montreal, I take the plane to Denver and make the three-hour drive—northeast at first, then due north through cattle country. The traffic in Denver worse every year, Denver itself submerged under a haze of brown smog, a paradise sinking under the weight of cars and people and money. I can see the fringe of blue mountains in the west, but if I take my eyes off the highway I'll be turned into road kill by an eighteen-wheeler. Bear down, concentrate on the road, watch for the exit where Interstate 76 forks northeast toward Nebraska. The country, eastern Colorado bleeding into Kansas, is so flat the Rockies hang in the rear-view mirror forever, marking the spot where the continental pinball machine hit "tilt" a few million years ago.

By the time I hit Brush the traffic has thinned some. I hang a left off the Interstate, the cities and freeways vanish, and I'm alone, driving straight north into God's country. For a full half hour on Highway 71 a little before suppertime on a Sunday afternoon, I don't see another car. Tammy Wynette and George Jones and Jim Reeves on the radio and it could be 1965, running 80 miles an hour and sometimes a little faster because there is nothing ahead but this ribbon of highway where the country opens out twenty miles ahead, driving hard through ranch country under a sky so high, so wide, so infinite it's like shaking hands with God. Ranch houses off in the distance in the shadow of the hills, a sprinkling of Black Angus or white-faced Hereford cattle grazing, a windmill or two. Two ranch kids in a big monster pickup come up fast; a flash of blue and the roar of a big engine and the road is empty again. Seventy miles and I'm over the state line into Nebraska, where the Highway 71 overpass crosses Interstate 80 with the traffic underneath streaming west to Cheyenne, trucks and buses and tourists in minivans hell-bent for the Rockies, cranky kids and exasperated parents wanting Denver or Steamboat Springs, anything but this Big Empty, missing God's country because they're in a hurry to get a pastrami sandwich at a crowded deli in Boulder.

Going home for the first time in fourteen years, the first time since our high school reunion in 1985. Going home looking for ghosts. Mom, Pop, my brother Red, Sonny, all gone now. And a long-lost version of myself, a boy who grew up out here loving this rough place like no other on earth.

About halfway between Kimball and Scottsbluff, on the fringe of the Wildcat Hills, there's a battered old roadside café at a place called Harrisburg where truckers and drifters and cattlemen used to sit around and drink coffee and talk about cattle and oil and drought. Pop and I trucked prairie hay from these hills—thousands of tons of it over the years. As soon as I was old enough to be some help I was out there with him and the hired hands. We'd pull into the Harrisburg café with a load of two hundred bales all tied down with thick ropes in sheep-shank knots I could never master, and go in for a hamburger and a malt with hay stuck to the sweat on our necks and faces and forearms. The cattlemen would look at me and say, "Is that your top hand, Jack?" and my father would say, "That's him, by gosh, and I'm gonna make a bronc rider out of this one. Look at them long legs. Time he's eighteen, he'll be able to ride anything on four feet."

The things that hit you hardest are those that have vanished most completely from your memory: I had forgotten Harrisburg, forgotten the café, forgotten those mornings with my father and George White Magpie, the big Crow Indian with the smallpox scars who rolled out of bed when I was sent into his shack to wake him in the morning still drunk and reeking of cheap whiskey. I would squeeze in between those two big men and listen to George chant in Crow while the old truck roared and Pop cursed his way through the gears.

Now I pull into the empty gravel parking lot of the old café and get out to look around. No sound but the wind, a smell of sage on the breeze, the café closed and shuttered.

The breeze stirs the dust. Pop steps down out of the truck in his cowboy boots and puts his hand on my shoulder. White Magpie walks ahead of us with that odd rolling gait. I march between them, ten years old and proud in my dusty cowboy boots, and sit down on the chrome and plastic stools at the counter. The ranchers and cowhands in the booths all nod to Pop. He orders me a vanilla malt and two burgers. The waitress makes the malt first and hands me the glass and the metal shaker, and I down it all and ask for another one. When the food comes, Pop nudges me in the ribs: "Now you get on the outside of that so you'll be good for all day." I nod and dig in. White Magpie has a cup of coffee and skips the meal. I know why, but I don't say anything to Pop: I saw George throwing up behind the truck after we got the first load on. I know this will be one of the days when he pours down water all day long and doesn't say much, when you smell the cheap whiskey as he sweats it out and know how it must hurt to be slinging seventy-pound bales in the heat after drinking all night. He will never complain, and at the end of the day Pop will give him ten bucks and he'll go buy a bottle and get drunk again. A big, strong Crow Indian who should have had a better life, drinking the sadness of the high plains people.

We leave the café, full and sleepy now. At the sugar factory we stagger out into the bright sunshine and unload seven tons of hay with the reek of cowshit and beet pulp all around and the doomed cattle nosing the load, fattened on the waste pulp left after they make the sugar, eating their way to a rich man's table in Chicago. When we're done, George pukes behind the truck again and slides in next to me with a wink.

"Let's go!" he says, imitating Pop, chuckling. "Let's go! Move hay!"

The old truck with its load of bales vanishes and it's silent again, just me and the wind and the sagebrush in this place that is almost a desert, and when I get back in the car the empty stretch of Highway 71 ahead swims in a sudden curtain of mist, a herd of buffalo grazing in the lengthening shadows along the north slope of the Wildcat Hills.

Coming down out of the hills now, with the North Platte Valley spread out below and that long line of bluffs on the western horizon, taking the new highway bypass that skirts west of town almost in the shadow of Scotts Bluff before cutting right through the land that used to be our farm. Past the spot where Pop had his corrals the year he was in the hospital and I had to fight that stubborn old cow Bess morning and night, beating her over the head with the milk bucket after she kicked it over, bringing home a dribble of milk for my mother and sisters. "Imagine that," my mother would fuss, "a boy twelve years old and almost grown, barely able to milk a cow." No cattle there now, just a realty office and a convenience store.

It's all beautiful and strange, every street and alley and back yard in this little town luminous with memory. It's still home. Everybody has one, a place where time plays strange tricks, where you shape-shift from the present to the past and back again so quickly that you're a little unsure which is which. You walk down a street in 1999 and you turn a corner and come to a place where it is 1956, and you stand there baffled on the playground of your old grade school, remembering how Grady Waugh dodged right here when you were playing pom-pom-pollaway and you dove to grab him and caught a chinful of gravel. That would be a dozen years before Grady and Randy Meisner from our high school rock group the Drivin' Dynamics went to California to make it big in the music biz, and Randy became one of the original Eagles and Grady went into the army and came out more confused than ever. Time ripples like that here, folds back on itself, leaves you spinning next to an old metal water fountain in a playground, taking you back so far your knees turn weak.

Down Broadway, the main street where Sonny and I would drive up and down all evening in my '59 Chevy, leaning out the window to talk to girls who could never quite be lured out of their daddy's car. Now the street is dead as a graveyard during the day, empty of cars at night, the life sucked out of the downtown by the big Wal-Mart and the mall out by the highway. Down Broadway and back, putting off the inevitable, the drive by our old house. Finally nothing to do but idle down West Overland, going slow, counting the blocks: Avenue A, Avenue B. Making the left turn at Avenue F, pulling up in front of the house on the corner, easing out of the car, almost afraid to look—but the old farmhouse is still here, right where it's supposed to be. The trucker who owns the place now has done a good job with it, painted it a neat gray, put on an addition that still leaves it a tiny home, sodded the yard and paved the driveway. There is no tangle of rusty farm machinery out back, no horses tethered to the front gate, no kids shooting marbles in the driveway or playing bows and arrows out back.

I knock on the door, but there's no one home. Walk around the house under tall trees my sister planted as saplings when we were in grade school. Head across the street, wanting to find the exact spot where Sonny and I waited for Charlie Starkweather, figuring it must be right about here, where the sidewalk is now, in front of the first house after the alley as you head down toward the river. Thinking: Lord, Sonny, I can see us right here, throwing rocks at the streetlights. And down there crouched over a circle in the dirt playing marbles, and over there trying to kill red ants with kerosene and firecrackers until Ronnie Bales ran home mad, calling us killers. I turn back to the little gray house, almost expecting Mom at the door, calling us in for supper, or Pop telling me to step on it because we have hay to move.

I wanted to come back in 1988 when my mother died, but I couldn't go home for her funeral because the Reagan White House had changed the rules. Someone in the Reagan administration found a way to get around the Ford and Carter amnesties (and cause some grief for a very few draft dodgers and deserters) by ruling that if you gave up your citizenship to avoid service in the military, you could be excluded from the U.S. It seemed backwards to me, and I argued that I avoided service first and gave up my citizenship later—but I lost the argument and had to get a waiver visa to go home again, and by the time the thing came in the mail six months later, it was much too late for her funeral.

My sister Linda comes down from Rapid City and we spend an afternoon driving around town, taking pictures of the old Midwest Theater, where we went to the movies almost every weekend and paid seventy-five cents for a ticket and twenty-five cents each for popcorn and soda. We go for a long walk along the river and talk about the winter when Pop was in the hospital when I was twelve, the winter I spent milking old Bess and we had so little money that we lived on cornmeal mush and cornbread for months. She remembers it as a good time, a close time. I remember it as a horror of poverty and fear and embarrassment, kids at school teasing us because our clothes were falling apart, standing in the principal's office too ashamed to admit that we were hungry when he asked if we needed free lunches. I remember the gifts the Elks Club brought in their rescue package for Christmas, the pocket knife with the seventy-nine-cent price tag still on it and the ugly hat with the flaps that pulled down over my ears and tied under my chin, and running out of the house and sitting alone in the tack shed with Pop's bridles and saddles crying because we were poor and everybody knew it. My sister remembers the apples and oranges in the box and how good they tasted that Christmas Eve.

Revisions and dreams and revisions of dreams, trying to work back over the warp of time, to bend my way through the ripples, find the thread, trust it and see where it leads. Knowing that every truth is only a version, every memory no more than a wedge through an old door.

On my last night in Scottsbluff, I have dinner with Sonny's sister Patty at a steak house in town. We sit there talking and eating, laughing about Sonny, kidding about things we used to do. She brings a stack of photos of him in Vietnam and later, the worst of the pictures we went through in 1969 missing. No one knows what happened to them. There are photos of Sonny back at the fire base near Cam Ranh Bay after humping the bush, with his M-16 over his knee and his shirt soaked with sweat, sitting around talking with his buddies, flopped on his bunk—the kind of photos you always see of soldiers in Vietnam, bored between periods of abject terror, sitting on sandbags, drinking beer, playing poker.

There is one photo Patty can't explain. It shows a Vietnamese girl who could be fifteen or twenty-five, a plain, studious-looking girl wearing cream-colored pajamas and rubber sandals, smiling shyly into the camera. Sonny's inscription on the back is cryptic: "Vo Thi By Oct 67," it says. "Killed Nov 67."

There is also a copy of a journal Sonny kept for a time when he was in alcohol rehab at the veterans' hospital in Cheyenne—brief, heartbreaking entries about the things he has to do to find a way to stop drinking and slip back into life again.

At the end drinking was about all Sonny did. He stuck to whiskey, nothing else. Sonny had a little apartment in Scottsbluff, and Patty would take food to him, but he didn't eat much. The day after Christmas 1996 he wasn't answering the phone, so Patty went over to make sure he was all right and found him unconscious on the floor. A window was wide open and the heat was off. It looked as if he might have got up to close it and collapsed. The temperature in the apartment was down near freezing, but Sonny was still breathing. There were fifty empty whiskey bottles in the apartment, and the food Patty had been taking him was still in the refrigerator, untouched. She called an ambulance and got Sonny to the hospital but he died ten hours later.

The official cause of death was listed as hypothermia, but the truth is Sonny just crawled down inside himself and drowned. He was fifty years old, and he never got over Vietnam. Patty's husband, another Vietnam vet, died a couple of months later.

We keep circling around the subject of the war, the way it knocked a hole in all our lives, the things it did to people. We worry at it, but that's about all we can do. Nothing is going to bring Sonny back, or Patty's husband, or Ron Bales. The war was a tragedy for two nations, one rich and one poor, the profligate expenditure of American and Vietnamese lives in pursuit of nothing at all. It was cruel and stupid, and when you're done worrying at it, it leaves you with nothing but a sadness that tastes like metal at the back of your throat.

I spend all the next morning up on the summit of Scotts Bluff, alone with the sagebrush and the yucca, the buffalo grass and ponderosa pine. The air is clear and I can see Laramie Peak in the Rockies, a hundred miles to the west. The bluff is a national monument but there are no more than a dozen tourists around this morning, and it's easy to find an outcrop where there's no one at all, where I can sit and listen to the silence, hearing nothing but the sound of the wind, and watch hawks soaring on the breeze a thousand feet above the valley. Holding my own private funeral for Sonny, cussing him a little because he could have called and he never did, cussing myself because I could have called and I never did. Looking down over the badlands where we hunted rattlesnakes, the river where we used to catch bluegill and catfish. Thinking about everything that has happened since that cold night in 1958 when we tried to kill Charlie Starkweather.

For a few good months in 1991, Mariela and I got back together again. Tom Clagg was out of her life, she was still in Miami, I went down on an assignment, and we hooked up again. Being with her was like it had been twenty-two years before, crazy and sweet and affectionate. We even made it down to Key West together, to a room much like the room I dreamed of in the army in the chilly winter of 1969. She was everything I remembered and more and it made all the lost years feel a little better, knowing there was something real there all along, even if we couldn't make it last. I thought I broke it off over mundane things like kids and distance and careers going two thousand miles apart, but looking back I think there was too much hurt in between, too many cold days scavenging Hastings Street for enough pop bottles to exchange for a bowl of soup, too many nights thinking about her with Tom Clagg, stuff I had pushed way down inside still gnawing at me so there was a bittersweet twist to every minute we had together, always thinking what might have been, unable to make something of what we had.

It has not all been harsh, or sad, or terrible. After fifteen years I went back to newspaper work, began traveling the world to write, pouring the years of silence into newspaper columns. There was no way to get the wasted years back, but I found my way again, found a thing I could do and a place where I could do it. Very late, I found a love that would last, a woman who could steady things and make the center hold while I went down to a place where I didn't want to go and worried at the past long enough to make this book. I have two good sons, and after too many years of separation when we saw each other too little, they moved in with me and stayed.

While doing the research for this book, my old friends Ray Brassard and Larry Grossman found thick wads of my old letters, passages from which I have quoted in this book. Most were written while I was living with Danielle in Outremont in the winter of '71–'72 or during the summer and fall of '72, when I was out in British Columbia and working hard at fiction and poetry without much success.

The letters bothered me. They had a surprising energy and verve—surprising because I tend to think of myself at the time as too depressed to be juggling so many projects at once—and I couldn't help but wonder what had happened to that young man. Of course, I know the answer. Exile wore me down. That sudden separation from all the things I knew and loved, the growing sense of powerful but unfocused guilt, the absurd decision to renounce my American citizenship, the diminished sense of self-worth that would finally lead to a disastrous and mutually destructive relationship—all these things took their toll. The effect of forced exile is felt not in any sudden tearing away but in the corrosive loss, over a period of time, of too many of the things that make you what you are. Another casualty of war? Perhaps that is putting it too strongly. But for my generation, Vietnam is the fault line. We were, most of us, very different people after we had passed through that fire.

Different—and yet not so different. I have spent half a life on each side of the border. I feel American and Canadian in roughly equal parts, knowing there's good and bad in both countries. But when I come down out of the Wildcat Hills at sunset, I know: the home you find at true north on the compass will always be here, for me, in this dry place out on the big toe of Nebraska. A lot of miles have slipped between us, and I imagine there aren't too many people out here who would care to claim me—but I grab a spot at a bar to watch a football game and start gabbing with the bartender, and my speech slips into that peculiar version of the western drawl they call the Platte Valley curse, and I'm as much at home as a horsefly on a Clydesdale.

From the north outcrop of the bluff I look down on two hawks riding the breeze eight hundred feet above the valley floor. The hawks have the whole sky to themselves as far as you can see in every direction, but they dive-bomb each other with beaks and talons anyway, shrieking as they soar into battle, fighting over that little patch of sky for no reason at all.

I feel as if I could sit here forever, looking out over the valley, the North Platte River down below, the sugar factory where we hauled all that hay off in the distance, wheat fields and badlands and herds of cattle grazing in distant pastures. Perched on the bluff, the hard clay pockmarked with the burrows of snakes and chipmunks, home to more wild things than a man can count. The only trees this high are ponderosa pines—gnarled and old, twisted into abstract shapes by the wind, trees that stand alone in a hard, dry place a long way from everywhere. Like our lives, the way they've been bent and battered and warped by wind and time.

I pluck a blade of buffalo grass and suck it between my teeth the way we did when we were kids trying to be like our fathers. Remembering a summer day a long time ago, Sonny and I chasing each other on bicycles, not watching where we were going, pedaling hard around a sharp curve on a dirt path onto a little wooden bridge with no railing. We had no time to brake or turn; suddenly we were airborne, tumbling a dozen feet down into chest-deep water, screaming all the way. Dragging the bikes out of a scummy pond, dripping wet and laughing, deciding it was so much fun we should go back and do it again on purpose, and then again, the ten-foot drop to the water as near as we would ever come to flying.

In fourth grade we spent months trying to figure out the secret, trying to fly like Superman. Every night I dreamed that we could do it; every day on the way to school we tried, running hard into the wind, our coats spread like wings, sure that if we could only run fast enough we would soar away like birds. It took two years, but we finally found a way to fly, racing our bikes off that old bridge.

The bluff is quiet now, a holy place. The Platte winds down from the Rockies on its way to the Missouri. The breeze strokes the wheat fields. The hawks take their battle farther west until they're nothing more than black specks in the distance. It's good to be home.

Acknowledgments

I am indebted to many books, read over a period of decades, for my understanding of the Vietnam War and that period in history. Foremost among them are Graham Greene's *The Quiet American,* Barbara Tuchman's *The March of Folly,* Neil Sheehan's *A Bright Shining Lie,* Frances FitzGerald's *Of a Fire in the Lake,* Bernard B. Fall's *Hell in a Very Small Place: The Siege of Dien Bien Phu,* Michael Herr's *Dispatches,* Tim O'Brien's *The Things They Carried* and *Going After Cacciato,* Bao Ninh's *The Sorrow of War,* and Philip Caputo's memoir, *A Rumor of War.* Stanley Karnow's *Vietnam,* the indispensable guide to the period, refreshed my memory of the events that formed the political and historical background to this book.

After I tried and failed to write this many times over a period of decades, the impetus to get it down at last came from my former agent, Jennifer Barclay, who has since moved. After her departure, Hilary Stanley stepped in with an intelligent eye for a manuscript. My Canadian editor, Iris Tupholme, made a single suggestion that saved me months of work.

My American editor, Elaine Pfefferblit, provided wise counsel, steady support, sharp editing, and that belief in the importance of a work without which a writer's best efforts can die on the vine. I only wish that all writers could have the experience of working with her.

While this book was being written, no one offered more help than Cheryl Tritt, my ally in the political and journalistic battles at the University of Nebraska in the late 1960s. Cheryl, now a busy lawyer in Washington, D.C., somehow found time to read most of the manuscript in its formative stages and to offer constant support and suggestions. I am also in debt to Catherine Wallace of the *Toronto Star*, Mick Lowe (who turned me against the war in the first place and helped with a critical section of this book thirty years later), Peter Burton and Peter Maly of the Vancouver committee, Pat Nagel, Bill Lever, Ken Spottswood, Eugene and Emma Marc, Mike and Penny Beerworth, John Simmons, my sister Linda Dittmar, my long-lost friend Bill Reedy, my sons Jesse and Tyler, Pat Walter Humphrey (who helped fill in some of the gaps in the life of her brother Sonny), and my late parents, Jack Carney Todd and Maxine Marguerite Morgan, who despite their extreme poverty supported me at a time when wealthier parents were disinheriting their sons for making the same decision I made.

I must thank in particular the five people who had the most influence on me during the period when the events in this book were reeling past at the speed of a road movie: Norm Wolfe, who first rescued me in Canada; Ray Brassard, who lived through many of the same experiences; Larry Grossman, who helped me through although our paths led in very different directions; my friend and mentor Dr. John Xiros Cooper of the University of British Columbia; and my childhood friend Sonny Walter, who once dreamed of writing this book with me.

If I was able to come to grips with the events of thirty years ago, it is above all because of the unwavering support of my talented wife, the singer Irene Marc, who somehow maintained her patience and good humor throughout.

Finally, I must thank the *Montreal Gazette* for the indulgence to work on this material and for providing a forum for my first, tentative efforts at remembrance.

Montreal
December 14, 2000